# Journey Through the Old Testament

# HARCOURT RELIGION HIGH SCHOOL

*Nihil Obstat*
Reverend Steven Olds, S. T. D.
Censor Deputatus
*Imprimatur*
✠ Most Reverend Thomas G. Wenski, Bishop of Orlando
April 13, 2005

The Ad Hoc Committee to Oversee the Use of the Catechism, United States Conference of Catholic Bishops, has found this catechetical text, ©2006, to be in conformity with the *Catechism of the Catholic Church*.

For permission to reprint copyrighted material, grateful acknowledgment is made to the following sources:

*Costello Publishing Company, Inc., Northport, NY:* From *Vatican Council II: The Basic Sixteen Documents,* edited by Rev. Austin Flannery, O. P. Text copyright © 1996 by Reverend Austin Flannery, O. P.

*International Consultation on English Texts:* English translation of the The Hail Mary and the Magnificat by the International Consultation on English Texts.

*National Council of the Churches of Christ in the U.S.A.:* Scripture quotations from the *New Revised Standard Version Bible: Catholic Edition.* Text copyright © 1993 and 1989 by the Division of Christian Education of the National Council of the Churches of Christ in the U.S.A.

*United States Conference of Catholic Bishops, Washington, D. C.:* From *The Challenge of Peace: God's Promise and Our Response* by United States Catholic Bishops. Text copyright © 1983 by United States Conference of Catholic Bishops. From *Sharing Catholic Social Teaching: Challenges and Directions* by United States Catholic Bishops. Text copyright © 1998 by United States Conference of Catholic Bishops.

Additional acknowledgments and credits can be found on page 236.

Printed in the United States of America

ISBN 0-15-901669-X

4 5 6 7 8 9 10    059    10 09 08

# Contents

**c. 1900** B.C.
Migration of Abraham
to Canaan

1900 B.C.

1500 B.C.

**c. 2000–1700** B.C. (perhaps later)
Stories of the ancestors
of the Israelites

# God and His Chosen People

## CHAPTER 1

"Make me to know your ways, O LORD;
teach me your paths."

*Psalm 25:4*

## Chapter Goals

In this chapter, you will:

- learn about the importance of the Old Testament.
- explore the purpose and meaning of God's Revelation to his people.
- come to understand the scope of salvation history as recorded in the Old Testament.
- analyze the structure, literary forms, and literary techniques of the Old Testament.
- learn about Blessed Mother Teresa of Calcutta.

**c. 1290** B.C.
Exodus of Israelites
from Egypt

**c. 1000–962** B.C.
Reign of
King David

**c. 960** B.C.
Bulding of
first temple

**c. 922** B.C.
Division of kingdom
into Israel and Judah

900 B.C.

# The Importance of the Old Testament

## Faith Sharing

### A Family History

This week, create a list of important times in the history of your family. Be sure to include celebratory events such as birth dates and vacations. Also include events that marked difficult times, such as moving to a new home or school, or the death of a loved one. Write a short summary describing how all of these events represent the story of your family.

## Faith Activity

**Favorite Stories** Write a few sentences noting the Old Testament stories with which you are most familiar. What meaning do these stories have for you? Who first taught you these stories? Share your responses with a partner. Then, as a class, determine which story is most popular, and locate the story in your Bible.

What do you first think of when you hear the word *old*? Do you think of wisdom and tradition? Or do you think of dullness and decay? If the word *old* is used to mean something that is no longer in use or without value, this sense of *old* certainly doesn't apply to the Old Testament.

Christians refer to the Jewish sacred writings in the Bible as the Old Testament to distinguish them from the Christian sacred writings of the New Testament. More recently, some Christians have preferred to call these writings the Hebrew Scriptures. One reason for doing so is to honor these Scriptures in their own right, not just as one part of the Bible used by Christians. The Old Testament is sacred to both Jews and Christians, and it remains a continuing source of inspiration to people of both religions today.

## A Connection Between Old and New

The Scriptures found in the Old Testament are basic to Christianity and Judaism. This part of the Bible establishes the foundation for the relationship between God and his people. It also sets forth the laws and practices of his people. These Scriptures present the history of the Israelites and the covenant that God made with them. In Genesis, God made his covenant with Abraham, the early ancestor of the Israelites. Abraham is the father of the Jewish people. The twelve tribes of the Israelites take their names from some of Abraham's descendants. The history and laws of the Old Testament continue to have ongoing significance and meaning for the individuals and community of Judaism. Their covenant with God is ongoing.

▶ Boy holding Torah at Bar Mitzvah.

Christians cannot fully understand God or their faith without understanding the Old Testament. The first five books in the Old Testament were central to the faith of first-century Jews, including Jesus. The Old Testament accounts of God entering into human events are an important part of the history of Jesus' followers and the traditions Jesus practiced. These writings are at the foundation of Jesus' teaching.

Therefore, it is essential to understand and appreciate the important connection between the Old Testament and the New Testament. "Old" does not imply that these scriptures are out-of-date. Rather, they are the record of **salvation history**, the saving action of God throughout human history. Together with the New Testament, these sacred writings are integral to our understanding of Jesus and Christianity. The New Testament has to be read in the light of the Old Testament. The Old Testament has to be read in the light of Jesus' death and Resurrection. The unity of the Old Testament and the New Testament comes from the unity of God's plan and his truth that is recorded in the Bible, both in the Old Testament and in the New Testament.

## A Shared Identity

The Old Testament, as a part of Sacred Scripture, holds a place of high honor in Judaism and Christianity—it is God's revelation and the story of salvation. The storytellers show us how God's promises to Abraham are later fulfilled in the time of David and Solomon. Israel's history is also integral to the identity of Jews and Christians.

In biblical times and texts, neither Jews nor Christians were terms that were used as they are understood today. Yet Jews and Christians today share the common history found in the Old Testament, which is also referred to as Hebrew Scriptures. The stories of the **patriarchs**, the ancestors of the Israelites, help people of faith understand God's commands and help them to implement God's commands in their lives and communities.

Jews and Christians are called into a reconciliation after many centuries of separation. The Second Vatican Council set forth the challenge of reversing centuries of hostile Christian teaching about Jews and Judaism. Since then, Jewish-Catholic relations have been based on a respectful exchange among people who share a faith in the same God and recognize the faith commitment of the other group.

The Catholic Church strives to educate her members about the faith of Jewish people. For instance, an understanding of Judaism can help us to better understand Christian liturgy. In other words, an understanding of the Jewish roots and practices will help us to better understand Christian beliefs and practices. Like Joseph, who reconciled with his brothers, Jews and Catholics are called to a sincere reconciliation.

## Break Open the Word

**Praise for God's Word**

Psalm 119 highlights the importance of God's word in the lives of his people. Read each passage below and write down what God's word can bring or do for those who believe in him.

Psalm 119:11
Psalm 119:105
Psalm 119:130

Then locate two more verses in Psalm 119 that describe God's word.

▲ Pope John Paul II meets Israel's chief Rabbi in Jerusalem, 2000.

# SABBATH AND THE LORD'S DAY

From the earliest days of the covenant, faithful Jews have followed the third commandment and kept holy the Sabbath (Shabbat or Shabbas). The Jewish community marks its days from sunset to sunset, so Sabbath starts on Friday at sunset and ends on Saturday at sunset.

The Sabbath commemorates the end of God's work of creation. On the seventh day, God finished the work he had begun, and he rested. God blessed and sanctified the heaven and the earth—all that he had created. In the Book of Exodus, we read that God blessed the Sabbath and made it holy. In the Book of Deuteronomy, we find that the Sabbath is also a day to remember Israel's liberation from slavery in Egypt. Thus, the Sabbath is a sign of the everlasting covenant God made with his people.

A striking characteristic of the celebration of the weekly Sabbath is that it is typically celebrated more at home than at synagogue. The celebration of the Sabbath begins with the ritual meal on Friday evening. Synagogue services are typically held Saturday mornings. The Jewish Sabbath is a day to stop business, to rest, and to appreciate God and his gifts.

**Christian Practice** Jesus and his first disciples honored the Sabbath and observed the Jewish holy days and celebrations. Jesus respected the holiness of this day, but he also interprets the Sabbath laws in a new light, teaching by his actions on Sabbath that being merciful, doing good, and saving lives bring honor to God and the holy day.

Jesus rose from the dead on the first day of the week, the day after Sabbath, on what we call Sunday. Jesus' Resurrection reminds us of the first creation, and his saving work brings about a new creation and a new life. The early Christian community gathered on Sunday for a ritual meal as Jesus had instructed during the Last Supper. They would break bread in his memory, read from Scripture, discuss Jesus' teachings, and celebrate Christ as their new Passover.

As Christianity spread, Jesus' Jewish followers continued to differentiate themselves from Jewish observances. The celebration of the Lord's Day became the manner in which Christians honored the command to keep holy the Sabbath.

Today, the Church continues to set aside Sunday as a special day to honor God in the celebration of the Eucharist, to rest from work, to spend time with family, and to do good works.

## Faith Activity

**Day of Rest** In small groups discuss all the ways Catholics keep holy the Lord's Day. Share anything special or different your family may do to set apart the day. Visit your parish's website or get a weekly bulletin, and find out what ways your parish celebrates on Sunday.

# God's Revelation to His People

To reveal is to disclose something that was hidden. **Divine revelation** is God's communicating of himself and of his plan of goodness throughout history. It refers to God's deliberate and gradual disclosure of himself to humans—his nature, his plan, his providence, and his expectations. The Bible is the written record of God's revelation. On different occasions God revealed different aspects of himself—love, power, glory, justice, wrath, mercy—that form a complex, evolving picture of his nature.

God remains the same, but the human understanding of him develops and deepens because God's gradual revelation in the Old Testament develops and deepens. Sometimes God's revelation deals with his plan of salvation for his people, as in his **covenant**, or sacred agreement, with Old Testament figures such as Noah and Abraham. Other times, such as when God revealed the **Ten Commandments**, God asks the Israelites to live in a certain way in order to remain his people.

## The Word of God

The Bible is referred to as the inspired "word of God." What does this mean? God inspired human authors to reveal his truths. He acted through them, and they used their own abilities to communicate God's word. **Biblical inspiration** is the process by which God the Holy Spirit assisted a human author in writing a book of the Bible. Because of this, God is the author of the Bible, and the truth that he willed us to know was conveyed without error. The inspired words of the Bible:

- are "a pure and unfailing fount of spiritual life" (*Dei Verbum #21*).

- can lead us towards a deeper love and understanding of Jesus.

- teach us about the power of the Trinity to spread the Good Word.

Biblical inspiration is rooted in God's dealings with the Hebrew people, where we find witness of God inspiring the entire Old Testament. The books of the Old Testament gave witness to how God and human authors worked together to produce a writing that can rightfully be called the word of God.

### Faith Activity

**Knowing God** How did you come to know about God? Write a paragraph on the people, places, or things that have helped you learn more about or grow closer to God the Father, God the Son, and God the Holy Spirit.

▲ Saint Matthew by Domenico Theotocopuli, c. 1610–14.

**The Canon** The Catholic Bible contains the faith story of the people of Israel—the Old Testament of 46 books—and of Christians—the New Testament of 27 books. These books are referred to as the **canon** of the Bible, that is, the official collection of inspired books of sacred Scripture that contain the witness and instruction for our faith.

*Canon* is rooted in the Greek word "kanon," which means "reed" or "measuring stick." The sacred canon of Catholic Scripture is the measure of authenticity that books are regarded to have as being revealed and inspired by God. The Old Testament and New Testament are the collection of books that are recognized by the teaching authority of the Church as the true measure of our faith.

The Old Testament was written in Aramaic or Hebrew. However, as a result of the Babylonian exile, many Jews were dispersed and living in a world influenced by Greek culture and language. Therefore, the books were translated into Greek, probably in the second century B.C. This translation is referred to as the Septuagint. *Septuagint* means "seventy." This word was used because some believe the Old Testament was translated by seventy scholars in seventy days.

Some Jews used the Septuagint to compose their own canon and selected books not considered part of the traditional Jewish canon. These books are the Wisdom of Solomon, Baruch, Judith, 1 and 2 Maccabees, Sirach/Ecclesiasticus, and Tobit. These books were probably chosen because of their Greek overtone. At times these books are referred to as the Deuterocanonicals (second canon). The Deuterocanonicals are included in the Catholic Bible.

The first Christians and the Church used the Greek version for the first fourteen centuries. However, Protestants rejected these books at the beginning of the Protestant Reformation when Martin Luther rejected all of the books not identical to the traditional Jewish canon. However, Catholics still maintain the deuterocanonicals.

Christians do agree, however, on the canon of the New Testament. These books hold the true message of Jesus as discerned through the Apostolic Tradition of the Church. The canonical books reflected the faith of the early Christians, a faith that preceded the writing of the New Testament. Therefore, the canon of Scripture reflects the faith of the Church.

The canon was developed with divine guidance. We must read and interpret the Scriptures with God's guidance and with the help of the Church in our own day. When reading the Bible, we enter into a tradition and a relationship with the earliest Christian communities responsible for writing and preserving the texts. Reading the Bible demands a respect for the faith of the Church and a respect for the inspiration of the Holy Spirit.

# The Covenant

From its beginning, Judaism has had a very strong, visible presence. It was unique in professing belief in only one God. The concept of **monotheism**, belief in one God, was almost unknown at this time. An equally unfamiliar idea was that a god would initiate a relationship with humans and take an active role in their lives. People who lived during this time usually made sacrifices to their gods in the hope that the gods would not interfere in their lives. Hebrew beliefs and practices set the Israelites, who later became known as the Jews, apart from the rest of culture.

| Core Beliefs |
|---|
| There is one God. |
| God created everything, including humans, whom he made in his image—male and female. |
| He chose a people with whom to share his revelation and to carry his blessing through history. These people were originally called the Israelites. After the fall of the Temple in Jerusalem, they became known as the Jews. They are also known as the Hebrews. |
| God made a covenant with the Israelites (Jews). The covenant, a sacred agreement between God and the Jewish people, began approximately 1,900 years before Jesus was born, when God selected Abraham to be the father of the *chosen* people. |

**Defining Moments** For the Jewish people, the Book of Exodus contains many of the defining moments in their journey with God. First is the story of the Passover. In this event, God's angel of death struck down the first-born of the Egyptians, but passed over the homes of the Israelites. They were protected because, at God's command, they had placed the blood of a lamb on the doorposts of their homes and eaten a meal of the lamb's flesh.

Following the Passover is the story of the **Exodus**. With the guidance of Moses, the Israelites passed through the waters of the Red Sea to freedom. Then, after the desert journey lasting years, Moses and the people made it to the Promised Land. God there made a covenant with his people. The Passover, the Exodus from Egypt, and the covenant at Mt. Sinai are central events in the history of Israel. For Jesus and his fellow Jews, these events were reminders of the tenderness of God's love for the people and their need to be faithful to the covenant.

## Faith Activity

**Expression of Love**
A *covenant* is ritualized through a specific action and involves obligations or promises from each party. For Jews and Christians, the covenant experienced with God is one of love. Name three ways you experience God's love in your everyday life. Name three ways you express your love to God in your everyday life.

**Names for the Law**
The Old Testament writers referred to God's law in many names. Read Psalm 19:7–10 and record all of the synonyms for the word "law" found in this passage. For each synonym include how the psalmist describes the law and its purpose in our lives.

**The Law** A fundamental element of the Old Testament is the establishment of God's relationship with his people through a sacred covenant. At first, God makes promises to his people, but he does not request any obligations from his people in return. This is evident in God's covenant with Abraham. God promises Abraham a nation and a people, but he asks nothing in return. With Moses, God's covenant includes obligations for the Israelites. God gives the major moral obligations and prescriptions of his Law in the Ten Commandments.

This is an example of God's revelation, which is more extensively experienced as God acts further in the entire history of the people. In the events and the Law, God gradually reveals himself and his relationship with his people. Through the prophets, God lets the people know what will befall them if they do not keep the Law and if they fail to be his people. For the Israelites, keeping the covenant with God began with following the Ten Commandments.

The Ten Commandments represent the basic prescriptive moral laws given by God. However, the Ten Commandments are understood to be a natural part of God's design. These laws are "engraved on our hearts." The **natural moral law** is a fundamental part of human nature. It is not outside of us, but within us. It is part of our human makeup and part of God's design.

Knowing right from wrong is intrinsic to our nature, even though God's revelation is needed to clarify human thinking corrupted by original sin. It is not simply a gift given to those who believe in the Bible. Whenever we are confronted with a difficult decision, we consider right and wrong. We use our ability to reason to search for truth. This is the way we solve problems and respond to God.

The natural moral law is also the foundation of moral rules and civil laws that we follow today. The U.S. Declaration of Independence is based on the natural moral law that people have "inalienable rights" which cannot be taken away. These basic human rights include "life, liberty, and the pursuit of happiness." Respecting these rights and working to make sure others are not denied these rights is understood to be what is good.

**The New Covenant**  Jesus was a Jew who preached the nearness of the kingdom of God to fellow Jews. He was influenced by the Jewish culture. Their relationship to Jesus drew the Jewish people deeper into divine revelation with God. Jesus fulfilled the Law of Moses by giving a new law of love and by teaching that God's covenant of love extends beyond the Chosen People to people everywhere. Jesus fulfilled the promise of the Old Testament prophets. As God's Son, his words and actions showed that God the Father was present in the world, actively healing, saving, and redeeming the people who had sinned and turned away. However, it is essential to realize that God has never revoked his covenant with the Jewish people.

Jesus, through his death and Resurrection, fulfilled the old covenant. The Church is the People of God and the Body of Christ, redeemed from sin by Jesus' death. The Israelites were called to be the People of God; now all people are called to be part of the new People of God in Christ. Through his sacrifice and death on the cross, Jesus became the Passover Lamb and the Exodus (the way out) for all of humankind to be released from the bonds of sin and death. Through his Resurrection, all are welcomed to the Promised Land of God's kingdom. Jesus gave himself as the ultimate gift of mercy, forgiveness, and love in his new covenant.

As we study the Old Testament and appreciate the meaning of its truth for God's chosen people, the Israelites, we also must remember that these defining moments in salvation history lead to *the* defining moment, the coming of the Son and the establishment of a new and everlasting covenant.

## Faith Activity

**Who Has Rights?**
Read the first few sentences of the Declaration of Independence. What connections do you see between these sentences and the natural moral law?

## Faith Activity

**Prayer**  Jesus taught his disciples the importance of prayer. He told his followers to ask his Father for all that they needed, and to trust that the Father knows what they need even before they ask. For what do you pray? Is there anything God can help you with right now? What do you have to be thankful for today? Say a silent prayer, then pray the Our Father as a class.

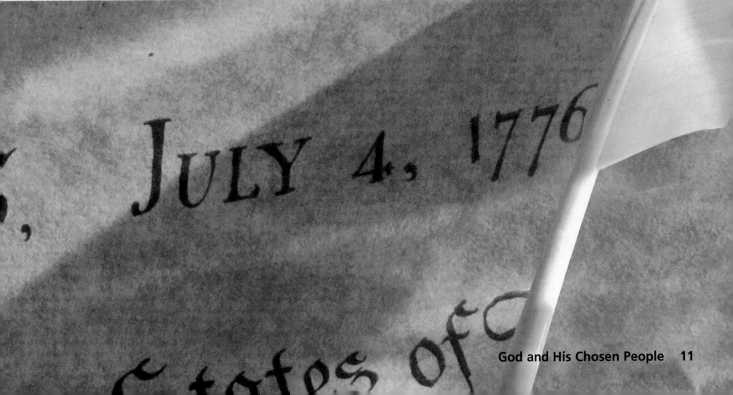

JULY 4, 1776

# OLD TESTAMENT PROPHECIES ABOUT JESUS

◀ Jesus Christ by Giotto and Cimabue.

In several passages of the New Testament, we find references to Old Testament prophecies. Often Jesus would speak of himself as fulfilling a prophecy from the Jewish Scriptures. In fact, the Gospel according to Luke records that Jesus began his public ministry in the synagogue in Nazareth on the Sabbath. Jesus did not select the Scriptures to be proclaimed; instead, he was given a scroll from the Book of Isaiah. He unrolled it, and read it aloud:

> "The Spirit of the Lord is upon me,
>    because he has anointed me to
>       bring good news to the poor.
> He has sent me to proclaim release
>       to the captives
>       and recovery of sight to the blind,
>       to let the oppressed go free,
>    to proclaim the year of the Lord's favor."
>                                     *Luke 4:18–19*

Jesus then told those gathered, "Today this scripture has been fulfilled in your hearing."

*Luke 4:21*

In this passage Jesus described some important parts of his mission. We know from the rest of the Gospels and the witness of the first disciples that Jesus spent his ministry doing what only the Anointed One could. He preached the Good News to the poor and helped people be free to really live. He performed acts of mercy and worked towards social justice. He celebrated and proclaimed the arrival of deliverance from sin. Unlike Isaiah, whom God communicated through to foretell the coming of a savior, Jesus was the Son of God and the savior who could make all of the prophecies come true.

### Break Open the Word

**Prophecies Fulfilled** The New Testament includes many other references to Old Testament prophecies and the way in which Jesus fulfilled them. How do these scripture verses relate to the life and death of Jesus?

Isaiah 7:14

Isaiah 11:2

Isaiah 53:3–7, 12; Zechariah 9:9, 11:13, 12:10

Psalm 69:21

# Recording Salvation History

The Old Testament narrates a rough historical sequence of events from the creation of the world to the kingdom of the Maccabees. However, the purpose of the Old Testament is to tell the story of God's relationship with his people. God is at work in the history and writings of the Israelites.

Many parts of the Old Testament present real events, but the intent and writings of the authors were not always historical, nor did the authors of the Old Testament have the resources of modern historians. As Thomas Cahill observes in his book *The Gifts of the Jews,* the Old Testament authors did not "have access to the card catalogue of the Library of Congress or the resources of the Internet." Some of the Old Testament is based on eyewitness accounts and written records of the events it records, but some parts are based on oral tradition and on written sources compiled centuries after the events.

## People and Places

The original audience of the Old Testament was the Israelites. The Israelites believed that their ancestors had entered into a special relationship with God—a covenant, by which they and their descendants had become God's chosen people. The histories, tales, poetry, laws, sermons, proverbs, and other writings that were eventually included in the Old Testament were intended in God's providence to serve as guidance to the Israelites on how to live in order to remain God's people. This story also has a specific relevance for Christians as part of the history of their faith. The values and lessons of the Old Testament provide universal truths of human experience and still apply today to people of all religions and of no religion.

The events of the Old Testament take place against the geographical background of the ancient Near East. This area was dominated by two major civilizations—that of Mesopotamia and that of Egypt. Mesopotamia is the valley of the Tigris and Euphrates rivers in what mainly is now Iraq. Mesopotamia formed one horn of the Fertile Crescent, a semicircle of rich farming and grazing land extending from the southeastern corner of the Mediterranean Sea to the head of the Persian Gulf. During this period, a long succession of peoples—Sumerians, Akkadians, Babylonians, Assyrians, and Persians—rose and fell in Mesopotamia. These groups invaded the Fertile Crescent from the surrounding deserts and mountains.

▲ Two boys carry a Torah by the Western Wall.

## Faith Activity

**Ancient Mesopotamian Cultures** Research one of the Mesopotamian cultures of ancient times (Sumerians, Akkadians, Babylonians, Assyrians, or Persians). What was life like for these people? Present your findings to the rest of the class.

Egyptian civilization, on the other hand, developed in the Nile Valley. Although also subject to invasions and periods of disorder, Egyptian civilization was far more stable than that of Mesopotamia. The lands of the Bible—modern Israel, Jordan, Lebanon, and Syria—formed the western horn of the Fertile Crescent. In ancient times, the coastline of this region was known as the "Way of the Sea," and formed the traditional route of armies moving north or south. Modern-day conflicts between the state of Israel and its Arab neighbors form only the most recent chapter in a long history of violence in this region.

## Key Moments in the Development of Israel

**The Patriarchs** The exact origin of the Israelites is unknown; according to the tradition recorded in the Old Testament Book of Genesis, the Israelites' ancestor Abraham migrated from the city-state of Ur in southern Mesopotamia along the Fertile Crescent to Canaan. This migration of the Israelites to Canaan took place sometime in the second millennium B.C. Abraham, his son Isaac, and grandson Jacob, who are referred to as the patriarchs, established themselves in Canaan. The wives of the patriarchs, Abraham's wife Sarah, Isaac's wife Rebekah, and Jacob's wives Rachel and Leah, also play important roles in the Old Testament narratives. They are the **matriarchs**, or founding mothers, of the people of Israel.

The Canaanites practiced **polytheism**, worshiping many gods; by contrast, the Israelites, led by God himself, practiced monotheism, worshiping a single god. The monotheism of the Israelites was a revolutionary concept in ancient times. The history of the Israelites was a long struggle to escape domination by their powerful neighbors and to preserve their political and religious freedom. We will learn more in later chapters about the people called the Israelites.

**The Exodus** According to the Old Testament, famine in Canaan forced the Israelites (Abraham's grandson Jacob and his sons' families) to migrate to Egypt, where they were eventually enslaved by the Egyptians. Sometime around 1290 B.C. the Israelites escaped from slavery under the leadership of Moses, who responded to a call by God and whose mighty deeds brought about the Exodus. Moses guided the people during a long period of wandering in the Sinai desert, which lies between Egypt and Canaan. It was during this period that the Israelites received on Mount Sinai their primary code of laws, including the Ten Commandments from God through Moses. The Israelites' departure from Egypt is referred to as the *Exodus*, from a Greek word meaning "a going out."

### Faith Activity

**In the Desert** Have you ever shared a "desert experience" with a group of people? That is, have you ever spent time away from home and experienced a challenge or hardship with others? What was the experience like? How did it affect your relationship with these people?

**The Conquest of Canaan**  The Old Testament Books of Joshua and Judges give different accounts of the Israelite conquest of Canaan. In Joshua, the Israelites conquer the Canaanite cities in a rapid series of assaults. Judges portrays the conquest as a gradual occupation over many years. Archaeological evidence and other ancient documents indicate that neither book is completely accurate historically. Rather, they are idealized pictures showing the underlying truth of the events—God fulfilled his promise to give the chosen people a land.

The occupation took place under the leadership of a series of charismatic military leaders known as the Judges. The conquest was completed during the reigns of Israel's first three kings, Saul (c. 1020–1000 B.C.), David (c. 1000–962 B.C.), and Solomon (c. 962–922 B.C.). The second king, David—one of Israel's greatest heroes—captured the city of Jerusalem, made it his capital, and relocated there Israel's holiest relic, the **Ark of the Covenant**, an ancient symbol of God's protection and presence. Israel was at the height of its power during the reign of David's son, Solomon, who further increased Jerusalem's importance as a religious center by building the first temple there.

**The Decline of Israel**  Under Solomon's successors, the united kingdom of Israel split into northern and southern kingdoms. The northern kingdom (Israel) was larger and stronger, but the southern kingdom (Judah) was more stable. In 722 B.C. the Assyrians conquered the northern kingdom and exiled its people. In 587 B.C. the Babylonians captured Jerusalem, destroyed Solomon's temple, and deported many of the people of Judah to Babylon. It was during the period of the divided kingdoms that the visionary reformers known as the prophets denounced their contemporaries, who deserted the pure worship of God and tolerated social injustice.

▼ Destruction of the Temple in Jerusalem by Francesco Hayez, 1863.

**Watershed Experience**
Why do you think that
the Jewish religion was
strengthened by the
experience of the
Babylonian Exile? In modern
times, the watershed
experience for the Jewish
people has been the
Holocaust, which nearly
destroyed the Jews of
Europe, but it also led to the
founding of modern Israel.
Discuss how the Babylonian
Exile and the Holocaust are
alike and unlike.

**Exile and Return** The Babylonian Exile (587–539 B.C.) was a watershed period in Old Testament history, during which the Jewish religion was refined and strengthened, and significant portions of the Old Testament were compiled. At the end of this period, in 539 B.C., the Persians, under the leadership of Cyrus the Great, conquered the Babylonians. Cyrus permitted the Jews in Babylon to return to Judah, although many Jews had prospered in Babylon and chose to stay there. In 515 B.C. the rebuilding of the Jerusalem temple was completed.

Around 333 B.C., Alexander the Great conquered the Persian Empire. Alexander's empire split apart after his death, and the Jews were ruled by his successors—first the Egyptian dynasty of the Ptolemies, then the Syrian dynasty of the Seleucids. Under the Seleucid rule, some Jews embraced the Hellenistic Greek culture of Alexander's empire, but the majority continued to worship the God of the Israelites. When the Seleucid ruler, Antiochus IV, forbade the Jews to practice their religion, the family of the Maccabees, a priest and his five sons, started a revolt. In 164 B.C. Judas Maccabeus defeated the Seleucid forces, liberated Jerusalem, and purified and rededicated the temple. Today, this event is memorialized in the feast of Chanukah.

## Sources of the Old Testament

From 1200 to 1000 B.C. the history and stories of ancient people were handed down orally from generation to generation by storytellers and poets. Thus, these stories were preserved through the oral tradition. In ancient times, written language was slow to develop. When it did, very few people could read or write. Groups of people gathered to learn about their history through poetry and storytelling. In a way similar to our festivals and poetry slams, ancient people gathered to tell their history and to share experiences. This method of communicating allowed tribes to share a common history and answered questions such as: From where did we come? Why is the world ordered the way it is?

The writers of the Old Testament histories relied on both oral and written sources. **Oral tradition** existed before the invention of writing (and continued afterward to some degree). In an oral tradition, historical chronicles, genealogies, laws, and other kinds of cultural lore are memorized and passed down from one generation to the next. There is striking evidence that complex records can be preserved by oral tradition over great lengths of time. For example, the oral historians of West Africa, the griots, preserved an oral epic of the deeds of the hero-king Sundiata, who founded the Mali Empire in A.D. 1200.

However, inconsistencies inevitably develop in oral traditions that are preserved over long periods; further discrepancies develop during the period in which a culture moves from oral tradition to writing. The written sources for the Old Testament histories were letters, memoirs, genealogies, palace and temple records, reports of settlements and military campaigns, and other documents.

Your family and friends may enjoy telling favorite stories about you. Have you ever heard stories about your first birthday, the day you learned how to ride a bike or swim, or a funny event on a vacation or at home? If you enjoy looking at photo albums, you probably associate certain events with the locations and events represented in the photos. Your family and friends might not have a written account of events in your life; however, these oral stories and pictorial recollections contain unique information about who you are. They also may be the only record of such events.

## Faith Activity

**Family Tradition** Record some examples of oral tradition—such as stories, rhymes, and sayings—that have been passed down from generation to generation in your family. What meaning does this oral tradition have for you? Why is it important or not important to you? You may want to share your memories with a partner.

▲ Apache man tells story to Apache girls.

**Biblical Parallels in Other Literature** While the Bible is unique and inspired by God, its first authors, the human writers of the Old Testament, were indirectly influenced at times by the other cultures of the ancient Near East, particularly those of Mesopotamia and Egypt. This is reflected in a number of parallels between the Old Testament and ancient Mesopotamian and Egyptian literature. In the early 1870s a scholar working in the British Museum made a startling discovery in examining some clay tablets from ancient Mesopotamia. The tablets revealed an account of a great flood that was remarkably similar to the story of Noah and the Ark in the Old Testament. The Mesopotamian account was part of *The Epic of Gilgamesh*, which was composed around 2000 B.C.

In 1901 archaeologists discovered a pillar engraved with the Law Code of Hammurabi, the ruler of Babylonia from 1792 to 1750 B.C. Many of the regulations in Hammurabi's code are similar to the laws of the Israelites in the Old Testament Books of Exodus, Leviticus, and Deuteronomy. The ancient Egyptians enjoyed collections of wise sayings, such as the teachings of Ptah-Hotep, the councilor of an Egyptian king who ruled around 2450 B.C. For example, Ptah-Hotep observes, "Good speech is more hidden than the emerald, but it may be found with the maidens at the grindstones." Ptah-Hotep's teachings are echoed in the Old Testament Books of Proverbs, Ecclesiastes, and Sirach (Ecclesiasticus).

## Connect to the Past

**Ancient Storytelling** This stele is typical of a Mesopotamian record of ancient stories. Ancient people recorded stories through illustration on clay tablets, wall paintings, and caves. In this way, they passed on to future generations insights that must have been very important to them. *What do you think this artifact illustrates and what is its importance? Create a panel of images to depict what you think future generations need to know about us.*

# Reading the Old Testament

## Structure of the Old Testament

Jews and Christians recognize God as the first author of Scripture. The Old Testament is a collection of books written by different human authors under God's inspiration. The Old Testament books were written at different times, and they include different types of literature. Some individual books, such as the Book of Psalms, are collections assembled over hundreds of years. However, the basic subject of all the books of the Old Testament is the same—God's role in shaping human events. Christians understand this to mean that the Old Testament also prepares for and declares in prophecy the coming of Christ, who is the redeemer of all humankind.

The books of the Old Testament fall into several large groups.

- The first five books form a group referred to as "the Law." Jews refer to the books of the Law as the *Torah* (from Hebrew, "law"); these books are also referred to as the *Pentateuch* (from Greek, "five books"). They provide accounts of the creation of the world, stories of the ancestors of the Jews, early Israelite history, and codes of Jewish law.

- The historical books give an account of Jewish history from the conquest of Canaan to the kingdom of the Maccabees.

- The wisdom books include poetry about religion and love, collections of wise sayings, and the Book of Job.

- The prophetic books include the visions and sermons of a group of Jewish religious reformers known as the prophets.

## A Collection of Books

| Books of the Law | Historical Books | Wisdom Books | Prophetic Books |
|---|---|---|---|
| Genesis | Joshua | Job | Isaiah |
| Exodus | Judges | Psalms | Jeremiah |
| Leviticus | Ruth | Proverbs | Lamentations |
| Numbers | 1 Samuel | Ecclesiastes | Baruch |
| Deuteronomy | 2 Samuel | Song of Songs | Ezekiel |
| | 1 Kings | (Song of Solomon) | Daniel |
| | 2 Kings | Wisdom | Hosea |
| | 1 Chronicles | (Wisdom of Solomon) | Joel |
| | 2 Chronicles | Sirach (Ecclesiasticus) | Amos |
| | Ezra | | Obadiah |
| | Nehemiah | | Jonah |
| | Tobit | | Micah |
| | Judith | | Nahum |
| | Esther | | Habakkuk |
| | 1 Maccabees | | Zephaniah |
| | 2 Maccabees | | Haggai |
| | | | Zechariah |
| | | | Malachi |

**Interpreting Scripture** **Biblical exegesis** is the explanation or critical interpretation of a passage of Sacred Scripture.

Trying to interpret the author's intention involves several steps:

- understanding the historical setting in which the author wrote,

- knowing the meaning of key concepts (such as sin or redemption) as the author uses them and not as defined in modern terms, and

- appreciating the literary forms chosen by the author.

The Second Vatican Council, especially in *Dei Verbum*, addressed the interpretation of Scripture. It says:

"Seeing that, in sacred scripture, God speaks through human beings in human fashion,[1] it follows that the interpreters of sacred scripture, if they are to ascertain what God has wished to communicate to us, should carefully search out the meaning which the sacred writers really had in mind, that meaning which God had thought well to manifest through the medium of their words.

In determining the intention of the sacred writers, attention must be paid, among other things, to *literary genres*.

The fact is that truth is differently presented and expressed in the various types of historical writing, in prophetical and poetical texts, and in other forms of literary expression. . . . Rightly to understand what the sacred authors wanted to affirm in their work, due attention must be paid both to the customary and characteristic patterns of perception, speech, and narrative which prevailed in their time, and to the conventions which people then observed in their dealings with one another."[2] (*Dei Verbum, 12*).

We concentrate on the intention of the human author when interpreting the Scriptures. In searching for the meaning of a Biblical text, discovering the author's intention becomes the central task. However, we need the guidance of the Holy Spirit, who first inspired the authors, to help us understand the truth God wishes to convey.

It is also important to consider the literary form used. The way a biblical text expresses the truth must first be understood in order to understand the truth it expresses. If the literary form is misunderstood, the message of the text may be misunderstood or even lost.

# Old Testament Literary Forms

Biblical scholars have identified numerous literary genres, or forms, in the Old Testament. Sometimes an inspired author wrote an entire book of the Bible in a single genre. In other instances, numerous genres were used to craft an individual book of the Bible. Some of the more commonly accepted literary forms found in the Old Testament follow.

**Origin Story** An **origin story** is an explanation of how something came to be. The narrative of Noah and the flood, for example, is in one sense an origin story because it explains the origin and significance of the rainbow.

**Short Story** A short story is a type of brief narrative in which characters and a plot are fully developed. Ruth, Esther, and Jonah are examples of short stories found in the Old Testament. You will read more about the stories of Ruth, Esther, and Jonah in later chapters.

**Psalms** Many of the **psalms** have been attributed to King David, who was a musician and poet as well as a political leader. His name is attached to more than 70 psalms; that is, the psalm was to, for, by, or in the style or spirit of David. Many of the psalm poems have a parallel structure and rhythm. In parallel structure, a numbered verse has several parts that continue, contrast, or overlap each other. An example of contrast is:

> "If I ascend to heaven, you are
> there;
> if I make my bed in Sheol,
> you are there."
>
> *Psalm 139:8*

The rhythm of the poetry was enhanced with musical instruments that accompanied psalm singing.

There is much we don't know about Hebrew poetic techniques since the original pronunciation has been lost and poetry depends so much on the sound of the words. There are also musical instructions at the beginning of many psalms, and their meanings have been lost as well.

**Epic** An **epic** is the detailed history of a hero who demonstrates both bravery and wisdom and goes through a series of trials. This hero is often a symbolic figure who represents the traits of an entire people. Epics usually are exaggerated and idealized in terms of character or events. An important epic found in the Old Testament is the story of Moses. Moses is an epic hero who represents the people of God.

**Folklore** Various elements of folklore are found in the narratives within the Book of Genesis. The term **folklore** refers to the composite of traditional customs, art forms, tales, and sayings preserved among a people—in this case, the people of Israel. An example of folklore is found in the story of Jacob and Esau in Genesis 27.

**Parable** A **parable** is a short illustrative story that teaches a moral or religious lesson, often through the use of comparisons. In the Old Testament, a parable can be a proverb, riddle, or allegory. A parable can often prove to be more memorable than other types

**Break open the Word**

**Jonah** Read the Book of Jonah. Identify the following elements of this story:
(1) God's command and Jonah's response,
(2) the crisis,
(3) the solution.
Then describe the character of Jonah. How does he change through the course of the story?

**Interpret the Art**

**The Pharaoh's Dreams** Joseph Explains the Pharaoh's Dreams by Marc Chagall, 1931. The Pharaoh was troubled by his dreams and consulted his high priests. They offered no answers to the visions of the Pharaoh, and at the prompting of one of his servants Pharaoh called for Joseph to interpret the dreams. *Which dream is shown here? What did Joseph interpret that the dream meant?*

of stories due to its accessible narrative style. Parables differ from fables in that a parable is told in response to a specific situation. The parable welcomes the listener to become involved with its message; it invites conversion.

**Oracle** An **oracle** consists of words of wisdom or advice given by God through a spokesperson. Note that the terms *oracle, oral history, oral surgery,* and *oration* all share the root word *oral,* which is related to the mouth.

**Narrative** A **narrative**, which can be either fictional or true, can illuminate a detail within a genealogy which might otherwise be overlooked. Some narratives either begin or end with a genealogy. Some narratives are stylistically framed by placing genealogies at the beginning and the ending of a story.

**Myth** A **myth** is a symbolic story that illustrates views of a particular people regarding the relationship between humans and the divine. You may think that a myth is entirely false, but that is not the case. A myth is true in the sense that it is universal. The story of a myth is universal, rather than mainly historical, and it provides insight into ultimate questions. It is a literary form often used by writers for a specific purpose, which is to communicate in symbolic language a reality that transcends experience.

## Work with the Chart

Forms are names given to the different styles of writing found in the Bible. Descriptions tell the characteristics of the writing style.
Choose one form from the table below and find an example of it in one of the Old Testament books.

| Literary Forms in the Old Testament | |
|---|---|
| **Forms** | **Descriptions** |
| Origin Stories | An explanation of how something came to be |
| Short Stories | Stories told to show how virtuous people live |
| Psalms and Canticles | Poems and prayers that were once sung |
| Epic | A long poem offering the detailed history of a hero |
| Folklore | Old stories changed and expanded by biblical writers to teach certain truths about God |
| Parables | Short stories told to answer a question or illustrate a deeper point |
| Oracle | Words of wisdom or advice given by God |
| Narrative | The telling of a specific detail within a person's genealogy |
| Myth | A symbolic story that illuminates views of a particular people regarding the relationship between humans and the divine |
| Historical Accounts | Accounts written to reveal God's activity in the world |
| Apocalyptic Literature | A form of writing that describes the destruction of evil and the coming of God's reign |

# Old Testament Literary Techniques

**Imagery**  **Imagery** refers to the concrete sensory details that make a literary work vivid and realistic. For example, before David goes out to face the giant Philistine warrior Goliath, the Bible says that David ". . . chose five smooth stones from the wadi, and put them in his shepherd's bag" (*1 Samuel 17:40*). Concrete details such as these help a reader visually imagine scenes in the Old Testament.

▲ David and Goliath, 1860.

**BReak OPeN** *the Word*

**Recollection**  In small groups discuss your recollections of the story of David and Goliath. Record main points and present them to the class. Then, read the account of David and Goliath in 1 Samuel 17:1–54.

- List the concrete details given about each of the two combatants.
- Describe the outcome of the events recorded in this passage.
- How does your group's recollection of the story compare to the real thing?

The sun "comes out like a bridegroom from his wedding canopy, and like a strong man runs its course with joy" (*Psalm 19:4–5*).

### Faith Activity

**Techniques in Action**
Examine Psalm 104 and find examples of imagery, figures of speech, and parallelism. Make a three-column chart, listing the literary technique, the verse or verses in which it appears, and the role it plays in the meaning of the psalm.

**Figures of Speech** **Figures of speech** are comparisons that are meant to be taken imaginatively, rather than literally. For example, there is a saying: "Tinsel is really snakes' mirrors." We all know that snakes do not possess mirrors, so we recognize the saying as figurative language. Figures of speech are common in Old Testament poetry. The two most common types of figurative comparison are the *simile* and the *metaphor*. A simile is a direct comparison, using the words *like* or *as*. For example, the speaker in Psalm 19 says that the sun rising and moving across the sky "comes out like a bridegroom from his wedding canopy, and like a strong man runs its course with joy" (*Psalm 19:4–5*). Similarly, a metaphor indicates a likeness between two things without directly stating a comparison. For example, the speaker in a love poem such as the Song of Solomon might praise his beloved's beauty in this way: "Your eyes are doves behind your veil" (*Song of Solomon 4:1*).

**Parallelism** The most evident feature of Old Testament poetry is **parallelism**, which can involve the repetition of words and phrases, or the repetition of thought patterns. For example, in the famous passage in Ecclesiastes 3:1–8 on the cyclic nature of life, the parallelism here involves similar phrases being repeated: "a time to weep, and a time to laugh; a time to mourn, and a time to dance." In Psalm 137:5–6, the parallelism involves repeated ideas, rather than phrases: "If I forget you, O Jerusalem, let my right hand wither! Let my tongue cling to the roof of my mouth, if I do not remember you."

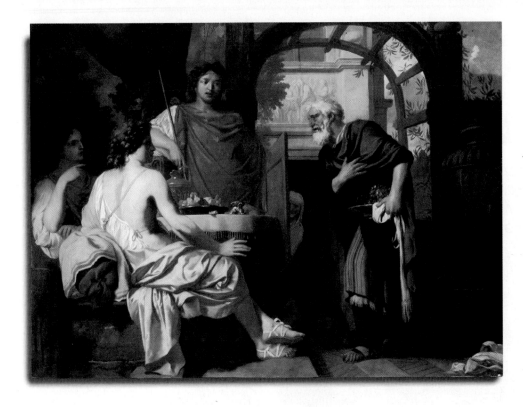

◀ Abraham and the Three Angels by Gérard de Lairesse.

**Irony**  **Irony** is a literary technique in which what is said or done is contrary to what is expected. For example, "I'd kill for a Nobel Peace Prize." Obviously, a person concerned with world peace would never kill. In the story in Genesis 18, three heavenly visitors announce to Abraham that he and his aged wife Sarah will have a son. Sarah, who is listening, laughs to herself at this improbable event (Sarah is well beyond child-bearing age). There follows a humorous exchange in which the Lord (one of the three) asks why Sarah laughed, she denies it, and the Lord insists that she did laugh.

**Symbolism**  Many stories in the Old Testament use symbolism, the representation of abstract or intangible things through symbols. In Western tradition, the snake is often a symbol for evil or trickery. In the temptation story in Genesis 3, the serpent is described as being "more crafty than any other wild animal" (*Genesis 3:1*). When God confronts the woman with her sin, she excuses herself by saying that the serpent tricked her. (See *Genesis 3:13*.) The symbolic nature of the serpent and its hostile relationship with humankind comes into play throughout classic literature. It is also important to note that in ancient times, some gods were represented as serpents. The Egyptians, for example, worshiped a serpentine god, Sito. Therefore, when Aaron's rod turns into a serpent and eats the Egyptian serpents, the situation represents the power of the God of the Hebrews over the Egyptian gods.

## Blessed Mother Teresa of Calcutta (1910–1997)

Mother Teresa believed that to change the world we must begin with our families: "Peace and war start within one's own home. If we really want peace for the world, let us start by loving one another within our own families."

Born into a working-class family in Macedonia to Albanian parents, Mother Teresa joined a missionary order and went to teach in the huge city of Calcutta in eastern India. There she saw the miseries resulting from the breakdown of the family and the inability of the society to provide the love and support families needed. Moved by the plight of the poor on the city's streets, she received permission in 1946 to leave her convent to study nursing and care for Calcutta's many sick and dying.

In 1948 Mother Teresa founded the Catholic Order of the Missionaries of Charity. She became an Indian citizen, and her order adopted the sari—the characteristic garb of Indian women—as the order's habit. Her order opened numerous centers to care for people who were blind, people with disabilities, lepers, abandoned infants and children, older people, and people who were dying. She eventually expanded her missionary order's work to countries throughout the world, and she was one of the pioneers in establishing centers to care for victims of AIDS.

Among the many notable aspects of her ministry was her care for the dying. In this work, perhaps the saddest cases she encountered were those who were dying who had been abandoned by their own families. Her concern was to bring comfort to these people by helping them to forgive those who had deserted them. In 1979 she received the Nobel Peace Prize. As Pope John Paul II observed after Mother Teresa's death in 1997, "She served all human beings by promoting their dignity and respect, and made those who had been defeated by life feel the tenderness of God."

The life of Mother Teresa is one of great care for others. Mother Teresa showed great mercy and love for her fellow people—all people, both great and small. She exhibited each of the seven key themes of Catholic Social Teaching through her ministry, most notably: Life and Dignity of the Human Person—in caring for the ill— and Option for the Poor and Vulnerable—by caring for those in one of the most poverty stricken areas of the world.

## Prayer

Begin by praying the Sign of the Cross.

**Leader:** O almighty and ever-present Lord and Father, we read how you always respected the covenant with the Israelites even when they had difficulty following it. We read how the first kings of the nation Israel were, at times, unfaithful and still you forgave them. Grant that we may always be true to the covenant and be close to you.

**All:** Amen.

**Leader:** Teach us your ways and guide us in your paths that we may always stay close to you and never depart from you.

**All:** Lord, teach us your ways.

**Leader:** Grant us humility and patience to journey with you and with our fellow members of your creation.

**All:** Lord, teach us your ways.

**Leader:** Reveal your Son and his loving teachings to us, so we may always live in love and unity with all your creation.

**All:** Lord, teach us your ways.

**Leader:** Pray in silence for yourself and your loved ones that you may stay true to the covenant…

**All:** (when finished) Amen.

**Leader:** Grant these and all blessings in the name of the Father, Son, and Holy Spirit.

**All:** Amen.

End by praying the Sign of the Cross.

1. What is another name for the Old Testament?
2. Which event stabilized the formerly tenuous relationship between Christians and Jews?
3. Describe the similarities between the Sabbath and the Lord's Day.
4. What does the term *canon* mean? How many books describe the canon of the Catholic Bible?
5. Detail the events of the first Passover.
6. How was the old covenant fulfilled? What is the new covenant?
7. What was the purpose of the Old Testament for its original audience?
8. What event does Chanukah memorialize?
9. Name an indirect source that may have influenced many Old Testament writers.
10. What are the four large groups under which the books of the Old Testament fall?
11. What are the main steps to understanding the author's intention in Old Testament writings?
12. Cite examples of three literary forms used in the Bible.

## Key Words

**Ark of the Covenant (p. 15)**—An ancient symbol of God's protection and presence; a portable throne in ancient times that included a seat that was believed to be occupied by God.

**biblical inspiration (p. 7)**—The process by which God the Holy Spirit assisted a human author in writing a book of the Bible.

**canon (p. 8)**—The official collection of inspired books of sacred Scripture that contain the witness and instruction for our faith.

**covenant (p. 7)**—A sacred agreement between God and his people.

**divine revelation (p. 7)**—God's communicating of himself and his plan of goodness throughout history.

**epic (p. 21)**—The detailed history of a hero who demonstrates bravery and wisdom and goes through a series of trials.

**Exodus (p. 9)**—Departure of the Israelites from Egyptian slavery under the leadership of Moses, who was led by God.

**figures of speech (p. 24)**—Comparisons meant to be taken imaginatively, rather than literally.

**folklore (p. 21)**—Composite of traditional customs, art forms, tales, and sayings preserved among a people.

**imagery (p. 23)**—Concrete sensory images that make a literary work vivid and realistic.

**irony (p. 25)**—A literary technique in which what is said or done is contrary to what is expected.

**matriarchs (p. 14)**—The founding mothers of Israel, particularly Sarah, Rebekah, Rachel, and Leah.

**monotheism (p. 9)**—The worship of one God.

**myth (p. 22)**—A symbolic story that illuminates views of a particular people regarding the relationship between humans and the divine.

**narrative (p. 22)**—A story that illuminates a detail within a genealogy.

**natural moral law (p. 10)**—The moral order that is part of God's design for creating the law that expresses the original moral sense, enabling people to discern good and evil through the use of reason.

**oracle (p. 22)**—Words of wisdom or advice given by God through a spokesperson.

**oral tradition (p. 17)**—Unwritten, memorized accounts of historical events and stories.

**origin story (p. 20)**—A story in which an explanation of how something came to be is given.

**parable (p. 22)**—A short illustrative story that teaches a moral or religious lesson.

**parallelism (p. 24)**—The repetition of words, phrases, or thought patterns.

**patriarchs (p. 5)**—The ancestors of the Israelites, particularly Abraham, Isaac, and Jacob.

**polytheism (p. 14)**—The worship of many gods.

**salvation history (p. 5)**—The saving action of God throughout human history.

**Ten Commandments (p. 7)**—The laws given by God to Moses that prescribe moral obligations for the Israelites as part of God's covenant with them.

## Teen to Teen

The United States Catholic Conference of Bishops has outlined seven specific areas of need that we should specifically direct our care. But these seven Catholic Social Teachings are just a starting point for what we must do to help our fellow men and women. If you could add another teaching that represents a serious need in your community, what would it be?

*"I would want to add a teaching about educating young children. The Catholic Social Teachings give a great place to start for people my age as well as adults, but young children need to be brought up with these teachings, too. That way they are living them all their lives.*

*Jill A.*

## Personal Challenge

"Our commitment to the Catholic social mission must be rooted in and strengthened by our spiritual lives. In our relationship with God we experience the conversion of heart that is necessary to truly love one another as God has loved us."

(*Sharing Catholic Social Teaching: Challenges and Directions,* USCCB, 1998.)

As Catholics we are called to love one another as God has loved us. There are many different ways in which we can help others and follow the New Commandment Jesus gave us. The United States Catholic Conference of Bishops has identified seven key themes that challenge us as Christians to live out the Catholic Social Teachings:

Life and Dignity of the Human Person
Call to Family, Community, and Participation
Rights and Responsibilities
Option for the Poor and Vulnerable
The Dignity of Work and the Rights of Workers
Solidarity
Care for God's Creation

These seven themes will be detailed in depth in each of the following chapters. Visit www.harcourtreligion.com for a link to the United States Conference of Catholic Bishops publication on Catholic Social Teachings and read the summaries for each of the key themes.

**Break Open the Word**

**Read Psalm 25:4,** the verse that opens the chapter. What aspects of the covenant does this verse convey? How can this verse shape and strengthen your spiritual life? Write four more lines to follow this verse that show your faith in the Lord.

**c. 2,000,000 B.C.**
First use
of stone tools

**c. 15,000 B.C.**
Lascaux cave
paintings

2,000,000 B.C.

1,500,000 B.C.

**c. 18,000 B.C.**
Ice Age

# The Creation of God's People

"All your works shall give thanks to you, O LORD,
and all your faithful shall bless you."

*Psalm 145:10*

## Chapter Goals

In this chapter, you will:

- examine the oral and written traditions of the Israelites and the authorship of the Pentateuch.

- discover the meaning and importance of the stories found in Genesis 1—11.

- consider the time period of the patriarchs described in Genesis 12—50.

- explore the stories of the patriarchs as faithful followers of the covenant.

- learn about Saint Francis of Assisi.

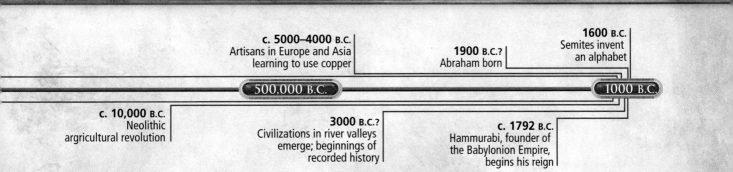

**c. 5000–4000 B.C.**
Artisans in Europe and Asia
learning to use copper

**1900 B.C.?**
Abraham born

**1600 B.C.**
Semites invent
an alphabet

500,000 B.C.  ·  1000 B.C.

**c. 10,000 B.C.**
Neolithic
argricultural revolution

**3000 B.C.?**
Civilizations in river valleys
emerge; beginnings of
recorded history

**c. 1792 B.C.**
Hammurabi, founder of
the Babylonion Empire,
begins his reign

# Understanding the Book of Genesis

As you read Genesis 1—11, you will learn about beginnings. Everyone has had a first day in a new place—at school, at a job, on a sports team. There will be many first days in your life because life is full of beginnings. The first stories in the Bible are attempts to explain big ideas—how the world began and the beginning of the relationship between God and his people. These stories are the first steps toward establishing the identity and purpose of God's people: From where did we come? How do we relate to God? Why are we here?

Many events described in the Old Testament seem unbelievable to us because they are unlike anything that occurs in our present-day surroundings. It is important to remember that what the Old Testament's stories teach us can be found at the heart of each story, not in the literal interpretation of the details. When we look closely, we see that while the circumstances may be different, the issues faced by humanity remain the same. Problems faced by our biblical ancestors are, in fact, very similar to modern-day issues we face today.

## Who Wrote the Pentateuch

It was very important to the Israelites to record events and deeds. Recognizing God's work in their history was central to the Israelites' identity as God's people. Their belief in one God set them apart from many of the people in the ancient Near East who worshiped many gods.

The oral tradition of the Bible is the first evidence of efforts to preserve and keep the stories of the Israelites alive. For many centuries, oral traditions continued to be passed down simultaneously with the drafting of written versions. Most ancient people could not read or write, and handwriting copies of the texts was very expensive and difficult. The written and oral traditions influenced each other and resulted in the interwoven text we have today.

If you were to follow the written path of the Old Testament, you would need a time machine to take you back and forth through different periods in history. The written history of the Old Testament is not linear. No single person sat down and wrote the Old Testament from start to finish. Authors wrote different books and different parts of the Bible at different times. Some of Genesis, the first book of the Bible, may have been written about 550 B.C., whereas parts of Exodus, the second book of the Bible, were probably written much earlier, in about 950 B.C. Biblical scholars often debate about these dates; no one is certain.

We call the first five books of the Bible—Genesis, Exodus, Leviticus, Numbers, and Deuteronomy—the **Pentateuch,** which in Greek means "five scrolls." The Hebrew word for the first five books is *Torah,* which means "the law." Most people once thought that Moses had written these books, but biblical scholarship shows that many authors wrote these books. The Pentateuch gives the religious history of humankind, particularly the chosen people, from the creation of the world to the death of Moses. The Pentateuch is often referred to in the New Testament as "the book of the law" (*Galatians 3:10*) or simply "the law" (*Romans 3:21*).

## The Four Traditions

God spoke through or inspired the human authors to compose the stories of the Old Testament. The many writers resulted in many different writing styles and forms in the Bible, composed over a period of several centuries. Each writer or school of writers contributed a piece or pieces in order to produce the story of God's people. For example, Genesis contains myths and poems, but it also contains other writing styles—narratives, speeches, hymns, parables, and historical accounts. Historians and scripture scholars continue to study the early texts today, like detectives trying to solve the mystery of authorship.

Most historians settle on four different traditions in the writing in the Pentateuch, but each of these traditions included many writers. Evidence of these four traditions can be seen in the other historical books, but the greatest influence is from the Priestly tradition, the final editors of the historical books.

In some cases, writers from two different traditions cover the same content or story. For example, in the first chapter of Genesis, we learn that man and woman were God's final creation. In the second chapter, we learn that God created trees and plants after creating man and woman. Thus, we find two creation stories in Genesis. When the writers and editors put the stories together, they chose to preserve material from both sources concerning the same story. The two accounts of the creation present different views, but the theology remains constant: God created the world.

### Faith Activity

**Verbal and Written Laws** Write a few sentences to explain when it is important to have written laws rather than verbal laws. When might you have trouble following laws that are only spoken laws? Why?

▼ Adam and Eve by Edward Munch.

The chart below shows how the different traditions, or sources, comprise the Pentateuch. You can refer back to this chart as you read the Pentateuch; however, remember that there is much disagreement among biblical scholars about the dates of different parts of these books. The dates given here are for your general reference. Remember that the larger the number B.C., the older the text is.

## Work with the Chart

**Continued Debate** Biblical scholars continue to debate about the traditions (sources) of the Pentateuch and when they were written. The "E" and "J" traditions are thought to have merged about 721 B.C. Some scholars believe the Priestly tradition was recorded about 587 B.C.

*What might cause archaeologists and scholars to continue to debate the sources of authorship?*

### The Four Traditions

| Tradition | Abbreviation | Period of Writing |
|-----------|--------------|-------------------|
| Yahwist | "J" | up to c. 950 B.C. |
| Elohist | "E" | up to c. 850 B.C. |
| Deuteronomic | "D" | up to c. 650 B.C. and later |
| Priestly | "P" | up to c. 550 B.C. and later |

**The "J" Yahwist Tradition (up to c. 950 B.C.)** To understand the text, scholars and historians study vocabulary, styles of writing, and common subjects or themes in the original writings. The Yahwist or "J" tradition source is notable for its use of the Hebrew name *Yahweh* for God.

- This tradition is called the "J" tradition after the German spelling of Yahweh, which is Jahweh. This name, Yahweh, has been thought to be too sacred to be spoken.

- At one time Yahweh was spelled "YHWH," without any vowels, since this is how the original Hebrew Torah was written.

- Centuries later, vowels were added. By this time, in speaking of God, people were substituting *Adonai*, meaning "Lord," for the name of God, so some of the vowels of the word *Adonai* were inserted in YHWH. Your Bible probably uses the word *Lord* throughout the Yahwist writing and in many other sections of the Pentateuch.

## Break open the Word

### The Yahwist Cycle

Give details of the Yahwist cycle, or pattern, of divine blessing, sin, punishment, and subsequent blessing or grace in one of the following scripture passages:
Genesis 2—3, the garden
Genesis 4, Cain and Abel
Genesis 5—8, the Flood
Genesis 9—10, Noah
Genesis 11, The Tower of Babel

Historians believe that the main "J" writer lived in the tenth century B.C., during the period of the United Kingdom of Israel, which was a proud time in Israel's history. People wanted a history written to show their national pride and national identity as God's special people. This writer created a foundational epic from earlier oral and written stories in order to express a national unity. The Yahwist writing includes the mythical stories of sin and God's promise.

Often, the "J" writers used **anthropomorphism**, the attributing of human characteristics to nonhuman realities, in describing God. For example, God speaks to the first man, the first woman, and the serpent. God also plants the garden in Eden. In the "J" tradition, God deals directly with humans in stories that are imaginative and dramatic.

**The "E" Elohist Tradition (up to c. 850 B.C.)** In this tradition, the writers refer to God as *Elohim*. This history was written during the time of the divided kingdom (c. 850 B.C.), and it is thought to have been created in the northern kingdom of Israel. After the northern tribes split from Judah in the ninth century B.C., the Elohist writers rewrote the traditional stories by focusing on the heroes from the northern tribes. The writers also included information about the covenant relationship, or pact, that God had made with his people. The Elohist writers presented God as a God of love, but also a God to be feared. He demands righteousness and justice, and his demands are not to be taken lightly.

The Elohist writers emphasize human responsibility, service, faithfulness, and obedience to God, and often include dreams or messengers. For the Elohist, God deals with humans indirectly and sends messages through angels and other means.

In parts of Genesis, the "J" and "E" traditions overlap; some scholars consider "J" and "E" traditions as one tradition, "JE." Another group of scholars believes that there was never an Elohist tradition, since the Elohist tradition is difficult to distinguish from the Yahwist tradition or the Priestly tradition.

► Moses Presents the Ten Commandments to the Israelites by Raphael, fifteenth century.

## Break open the Word

### Style and Focus
Find examples of the Deuteronomic writers' style (long sentences) and the writers' focus on law in Deuteronomy 12—26 and Judges 2:6–20.

## Faith Activity

### An Important Practice
Imagine you have been asked to describe an important practice of the Catholic Church that involves rituals and rules. How would you convey the reason the practice is important to our country as well as the manner in which the practice should occur? Choose one of these four traditions and describe the practice and its purpose in that style.

**The "D" Deuteronomic Tradition (up to c. 650 B.C. and later)** This tradition of writings includes updates to the religious laws from Moses' time. This was called the second giving of the Law—*deuteros* means "second"; *nomos* means "law." This tradition of writers encourages people to obey laws out of love, not just out of duty. The success or failure of Israel depends upon Israel's observance of the Law. These writings began around the eighth century B.C. and are noted for their long sentences.

Most of the subject matter focuses on the covenant with God. For example, Moses gives speeches to urge Israel to follow the Torah. Other than the Book of Deuteronomy, not a great deal of the Deuteronomic style exists in the Pentateuch. However, the Deuteronomic writers did work with the Books of Joshua, Judges, Samuel, and Kings.

**The "P" Priestly Tradition (up to 520 B.C. and later)** This tradition is found in the Book of Genesis and in other places in the Old Testament. These authors, actually a school of priests, wrote about God calling things into existence, and they gave other examples of the power of God's word. Many scripture scholars believe that in about 587 B.C. the writers of the Priestly tradition developed the final version of the Pentateuch. They sought to unify the people by documenting the laws of the cult, the religious practices during the time of Moses, and the Tribal Confederacy.

The priestly writers wrote the final version of the Pentateuch after the Israelites' return from the Babylonian Exile, during the period of resettlement and rebuilding. The Priestly tradition writers believed that the people had lost touch with their past, so the writers saw the need to purify religious concepts and revive basic religious practices. The stories in this tradition reteach the beliefs and practices that the people lost while they were separated and divided or exiled. The writers give special emphasis to subjects important to priests. For example, the Priestly tradition mentions special religious ceremonies and cultic rituals, such as circumcision.

# The Stories of Genesis

The stories presented in Genesis 1—11 are not history in the modern sense. This part of Genesis concerns a period of time called *primeval history*, which means before the recording of historical dates, facts, and events. The stories are not tied to any specific dates or periods. Primeval history, also called prehistory, records human events before the invention of writing. Historians believe many great accomplishments took place in ancient times. Archaeologists and scientists have found tools, paintings, fossils—even jewelry—from these ancient times. These historical artifacts represent evidence of this time period and help us piece together parts of early human history.

## Creation

The writers of the first chapters of Genesis accepted an enormous responsibility when they attempted to craft and document the origins of the world. Imagine yourself in their position: How do I explain the beginnings of the world? How will my reader understand the first humans and their actions? These writers worked to craft the centuries-old oral traditions into a written format that their readers could understand. If you were given the responsibility of explaining something that exists in the natural and historical world, where would you begin? For example, imagine writing an essay explaining what makes your family a family—is it the experiences you have, the home you maintain, or the emotions you share? How do you prove that you have a true family or that you truly love another person? Abstract concepts are difficult to explain.

The first story in Genesis describes the creation of the universe, a world that is all good. The writers of this story present an explanation of the universe that is neither based on historical events, nor is it based on facts of natural science. The writers present a religious truth, but not a literal truth, because the writers' focus is God—not cultures and peoples, and not nature or science. God creates the first man and woman in his image as beings with dignity and free will who share in creation through their own work. This creation story describes how humans entered the world in the image of God and how they have a special role to protect that world. For us, the religious truths presented here are more important than the literal accuracy of the details of the stories: God created the world and all that is in it; how he made it is not as important.

This story also sets up the relationship between God and his people. Human life is lived in relation to God and in relation to other people and nature. This is often described as "right relationship with God." *Right relationship* is an acknowledgment of the covenant and its giver. It is the way to live as prescribed by God—as first revealed when God spoke to the

## Faith Activity

**Original Goodness**
God created humans to live in happiness with him, to be in harmony with one another, and to respect and care for all of his creation. What are some ways people in today's world live up to God's original hope for us? What are some things you could change in order to live in happiness with God and harmony with your family and friends?

## Break Open the Word

**Compare Accounts**
With a small group, read Genesis 1:1–31 and Genesis 2:1–25. Make a list of what is similar between the two creation accounts and what is different. Share your list with another group. Then together decide what three important truths are communicated in both accounts.

first humans (according to the first creation story). God chose to have a special people and made a covenant with them. These were God's plans arising from his loving goodness.

**Religious Truth** The stories of creation are included in an ongoing debate about how to interpret the Bible. *Creationism* is the teaching of the origins of the world through a literal interpretation of the creation stories in the Bible. Evolution seeks to explain the origins of humans through science. Evolution and its understanding of the world and its understanding of the origins of humans relies on science, but it neither excludes nor contradicts religious belief in a Creator, in God.

The important truth in the Bible is religious truth. It is important to know that God made the world and all that is in it. It is less important from a religious point of view to know how he made it.

In reading the story of creation, we need to consider the culture, literary forms, and the authors' purpose in telling or writing the story. Our scientific knowledge was unknown and unimportant to the writers of the creation stories. Today, the natural sciences enrich our knowledge of the development of life on earth, the appearance of humans, and the structure of the world. For us, the physical origins of life on earth explained by the natural sciences are important, as is the religious meaning underlying the stories in Genesis.

# ANCIENT CREATION STORIES

Genesis contains myths about the origins of the Jewish people. These stories contain the explanation of the creation of the world. The most closely related myth to Genesis is a Babylonian epic called *Enuma Elish*. This is a collection of stories with answers to big questions about people and the world in which they live: From where did we come? Why is the world ordered the way it is?

The stories in *Enuma Elish* date from 2000 to 1800 B.C., although the only existing manuscripts date from after 1000 B.C. The myth includes the accounts of many gods competing for power with poison and monsters. In *Enuma Elish* the chief god, Marduk, defeats his enemies and establishes his power forever. Then he creates the world—one part to be high as the heavens, the other part to be Earth.

The originators of the first creation story in Genesis knew the Enuma Elish myth, but they told their story with details that fit their under- standing of the world and of God. The story- tellers wanted to explain the idea of creation dif- ferently. They focused on the God of order—not on chaos. God is the being who makes everything that is good: God commands and gives things their identity.

Those who told and wrote the stories in Genesis 1—11 also would have been familiar with the famous epic of *Gilgamesh*. This is one of the oldest and greatest epics in literature. The first records of this story were found on stone tablets, and copies of the story have been found in Syria, Turkey, and the Near East. The hero of the story is Gilgamesh, who was thought to be the king of Uruk, a city.

The story of Gilgamesh chronicles serious life-and-death problems of the hero. In the course of the story, Gilgamesh and his friend Enkidu (who is made from clay) triumph over the forces of evil—and often encounter dragons and monsters. In one section of the epic, the gods try to destroy humankind with a flood. The god of wisdom tells one of the characters, Utnapishtim, to build a large boat with which to carry the seed of all living things.

## Interpret the Art

**Gilgamesh and Creation** This is a statue of a hero, possibly Gilgamesh, taming a lion. The epic creation story of Gilgamesh includes many references to Gilgamesh dominating creation. *In which verse in Genesis does God grant Adam and Eve the same dominion?*

# The Fall

In the highly symbolic story of the fall, the first humans eat the forbidden fruit, and, in this act, they disobey God. They choose to replace God with themselves. After they sin, they feel naked and ashamed, and they hide. This first sin has effects for the remainder of human history.

What is sin? **Sin** is something spoken, a deed, an attitude, or a desire contrary to God's law. Sin is an offense against reason, truth, and right conscience; it is failure in genuine love for God and neighbor. In this story, sin is the act of the will in revolt against God. The first humans break their relationship with God by disobeying him and by acting contrary to his law. The fall is the first sin of human history, or the **original sin**. This initial sin is an act of arrogance that leads to other sins. But God does not abandon his creatures; rather, he offers them the promise of salvation after the fall from grace.

**Cain and Abel** Chapter 4 of Genesis introduces the reader to a second story about sin. Cain and Abel, two brothers, are the sons of the first humans. The brothers represent the two major occupations—farming and herding. Cain works in the fields. Abel is a shepherd. They make sacrificial offerings to God, but Abel offers the finest and fattest of his flock, while Cain offers less than the best produce. God is pleased with Abel's offering. This angers Cain, and he murders Abel. Cain's sin is a personal sin. This story presents an important point: The first sin is followed by a continuation of sin, and within a short time, other forms of **personal sin**, the free choice of humans to disobey God, enter the world—the murder of a brother being one of the worst. The original sin affects the children of the first humans and, indeed, of all the human family.

## Interpret the Art

**Cain and Abel** Italian Baroque Painting Depicting Cain Killing Abel and Cain's Banishment. This painting shows Cain fleeing into the wilderness after the killing of Abel. God "marks" Cain so that whomever kills him will be cursed sevenfold.
*How can God's actions be interpreted as an indictment on capital punishment?*

# Noah and the Great Flood

As the descendants of the first humans grew in number and disseminated into other regions, the sins of humankind continued. God saw the evil humans had done and was sorry that he had created humankind. In the story of Noah, God chooses a good and honest man. God intends to destroy every living thing he has made, but he will save Noah and his family. He gives Noah instructions for building a giant ark, stocking it, and preparing for the flood. Noah's acceptance of God's instructions is an act of faith, and in this he becomes an example for all of us.

▲ Noah's Ark by Malcah Zeldis, 1978.

## scripture

"Then God said to Noah and to his sons with him, 'As for me, I am establishing my covenant with you and your descendants after you, and with every living creature that is with you, the birds, the domestic animals, and every animal of the earth with you, as many as came out of the ark. I establish my covenant with you, that never again shall all flesh be cut off by the waters of a flood, and never again shall there be a flood to destroy the earth.' God said, 'This is the sign of the covenant that I make between me and you and every living creature that is with you, for all future generations: I have set my bow in the clouds, and it shall be a sign of the covenant between me and the earth. When I bring clouds over the earth and the bow is seen in the clouds, I will remember my covenant that is between me and you and every living creature of all flesh; and the waters shall never again become a flood to destroy all flesh. When the bow is in the clouds, I will see it and remember the everlasting covenant between God and every living creature of all flesh that is on the earth.'"

*Genesis 9:8–16*

After forty days and nights of rain, every living thing on earth is destroyed, except for Noah and the others on his ark. Noah builds an altar in thanksgiving to God.

God's covenant with Noah foreshadows God's covenant with the Israelites through Abraham. As events transpire in the Bible, the Israelites experience God's covenant over and over again. Christians believe God's covenant with his chosen people was fulfilled in Jesus and extended to all people.

In the fall and flood stories, the reader may notice that God punishes sinners justly, yet he continues to love and care for them. The first humans must leave the garden, but God provides clothes when they find they are naked. Cain is forced to wander, but God marks him to keep him from harm. God gives Noah instructions for building the ark, thus ensuring that not all humans will die. These are all examples of God's mercy. God enters human history and saves them through his mighty deeds. These occurrences of divine intervention make up salvation history.

▲ The Tower of Babel by Pieter Brueghel the Elder, 1563.

## The Tower of Babel

The last story in primeval history (Genesis 1—11) is the story of the Tower of Babel. The descendants of Noah multiply and settle in a plain. Once again, humans commit personal sins and the effects of the original sin continue. According to the story, the people of the different nations try to build a tower to the heavens—a tower that will make them famous. But because of their sins, these people seek power without recognizing or remembering their relationship with God. God sees that this is not good and can see that there will be no limit to what the people will want. God halts the efforts of the people of different nations by confusing their speech.

The building of the Tower of Babel is a **social sin**, a collective, societal act or sign that society has distanced itself from God. The people build a tower independent of God. *Babel* is similar to the word "babble" in English, which you may know means to talk nonsense or to make no sense. In the end, the story gives people an explanation for the many languages they hear and the inability of different nations to work together because of their language differences.

### Faith Sharing

**Keeping God's Covenant** With your group discuss examples of people keeping God's covenant by honoring him, other people, or his creation. Then come up with some examples of the effects of original sin. During the week, review newspapers, watch the news, or read the news online to find specific examples of both. How can your choices lead you to either keep God's covenant or to fall to temptation and to turn from God? Discuss your findings and your thoughts with your group.

# Protecting the Environment

According to the Genesis story, humans were given dominion over all the animals of the earth. Further, they were expected to take care of the garden in which God placed them. From earliest times, the earth's resources have seemed unlimited and there for the taking by humankind. Having dominion has been interpreted to mean control and consumption.

Today we have a different picture. Nature deserves respect as God's creation. Natural resources—animal, vegetable, and mineral—are limited, and many are nonrenewable. Many animal and plant species are endangered, and many have become extinct. Fossil fuels are being exhausted. Air and water are polluted. Natural cycles have been disturbed. In many regions, environmental deterioration has resulted in poverty, hunger, thirst, illness, and even death.

For the sake of future generations enjoying the riches of the earth, we must change our habits. Pope John Paul II made it clear that our individual lifestyles and national patterns of consumption must change.

"Modern society will find no solution to the ecological problem unless it takes a serious look at its lifestyle. In many parts of the world, society is given to instant gratification and consumerism while remaining indifferent to the damage which these cause. . . . The seriousness of the ecological issue lays bare the depth of our moral crisis. . . . Simplicity, moderation and discipline, as well as a spirit of sacrifice, must become a part of everyday life, lest all suffer the negative consequences of the careless habits of a few." (*The Ecological Crisis: A Common Responsibility,* #13).

Each of us should accept responsibility for life, respect the environment, and be caretakers of the world that God created. The choices made by our parents and grandparents have affected our present. The choices we make today will affect the future. Every time we are involved in a give-and-take situation with the environment, there is an effect. Actions have consequences; some consequences are good and some consequences are not so good.

## Faith Activity

**What the Bishops Say** Research the U.S. Catholic Bishops' statement *Renewing the Earth: An Invitation to Reflection and Action on Environment in Light of Catholic Social Teaching* (1992). What does this document teach about how attention to environmental issues affects our neighbors in our community and the world? If the bishops' statement were being written today, how might it be different? Explain your answer.

# The Time of the Patriarchs

## Break open the Word

**Important Figures in Genesis** In pairs or small groups, read the following passages and Identify the important figures and their roles in salvation history.

Genesis 11:27—12:3

Genesis 13:14–17

Genesis 17:1–8

## Faith Activity

**Friend in Faith** Think about someone who has been a model of faith for you, someone who has helped you have faith and understand what God wants for you and from you. If you can, write that person a letter thanking him or her for going before you in faith.

The Book of Genesis provides stories of important figures in the early stages of our religious history. This biblical **genealogy**, or account of our ancestry, shows the succession of generations and illustrates that we are descendants of many faithful followers of God. The genealogies found in Scripture show how the Israelites saw themselves as being related to the surrounding peoples. They gave the Israelites a stronger sense of God's **providence**, or divine guidance and care, and of their rootedness, which was important during the Exile when the Pentateuch was probably written.

One of the prominent figures in our biblical genealogy is Abraham. He was the first great male leader, or **patriarch**, of the people of Israel. Leadership passed from Abraham to his son, Isaac, to Isaac's son, Jacob, and then to Jacob's sons and grandsons. The heads of the twelve tribes of Israel—the twelve male descendants of Abraham—are also considered patriarchs. The female ancestors of Israel, such as Sarah, Rebekah, Leah, and Rachel, are called matriarchs. Studying the narrative of Abraham and his family provides us with a sense of our spiritual ancestry and an example of the power of faith.

## The Middle East at the Time of the Patriarchs

The Genesis storytellers included details that are based in historical fact. Ancient ways of life, laws, and some events are similar to those in the stories of the patriarchs. It was later during the monarchy and exile that the stories were written down and compiled. A major concern of this later time was God's promise of a land for his people, and this is reflected in the stories.

The story of Israel's patriarchs begins in earnest with Abraham and includes his son and grandson, Isaac and Jacob, and Jacob's sons and grandsons. Twelve of Jacob's male descendants (ten sons and two grandsons) were the basis for the twelve tribes of Israel. These tribes were more like clans than political units. These tribes, and other peoples that populated the ancient Middle East, are known ethnically as Semites. This group included many different peoples—Arameans, Assyrians, Babylonians, Canaanites, and Phoenicians.

**Geography** You have learned that Genesis 1—11 is rooted in prehistory. Genesis 12—50 has a more historical basis in the sense of being related to the known history of the ancient Middle East. Unlike the primeval history in Genesis, considerable archeological evidence exists that, in part, connects the history of the ancient Middle East to the time of the patriarchs. The geography of the ancient Middle East contains an area known as the Fertile Crescent that stretches roughly from modern-day Iraq into Egypt and contains the Tigris, Euphrates, and Nile rivers. These rivers provided a source for agriculture and trade, which enabled cities to grow and civilizations to flourish. Remains of these cities exist today. Customs and laws of the ancient Middle East are evident in the story of the patriarchs.

The city of Ur is the birthplace of Abraham. Ur was in Sumeria in the far eastern fertile plain between the Tigris and Euphrates rivers. The kingdom of Ur collapsed when the people who dwelled in the mountains above the Mesopotamian plain, the Elamites, attacked. For 200 years, struggles persisted among the smaller city-states in Mesopotamia, then the Amorites, a semi-nomadic Semitic group, came into power. During this period, known as the First Babylonian Dynasty, the center of power transferred from the northern city of Mari to Babylonia.

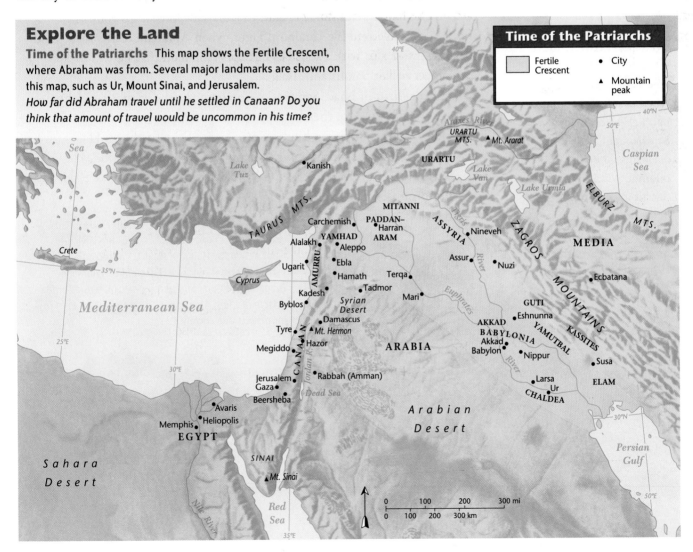

## Explore the Land

**Time of the Patriarchs** This map shows the Fertile Crescent, where Abraham was from. Several major landmarks are shown on this map, such as Ur, Mount Sinai, and Jerusalem.
*How far did Abraham travel until he settled in Canaan? Do you think that amount of travel would be uncommon in his time?*

**Time of the Patriarchs**

- Fertile Crescent
- • City
- ▲ Mountain peak

**Laws & Customs** Hammurabi, this dynasty's greatest king, reigned from 1792 to 1750 B.C. Around this time, the epics *Enuma Elish* and *Gilgamesh* were written. The Code of Hammurabi—a collection of laws that encompass economic, family, criminal, and civil matters—was also compiled. The Code of Hammurabi was based on laws and customs that had existed in Sumerian communities for centuries. As has been noted, it is likely that this code provided the basis for parts of the Israelite law codes.

Ancient inheritance laws and the custom of sacrifice are crucial in the stories of the patriarchs. Ritual sacrifice was an integral part of the Sumerians' religion, and they would offer sacrifices of grain, animals, or wine to the god or goddess particular to their city-state. For the patriarchs, sacrifices intended for God were considered an act of petition or thanksgiving and had the power to bring two parties together.

**Privileges under the Code** In order to ensure the survival of the tribe, it was not an unusual custom in the ancient Middle East for a man to take a second wife, or a female servant—a *concubine*—to bear children. The Code of Hammurabi states that a wife may give her husband "a maid-servant as wife." The writers used these details for the story of Abraham, Sarah, and Hagar. (See *Genesis 16:1–4.*) When Abraham's wife, Sarah, is unable to conceive, she offers her slave, Hagar, to Abraham. Hagar gives birth to Ishmael, who is loved by Abraham. Later, when Abraham learns from God that Sarah will also bear a son, God assures Abraham that he will bless Ishmael as well as Sarah's son, Isaac.

After the birth of Isaac, Sarah asks Abraham to send Hagar and Ishmael away. Abraham does so, thereby placing Isaac in his predetermined role in salvation history and giving him the privileges of the firstborn. Hagar, in her distress at having been cast out, is prepared to abandon her child. However, an angel of God speaks to her and promises that God will make of Ishmael a great nation. Muslims believe that they are the descendants of Ishmael and, therefore, believe themselves to be children of Abraham and the great nation promised by God.

### Faith Activity

**Conflict in the Middle East** Find a current article about political, ethnic, or religious tensions in the Middle East by looking in a newspaper, in a magazine, or on the Internet. Write an essay describing one conflict in the area. Include a description of the groups involved in this conflict.

## Connect to the Past

**The Code of Hammurabi** The Codex Hammurabi, Babylonian inscription, 1790 B.C. This codex represents a small portion of the laws and rules set out by Hammurabi that guided criminal, civil, and social conduct in ancient Babylonia. *Research the Code and determine which rules or laws exist in modern American society and which exist in modern Israeli society.*

Mesopotamian law codes gave protection to children born of a female servant. Hammurabi's code states that if a man's wife bears children, yet the man "adopts the slave's children, then his household shall be divided evenly between the children of both." Another ancient custom and law present in the story of the patriarchs is that the firstborn son of a man's first wife is to be the principal heir. Hammurabi's code states that the household will be evenly divided among children after the "firstborn son receives the preferential share." This custom has been known to cause conflict. The Old Testament writers dramatize such a conflict when Isaac's intentions for blessing his firstborn son, Esau, are upset by Jacob's trickery.

Genesis tells the stories of Abraham. Sometime in the second millennium B.C., Abraham led his people westward out of Ur in Sumeria and eventually settled in Canaan, later called Palestine. The Hyksos people who came from Palestine were a predominantly Semitic people who entered Egypt about 1720 B.C. This immigration occurred after the Thirteenth Dynasty, during which there had been civil unrest in Egypt while provincial governors vied for the pharaoh's throne. The immigrants took control and the Egyptians eventually became subject to the Hyksos. Slavery was common in the ancient Middle East. In fact the Code of Hammurabi has a section of laws dedicated to stealing or housing others' slaves, the consequence for runaway slaves, and the reward for returning slaves.

The writers of the Old Testament included historical details and were influenced by existing laws and codes. Floods, drought, and irrigation were ever-present factors in the way of life in the ancient Middle East. When the seven-year famine occurred in Egypt, the Egyptians fared well, as did the Hebrews. However, some historians say that the pharaohs of the Eighteenth Dynasty expelled the Hyksos and enslaved the Hebrews.

# THE TWELVE APOSTLES & THE TWELVE TRIBES

As a faithful Jew and a son of the house of David, Jesus must have had an understanding of the significance of the number twelve in the life of God's people. Of greatest significance are the twelve sons of Jacob and the twelve tribes of Israel.

At the beginning of his public ministry, Jesus called ordinary men to follow him: fishers, tax collectors, brothers, and friends. From among his disciples, Jesus chose twelve to preach, teach, and heal in his name. These were the Apostles, whom many knew simply as *The Twelve*.

The Gospels according to Matthew, Mark, and Luke list The Twelve, and all three Gospels refer to them as Apostles.

Simon, whom Jesus named Peter

Andrew, brother of Simon Peter

James, son of Zebedee

John, brother of James

Philip

Bartholomew

Matthew

Thomas

James, son of Alphaeus

Simon the Cananaean, also known as
    the Zealot

Thaddaeus

Judas Iscariot, who betrayed Jesus

▲ Stained glass window in Galway that depicts Jesus and the twelve Apostles.

In Matthew 19:28 and Luke 22:30, we read of Jesus' assurance to his Apostles that they will sit on the twelve thrones and judge the twelve tribes of Israel. In these references, it seems that Jesus considers his Apostles the foundation of the new Israel—what would become his Church.

# The Story of the Patriarchs

Genesis 11:27—50:26 establishes critical foundations about the ancestors of Israel and the dynamic relationship between God and his people. In these stories, God makes a covenant with Abraham in which he promises a home for his people—the Promised Land. Although God's people struggle with their faith, the obligation of the covenant is with God alone. God puts no obligations on the people, and Abraham does nothing to merit God's promises. God will make Abraham's descendants a great nation, even if they don't deserve it.

## Abraham

The first story of Abraham (See *Genesis 12—15.*) illustrates promise and faith. This story represents the cycle that is common to all of the Abraham stories. In all circumstances, even when people fail, God is always faithful to his promise. As you read, follow the events as God fulfills his promises to Abraham and Sarah.

You will note that names are very important and significant. Abram is changed to Abraham when he is assigned a mission—to be "the father of a host of nations." Sarai, too, receives a change of name—to Sarah.

Abraham and his wife Sarah do not have any children. Among these nomadic people, barrenness was considered a terrible curse. Children were a sign of God's blessing. God visited Abraham and told him to move to a place where God would bless him and make of him a great nation.

This is an example of God's covenant with his people, his promise to give them land—a home and a great nation. Abraham responded to the covenant with faith and obedience to God's commands and promises. He shows his trust in God by leaving his home and setting out for the unknown, relying on God to be faithful to his promises to him.

### Faith Activity

**Name Changing** Why do you think God changed Abram's and Sarai's names? Peoples' names have significance in many ways. When are names given to people? When do people choose to change or add to their names? What significance does the action of naming have in each case? What does your name mean to you?

### scripture

"After these things the word of the LORD came to Abram in a vision, 'Do not be afraid, Abram, I am your shield; your reward shall be very great.' But Abram said, 'O Lord GOD, what will you give me, for I continue childless, and the heir of my house is Eliezer of Damascus?' And Abram said, 'You have given me no offspring, and so a slave born in my house is to be my heir.' But the word of the LORD came to him,

'This man shall not be your heir; no one but your very own issue shall be your heir.' He brought him outside and said, 'Look toward heaven and count the stars, if you are able to count them.' Then he said to him, 'So shall your descendants be.' And he believed the LORD; and the LORD reckoned it to him as righteousness."

*Genesis 15:1–6*

**God's Covenant** Read Genesis 15, the story of God's covenant with Abram. List the terms of the covenant as described there. Then put the terms in your own words. Compare your list and your rephrased terms, to that of your classmates.

**Abraham's Willingness** In small groups, discuss the moving story about Abraham's willingness to sacrifice Isaac. What in the story surprises you? Why is this considered the ultimate test of a person's faith in God? In smaller ways, our faith is tested, too. What are some ways your faith is stretched and you trust in something that is unknown?

When Abraham and his nephew, Lot, decide to part, their choices for land in Negeb influence their individual futures. Abraham and his people ventured into the land of Canaan while Lot settled in the city Sodom—a place we associate with many sinners. Lot did not choose the Promised Land.

God and Abraham renew their covenant in a sacrificial ceremony. Abraham takes a cow, a female goat, and a ram, and he cuts them in half. He then kills a turtledove and a pigeon—leaving them whole. These acts were ritual demonstrations of Abraham's obedience to God. After Abraham made his sacrifices, God restates his promise to Abraham.

## The Sons of Abraham

Sarah believed that she was too old and, therefore, unable to bear children. Following the custom of the time, she gives her servant Hagar to Abraham and tells him to treat Hagar as his wife. Hagar bears Abraham a son, named Ishmael, who eventually had many descendants. This son is not the child of the Promised Land, however. God promises a son for Abraham and Sarah. God continues to make this promise to them even though Sarah and Abraham deny the possibility that it will happen. Sarah's harsh treatment of Hagar raises an important point for later generations. Even though the nearby Arabic tribes are closely related to the Israelites, they have not received the same promise. God does protect and bless them, however, which illustrates a part of the promise to Abraham: Through him all nations will be blessed.

The history of God's promise continues in the event of Isaac's birth when, against all odds, Sarah and Abraham have a child. Their God is indeed powerful. But in the very next chapter of Genesis, Chapter 22, another important story is told. Abraham's faith is tested when he believes God is commanding him to sacrifice his son by Sarah. This was to be the promised son, but Abraham prepares to sacrifice him. The storytellers fill the story with great tension by emphasizing the lengths to which Abraham is asked to go to show his devotion. At the last moment, God intervenes and stops Abraham. Abraham proved his faith in God by his willingness to sacrifice Isaac. This story also presents a strong statement against human sacrifice, which was practiced by some groups in the Middle East. Abraham's unselfish faith in God—his willingness to give up his son of the promise at God's command—is a sacrifice in itself.

**Isaac** God guides a servant's journey to find the right woman for Isaac. The search leads the servant to Rebekah. Rebekah gives birth to Jacob and Esau, who were known to constantly battle with each other. Even in the womb, they struggled with one another. The storytellers included this to foretell the struggle between the nations in later stories. In Genesis 32, you will see that Jacob is given the name Israel. In Genesis 36, Esau is Edom—the enemy of Israel. The descendants of Jacob represent God's plan to create a people great in number, such as that of a nation.

▲ Peregrination of the family of Abraham by Giovanni Benedetto Castiglione.

 **BREAK OPEN** *the Word*

**Isaac and Rebekah** In Genesis 26:6–11, Isaac asks Rebekah to call herself his sister, not his wife, while they are in Gerar. This parallels his father's request of Sarah in Genesis 12:10–20. Compare the two passages. What might be the significance of this parallelism?

**break open**
*the* **Word**

**Struggle Between Siblings** Read Genesis 21 and 1 Samuel 16. Compare the two passages. How do these stories present the struggles between siblings? What makes the two stories similar?

**Jacob and Esau** You have read about the importance of inheritance laws and the rights of sons. In Genesis, Jacob manipulates his brother Esau, who is the elder of the two sons, out of his birthright. Then their father, Isaac, is fooled and gives his blessing to Jacob—instead of Esau.

These are the first of many examples of Jacob's trickery. Remember the overall purpose in these stories is to show God's promise despite all obstacles. Try to imagine Israel's ancestors telling these stories around a campfire. They probably presented Jacob as someone who outsmarted the others and wins. The younger son obtains the privileges meant for the older son. The writers present exciting events to keep the stories lively and to show God at work in human history, unhampered by the customs of the time.

The story of the struggle between Jacob and Esau is one of many elder son/younger son stories in the Old Testament, such as Isaac in Genesis 21, and David in 1 Samuel 16. The Israelites viewed themselves as the struggling "younger son". They had few natural advantages compared to the nations around them, and they became successful only because of God's blessings. The trickery of Jacob is also a reminder that the chosen people are not blessed because they are better people than their neighbors are. They are blessed because God has chosen them.

▲ Isaac and Jacob by Jusepe de Ribera, 1637.

As the situation develops, Isaac cannot take back his blessing, but he does give Esau another blessing. The storytellers portray Rebekah as being aware of the continuing struggle between her two sons and of God's plan for Jacob. Her actions on behalf of Jacob point to her willingness to be a part of God's plan to fulfill his promise.

On his journey to Haran, as he escapes his brother's fury, Jacob has a dream and is visited by God. God restates the covenant he made with Abraham: "I am the LORD, the God of Abraham your father and the God of Isaac; the land on which you lie I will give to you and to your offspring" (*Genesis 28:13*). Repeatedly in the stories of the patriarchs, the writers remind the reader of God's promise in the midst of struggle. The faith of each patriarch in turn is tested.

After Jacob marries and becomes quite wealthy, he decides to leave Haran. He sends a message to Esau that he is on his way home and that he hopes to reunite with him, but he still worries that Esau will kill him. On his journey, he meets a man and wrestles with him until daybreak. In this struggle, Jacob demands that the man bless him. Through his blessing, it becomes clear that Jacob has been struggling against God. The man gives him the name Israel, and Jacob walks away from this struggle limping. The name change marks Jacob's prevailing in his struggle; so, too, will the people of Israel prevail in their struggles.

The writers included several details in this story that call forth different interpretations. God is a mystery even when he reveals himself to humans. Jacob has two struggles—one with his brother and one with God. Jacob had been away for fourteen years and did not know what he would find upon his return. He returns to the promise that was given to his father and his grandfather a long time ago—the Promised Land and a great people, God's chosen people.

## Interpret the Art

**God's Promise** Jacob Wrestling with the Angel by Eugene Delacroix, 1850. Jacob wrestles with a strange man and subdues him. Jacob then discovers this man is an angel and demands a blessing. The angel blesses him, and gives him a change in name to Israel.

*Find another example of a name change signifying an event of great importance and compare it with Jacob's story.*

**Break open the Word**

**Famine and Slavery**
Read Genesis 37—50. Find three examples of the writers using famine and slavery to add drama to the stories of Joseph.

**Joseph** Joseph, the favored son of Jacob, endures mistreatment at the hands of his brothers and, in Egypt, by Potiphar's wife. These are difficult challenges, but God is with him and ensures his favor with the chief jailer. Inspired by God's support, Joseph shows great courage, honor, and integrity. The stories of Jacob that conclude the Book of Genesis illustrate the truth that despite evil acts on the part of humans, God is present to them with loving goodness. He works for the good in all things. Joseph gains the favor of the pharaoh by his good deeds in prison and by interpreting the pharaoh's dreams. As a result, Joseph becomes the governor of Egypt.

In Egypt, Joseph's brothers are brought in to see the governor. Joseph knows them, but they do not recognize him grown up and in a position of power. Joseph puts one brother, Simeon, in jail and tells the brothers that they must return home to get their youngest brother. Upon hearing this story, Jacob is distraught over the loss of yet another son. Jacob reluctantly sends his other favorite son, Benjamin, as a sort of sacrifice to save Simeon. This story recalls the sacrifice Abraham attempted to make of his son Isaac.

Finally, when all of his brothers are together, Joseph reveals his identity and tells them that God has drawn good out of their horrible acts against him. This is a tale of reconciliation, as Joseph reunites with his family. Joseph interprets their past actions (just as he interpreted dreams)—all the past events were part of God's plan to save his people from famine. In this story Joseph also brings security and prosperity to his people. The blessing of God is shown through the perseverance and strength of Joseph. Despite the acts against him, Joseph obeys God and keeps the covenant.

The stories of the patriarchs remind us that God is our ultimate goal and that our faith in God is well-placed because he is Truth and Love. The generations described in the stories in Genesis are examples of how God perpetuates the covenant with every generation. God gifts us with faith to respond to him.

▶ Joseph and the Pharaoh, c. 1300–c. 1330. Clockwise from the top left, Joseph is interpreting the pharoah's dream, the pharoah is dreaming of the fat and thin cattle, Joseph with his brothers, and a man orders a second man to be bound and led away.

# LIVING OUT PROMISES

The stories of the patriarchs contain many examples of faith being tested by the trials of life. By prevailing through these hardships, each of the men and women in the stories fulfilled a specific role in their families and communities. Abraham was the father of a people; Sarah was the mother of Isaac—the child of the promise, and Rebekah helped Jacob gain his father's blessing and escape to Haran. God chose these people, communicated to them, and made a covenant with them. His promise and covenant with them continued through the ages because God is faithful even when his people fail. God always calls his people back to a covenant relationship.

Who makes promises to you? Your family members make a promise to love and care for you. To whom do you make promises? You have an obligation to care for and to love your family as well. If you contribute to your household, you are building up your family. Small sacrifices might come in the form of giving up something that you would enjoy in order to help someone in your family. In such ways you live in faith.

Like the patriarchs, you face small and sometimes large tests of your faith every day. If someone hurts you verbally or physically, you face a decision. You can respond in a hurtful way, or you can find a peaceful way to end the conflict. At these times, it may be difficult to see how to maintain right relationships with God and with

other people. Remember the example of those who have gone before you. Abraham trusted God and was blessed with a destiny beyond his wildest dreams. Joseph was faced with the misdeeds of his brothers and Potiphar's wife. He showed strength and integrity and persevered on a path that put him in the position of saving his family.

People in your school and community make promises to you, but sometimes the fulfillment of these promises is difficult to notice. More often you may simply neglect to acknowledge how well people keep their promises. Teachers make a commitment to you and to your education. Firefighters, police officers, and hospital workers make commitments to care for the community within which they work. Maybe your friends do special things for you when you have a tough day. When you live within the laws and customs of your community and help other people become their best, you are living the commitment to which you are called. You are being faithful.

 *Faith* **Activity**

**Promises You Make**  What kinds of promises do you make to your family and friends? How do you keep those promises? Do you sometimes fail to keep them? How do others respond if that happens? How does keeping your promises and being faithful help you to be a member of your family and community?

## Saint Francis of Assisi (1182–1226)

Francis was born in Assisi in central Italy and was christened Giovanni, or John. His name was changed later to Francesco, or Francis, likely because of his father's extensive trade with France.

His father was a wealthy cloth merchant, and young Francis lived a privileged life because of his family's wealth. However, a series of life-altering experiences—being a prisoner of war, becoming ill, and encountering a leper—led him to a conversion experience.

At San Damiano church, Francis experienced a call from God to repair the Church. Misunderstanding the call, Francis first removed and sold goods from his father's warehouse to finance the renovation of the church of San Damiano. When brought to trial for the theft, Francis publicly disrobed and returned his clothes to his father, understanding at last that God was calling him to reform God's Church.

Francis no longer cared about what he wore or ate, and he focused on following Jesus' example of trusting that God would provide for him. Francis was frequently seen begging for food in the streets, visiting the sick in hospitals, preaching a message of peace and purity in the streets, and caring for those neglected by others. Francis lived a simple life, and he was not afraid to work with people, in the fields, and among the animals.

In 1210 Francis' community journeyed to Rome to seek the approval of Pope Innocent III for its religious rule and order. In an age of wealth, Francis favored the poor; in an age of crusades and battles, he stood for nonviolence and peace; in an age of male domination, he helped form a religious community for women, the Order of Saint Clare.

Francis spent a great deal of time out of doors as a result of his chosen lifestyle of poverty. A passage from Scripture that inspired him was "Consider the lilies of the field, how they grow; they neither toil nor spin, yet I tell you, even Solomon in all his glory was not clothed like one of these" (*Matthew 6:28–29*). He respected water because it was used in Baptism, rocks because God was called The Rock, and trees because Christ was crucified on the wood of a tree.

Saint Francis of Assisi was a man who had a profound love for God's creatures. In art, he is often depicted with arms outstretched preaching to the birds and beasts of the forest. Francis regarded both animate and inanimate realms of creation as members of his family. And as Francis regarded all creation as his family, so should we, too. The Care for God's Creation calls us all to respect life in all its forms.

## Prayer

Begin by praying the Sign of the Cross.

**Leader:** O peace-loving Lord, we seek to be more like your Son, Jesus. Let us remember to care for all of God's creations—whether they are animate or inanimate—and show our love for them however we can. Teach us to follow in the footsteps of your Son and in the footsteps of Saint Francis of Assisi. Saint Francis lived a life of peace and dedicated love for all your creations, O Lord. Be with us as we pray the prayer that faithfully captures the wisdom of Saint Francis.

**Leader:** Lord, make me an instrument of your peace;
where there is hatred, let me sow love;
where there is injury, pardon;
where there is doubt, faith;

**All:** Lord, make me an instrument of your peace.

**Leader:** where there is despair, hope;
where there is darkness, light;
and where there is sadness, joy.

**All:** Lord, make me an instrument of your peace.

**Leader:** Grant that I may not so much seek
to be consoled as to console,
to be understood as to understand,
to be loved as to love;

**All:** Lord, make me an instrument of your peace.

**Leader:** for it is in giving that we receive,
it is in pardoning that we are pardoned,
and it is in dying that we are born to eternal life.

**All:** Lord, make me an instrument of your peace. Amen.

End by praying the Sign of the Cross.

## Review

1. What are the four traditions that comprise the Pentateuch?

2. What is the main focus of each of the traditions?

3. Who was originally thought to be the author of the Pentateuch?

4. What is the common theme found in the stories of Cain and Abel, Noah, and the Tower of Babel?

5. Describe the differences between the creation story of Genesis, of Gilgamesh, and of *Enuma Elish*.

6. Why does Cain murder Abel? What important point is presented in this story?

7. List the twelve Apostles. What were some occupations they held before becoming Apostles?

8. What is the Code of Hammurabi? On what is the Code of Hammurabi based?

9. Why does Abraham send Ishmael and Hagar away? What happened to Ishmael?

10. How does Abraham prove his faith in the Lord?

11. What were the names of Isaac's two sons? How is God's covenant represented in the stories of each of Abraham's two sons?

12. How does Joseph bring security to his people? In spite of the terrible things that happened to Joseph, why was he kind to his brothers when they are brought before him?

## Key Words

**anthropomorphism (p. 35)**—The attributing of human characteristics to nonhuman realities.

**genealogy (p. 44)**—An account of ancestry.

**original sin (p. 40)**—The human condition of the need for salvation based on the first humans' choice to disobey.

**patriarch (p. 44)**—Male leader of a family or tribe.

**Pentateuch (p. 33)**—The first five books of the Old Testament; the Torah.

**personal sin (p. 40)**—The free choice to disobey God; to do something that is the opposite of the good.

**providence (p. 44)**—Divine guidance and care.

**sin (p. 40)**—Something spoken, a deed, an attitude, or a desire contrary to God's law.

**social sin (p. 42)**—A collective, societal act or sign that society has distanced itself from God.

## Teen to Teen

In many suburban and urban areas there are programs that communities institute to help the environment. Among them are recycling programs, adopt-a-road programs, river and lake clean ups, and carpool programs. Are there any programs like this in your community that you or your classmates participate in? If not, are there any that you can help get started in your community?

*"My friends and I joined the Environmental Club at my school this year. With our membership fees we adopted a small stretch of road by the school, and we clean it up once a week after our meetings. There are a lot of us, so it doesn't take much time. We noticed that after a few months of cleaning up the road has been much, much cleaner on a daily basis. We plan on doing some fundraisers to take part in more road adoptions near our school so that the whole area will be clean and beautiful."*

*Tarik L.*

## Personal Challenge—Care for God's Creation

"On a planet conflicted over environmental issues, the Catholic tradition insists that we show our respect for the Creator by our stewardship of creation. Care for the earth is not just an Earth Day slogan, it is a requirement of our faith. We are called to protect people and the planet, living our faith in relationship with all of God's creation. This environmental challenge has fundamental moral and ethical dimensions that cannot be ignored."
(*Sharing Catholic Social Teaching: Challenges and Directions,* USCCB, 1998.)

Have you ever bent down to pick up a stray candy wrapper? Or picked a can out of a stream or lake? These are small steps in the right direction if we are to be stewards of God's creation. As the U.S. Catholic Bishops point out, not only must we protect the planet, we must also protect our fellow humans. Sending food, water, supplies, or money to people who have recently suffered through a natural disaster shows great care and compassion. But do not forget to send aid to those who are in need at all times. Consider the life of Saint Francis of Assisi when sending aid. Saint Francis willingly gave all he had for the sake of people, animals, and the environment around him.

### Break Open the Word

**Read Psalm 145:10,** the verse that opens the chapter. Consider all the works that the Lord has created on earth and the heavens. This verse speak of the glory and splendor of the kingdom, as well as the wondrous deeds God has done for us. How can we learn from this verse to better care for all that God has granted us?

**c. 1850–1700** B.C.
Famine drives Israelites
to Egypt

**c. 1550–1200** B.C.
Egyptian rule over Canaan

**c. 1290–1224** B.C.
Reign of Ramses II;
expansion of Egyptian territory

1900 B.C.

1500 B.C.

**c. 1792–1750** B.C.
Hammurabi rules;
Hammurabi's Code produced

**1333–1323** B.C.
King Tutankhamen rules

**c. 1290–1250** B.C.
The Exodus: Moses leads the
Israelites back to Canaan

# God's People and the Promised Land

"You let people ride over our heads;
we went through fire and through water;
yet you have brought us out to a spacious place."

*Psalm 66:12*

## Chapter Goals

In this chapter, you will:

- learn about the remaining books of the Pentateuch and the various peoples who came to be the Israelites.
- examine the Israelites' search for the Promised Land.
- analyze the Israelites' settling of the Promised Land.
- explore Israel under the judges.
- learn about Saint Joan of Arc.

**c. 1187–1156** B.C.
Reign of Ramses III

**994–962** B.C.
David is king
of all Israel

1000 B.C.

500 B.C.

**1020–1000** B.C.
Saul rules the
people of Israel

**c. 586–587** B.C.
Temple at Jerusalem
destroyed by Babylonians

# Who Were the Israelites?

▲ Moses Smashing the Tables of the Law by Rembrandt Harmensz van Rijn, 1659.

## BREAK OPEN the Word

### The Ten Commandments

Working in a small group, read Exodus 20 and Deuteronomy 5, and compare the two versions of the Ten Commandments. Explain how such a comparison supports the existence of different sources.

The remaining four books of the Pentateuch have great focus on cultic material such as genealogies and laws. They tell the story of how the people of Israel became an independent nation and the gradual development of the Israelites' faith in God. These adjustments were not always easy to make. But God was present in the formation of the people of Israel, helping to guide them along the way within the stories of the remaining four books.

In these books, you will find great drama, a hero, and the real goal of God's people—to keep their part of the covenant so that they will reach and occupy the Promised Land. This text also includes richly detailed stories (some taken from Egyptian and Palestinian folklore). A rod changes into a serpent, bread falls from the heavens, and other signs of God's action are shown within the stories of the remaining four books.

## The Books of Moses

Genesis is the first book of the Pentateuch; Exodus, Leviticus, Numbers, and Deuteronomy are the other books. The dominant theory of biblical scholars is that the Pentateuch is a composite record of many generations of oral narrators and that it was written by many people. Each writer provided a different link in the chain that would become the record of the spiritual history of Israel.

The different schools, or traditions—Yahwist (J), Elohist (E), Priestly (P), and Deuteronomic (D)—were discussed in depth in Chapter 2. At one point, Moses was thought to be the sole author of the Pentateuch. But scholars and historians then pointed out parts of the narrative that speak of Moses in the third person, as "he" or "Moses", and the fact that some of the events in the Pentateuch occur after the death of Moses. When scholars were able to isolate sections and verses that came from the four sources, they provided an explanation for why there are two versions of a number of items within the Pentateuch. For instance, there are two versions of the Ten Commandments; one in Exodus 20 and one in Deuteronomy 5. Regardless of the source, however, Moses is at the heart of the Pentateuch. Thus, the books are considered the "five books of Moses."

**Legal Documents** The Pentateuch is a combination of narratives and law codes which cover time from the creation of the universe to just after the death of Moses. The Pentateuch also provides instructions regarding the punishments for certain crimes. In a religious society, religious laws included civil laws. Civil laws governed private citizens and were mandated by the nation or state. People who did not obey the laws were punished accordingly. It was once believed that the laws found within the Old Testament were unique in ancient times. However, the discovery of legal documents such as the Code of Hammurabi and Hittite laws proves that law codes were not uncommon during that time. The writers of the Old Testament would have been familiar with the language used in other covenants. Therefore, the discovery of Hittite laws and others like it help us place the covenant between God and the Israelites under Moses in its historical context.

## The People of the Exodus

Historical evidence shows that during his reign, Pharaoh Ramses II (c. 1290–1224 B.C.) undertook an ambitious construction program. A new palace and two new cities were constructed during his reign. Besides needing labor for construction, the building program required other workers to produce food for the laborers and to maintain the pharaoh's armies. Slaves made up this extensive workforce. In the Exodus story, Ramses II is believed to be the pharaoh who enslaved the Israelites, as well as the one on whom the ten plagues were inflicted.

These plagues, and how Moses led the enslaved Israelites out of Egypt, is in part a fulfillment of the promise that is made by God to Abraham, Isaac, and Jacob, which is recounted in Genesis. However, no mention of the Exodus or the enslavement of the Israelites exists in Egyptian historical records. The Book of Exodus is probably based on a real escape from slavery in Egypt, but it most likely involved a relatively small group of people unworthy of mention in the official records. The numbers in Exodus 12:37–38 are surely an exaggeration typical of the epic style. Nonetheless, archeological and textual evidence—from texts other than the Bible—convey a history of who the Israelites were.

▲ Ramses II seated on his throne, 1304–1237 B.C.

# Explore the Land

**Exodus and the Fight for Canaan**  This map shows the probable route that Moses and the Israelites took on their long quest that ended in the Promised Land, Canaan.

*How many square miles would you estimate were controlled by ancient Israel? How many square miles does the present state of Israel control?*

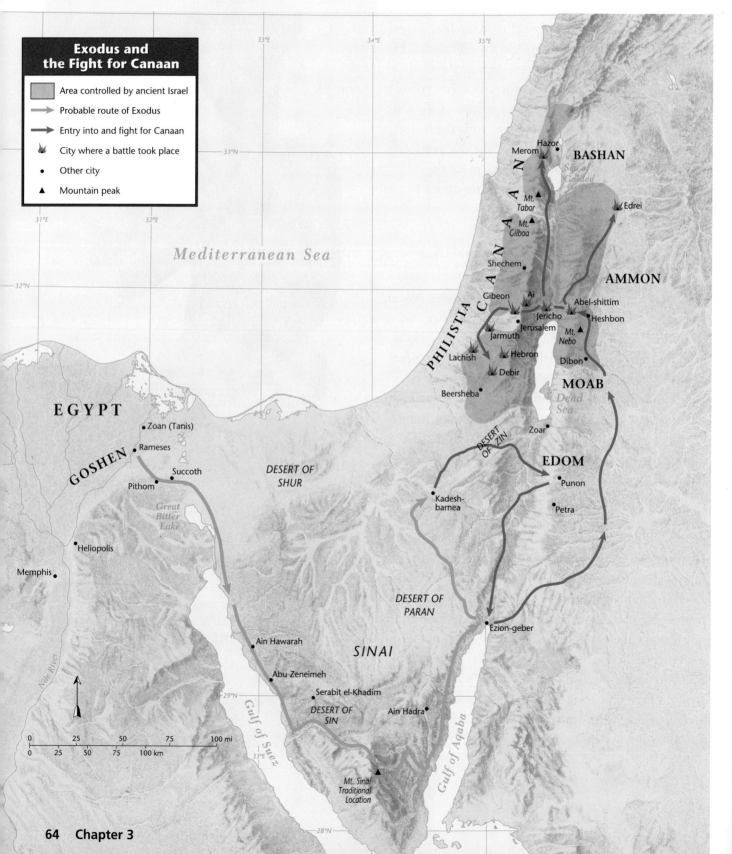

## Exodus and the Fight for Canaan

- Area controlled by ancient Israel
- Probable route of Exodus
- Entry into and fight for Canaan
- City where a battle took place
- Other city
- ▲ Mountain peak

Mediterranean Sea

BASHAN
Hazor
Merom
*Sea of Galilee*
Mt. Tabor ▲
Edrei
Mt. Gilboa ▲
Shechem
AMMON
Gibeon
Ai
Abel-shittim
Jericho
Heshbon
PHILISTIA
Jerusalem
Mt. Nebo ▲
Jarmuth
Lachish
Hebron
Dibon
Debir
MOAB
Beersheba
*Dead Sea*
Zoar
C A N A A N
DESERT OF ZIN
EDOM
EGYPT
Zoan (Tanis)
Rameses
GOSHEN
Succoth
Pithom
DESERT OF SHUR
Punon
Heliopolis
*Great Bitter Lake*
Kadesh-barnea
Petra
Memphis
DESERT OF PARAN
Ezion-geber
Ain Hawarah
SINAI
Abu Zeneimeh
Serabit el-Khadim
DESERT OF SIN
Ain Hadra
*Nile River*
*Gulf of Suez*
*Gulf of Aqaba*
Mt. Sinai Traditional Location

0   25   50   75   100 mi
0   25   50   75   100 km

The people who eventually became the Israelite nation probably included more than the descendants of the slaves who left Egypt. Quite likely, the **Israelites** who became a great nation included Canaanites, hapiru, shasu, and Sea Peoples, along with the original Hebrews.

**Canaanites** Scholars agree that the land of Canaan was a place populated by many different peoples, including the group that would come to be known as the Israelites. Canaan, which later became part of Israel, was under Egyptian rule for many years (c. 1550–1200 B.C.). During this time, Canaanite kings were often at war with one another, and there were many rebellions against Egyptian authority. A war with the Hittites, shortly after 1300 B.C., weakened the Egyptian empire, and a time of transition began in Canaan. During this transition, the many peoples who had settled in Canaan began establishing themselves as independent ethnic groups, rather than remaining part of the composite ethnic group known as the Canaanites. The culture and religion of the Canaanites had a large influence on all of the cultures that developed from it.

**Hapiru** Historians have noted a connection between the word *Hebrew* and a people called the **hapiru**—one of the peoples who inhabited Canaan. The hapiru are mentioned in the Amarna letters, written in the fourteenth century B.C. and excavated in Egypt in the late 1800s. The letters, written by Canaanite kings under Egyptian rule, record the kings' complaints about the hapiru who raided their villages and fields. The Canaanite kings, who paid tribute to Egypt, asked for protection from these people. In the letters, the hapiru do not seem to be an ethnic group, but rather people living on the fringe of society. One letter refers to the hapiru as former slaves. Therefore, the hapiru may have been ancestors of the **Hebrews**, peoples enslaved in Egypt who eventually became the community known as Israel.

A number of references to marginal or fringe groups appear in the Old Testament. In Genesis 23:4, Abraham says to the Hittites, "I am a stranger and an alien residing among you. . . ." Deuteronomy 26:5 presents Jacob as "a wandering Aramean" who "went down into Egypt and lived there as an alien, few in number, and there he became a great nation, mighty and populous." Verses such as these provide support for the theory that the hapiru were ancestors of the Hebrews. The term *Hebrew* was used to distinguish the early Israelites from other peoples of the ancient Near East, particularly the Egyptians and the Philistines.

**Shasu** Still other groups of people who dwelled in Canaan may have been related to the Israelites of Exodus. The nomadic shasu's flocks frequently disturbed Egyptian land. Egyptian records mention that the shasu were sometimes taxed, but more notably the military records indicate that they were enslaved—like the Israelites.

**Faith Activity**

**Diversity in Your Life**
Reflect on the different backgrounds of the people who make up your class, school, parish, and regional communities. What are some of the similarities and differences in the people who are part of your every-day life? How is your social environment different or similar to that of the ancient Canaanites?

## Faith Activity

**Working Together** In small groups, make a list of countries today where two or more groups of different religions or ethnic backgrounds are having difficulty working together as one nation. For each example, name the core of the problem and discuss possible solutions.

**Sea Peoples** Historians also recognize that the different groups that migrated from the Aegean Sea, who were collectively known as the Sea Peoples, may also be part of the combination of peoples who came to be known as the Israelites. In a mortuary temple of Ramses III, who reigned c. 1187–1156 B.C., there is a mural, or relief, of battles being fought with the Sea Peoples on sea and land. Accompanying these images are women, children, and oxcarts—an indication the Sea Peoples were not just an invading army, but people coming to settle in Canaan. The Israelite tribe of Dan may have come from the Denyen, one of the Sea Peoples' groups. On the other hand, another group, the Philistines, became a major enemy of Israel.

**Israel: A People** Canaan was certainly a place of mixed peoples. It was also an area that included different ways of life—farming, herding, fishing, and trading—in rural areas and cities. Despite the different lifestyles in Canaan, a similar material culture is found there, indicating that different groups shared similar traits. At the end of the Iron Age, the stability of Egypt came to an end and, in the highlands above Canaan, a decentralized, tribal society came into existence—Israel. The first appearance of the word *Israel* occurs in writing on a stele (a stone with carved writing) telling of the military victories of Merneptah, king of Egypt. The stele reads, "Israel is laid waste, his seed is not." This is significant because the word *Israel* is written with the Egyptian symbol meaning people, not country or city.

**Jews** Hebrews, Israelites, and Jews share a common history. Hebrews are the ancestors of the Israelites. The term *Jew* comes from the word *Judah*—one of the twelve tribes of Israel. Judah was also the name of an independent kingdom that formed after the nation of Israel split in two (922 B.C.). Babylonians destroyed Judah around 587 B.C. and took its people as prisoners. After the Babylonian Exile, these former prisoners returned to what was the land of Judah. They became known as **Jews** from that point in history.

# JEWISH PEOPLE TODAY

From the time of the Diaspora, approximately 2,000 years ago, until 1948, Jews had no country of their own and, therefore, formed communities worldwide. Today, Jews live in Europe, Asia, India, Africa, Australia, and the Americas. The Jewish religion is a living faith; it is a continuing religion and people. The essential element of the Jewish faith is the belief that Jews are God's chosen people. God spells out this relationship in Exodus 19:5: "Now therefore, if you obey my voice and keep my covenant, you shall be my treasured possession out of all the peoples." God is faithful and has not revoked his covenant with his chosen people. Likewise, his people understand themselves to be obligated to keep his law, an obligation reinforced throughout Jewish liturgy.

The covenant of God was made with the descendants of Abraham. For this reason, the Jews see themselves as a nation, sharing a particular ethnic heritage, as well as a faith. Although marrying outside the faith is discouraged, doing so will not cause a Jew to fall out of the covenant relationship with God. He or she has to deliberately convert to another religion in order to step outside the bounds of the covenant.

## Orthodox and Non-Orthodox Judaism

Within the Jewish faith, there are many different branches—Orthodox, Hasidic, Conservative, Reconstructionist, Reform, and Humanistic. The separation of Jews into these groups is based on differences in interpretation of the Scriptures and the daily application of them.

Even within these branches, there are many differences in belief and practice between individuals.

Orthodoxy is a strict, traditional observance of the law in which emphasis is placed upon diligent study of the **Talmud**—a collection of Jewish oral law and commentary. Hasidism is a branch of Orthodoxy in which personal piety and spiritual devotion are stressed, and worship is more mystical and joyful.

Conservative Judaism maintains that while some biblical traditions are permanent, others were meaningful during a certain period of time. Followers of Conservative Judaism believe in responding to the changing times. For example, as of 1983, women can be ordained as Jewish teachers and spritual leaders known as **rabbis** within the Conservative movement. Reconstructionism, which grew out of Conservative Judaism, retains many traditional practices but does not impose a belief in the divine revelation of the Scriptures.

The Reform movement called for dispensing with what followers considered to be outdated rituals in order to focus on a more purely ethical way of life. Reform Jews believe in the equality of men and women and many Reform temples have female rabbis. Humanistic Judaism developed out of the Reform movement and, like Reconstructionism, believes that Judaism is a human creation, rather than a religion inspired by a divine being. Humanistic Judaism embraces a variety of beliefs and practices.

# The Life and Times of the Israelites

To understand who the Israelites were, it is important to look at the history of the ancient Near East as revealed through archeological and textual evidence. Scholars use textual and archeological evidence to construct a picture of the ancient Near East.

- Archeological evidence can provide a record of material culture. Material culture includes artifacts like pottery or tools, as well as food and refused remains found in a collection of garbage or in a fire pit.

- Textual evidence provides other sorts of information, such as dates. The purpose for which a text was written should be kept in mind. For example, information could be presented in a particular way to portray a person or event in a particular light.

**Near Eastern Customs** The Books of Exodus, Leviticus, Numbers, and Deuteronomy exhibit evidence of how the Israelites and their way of living were a part of the Near Eastern world and its people, but also unique to it and distinct from the Near Eastern world.

Scholars believe that **Passover**, the event of the Israelites being "passed over" by the angel of death, actually coincided with a spring festival that had its roots in a shepherding culture. This celebration would have coincided with either the annual spring change of pasture or the sacrifice of the firstborn animal to ensure fertility. Other evidence is that the spring festival, like Passover, would occur in the evening at the time of the full moon. The Seder meal celebrated during Passover recalls the entire Exodus event. All the groups who became part of Israel adopted the Exodus group's story as their own. They may have all formerly been under Egyptian rule, so the story of escape from Egyptian oppression would have appealed to them. In a sense, it was also their story.

## Connect to the Past

**Vessels** Both of these vessels are from between the fifteenth and thirteenth centuries B.C. The bull shaped vessel was created by a Jewish artisan and represents the most sacred animal that a Jewish high priest could sacrifice. The other vessel was created by the Phillistines and was likely used for transporting water. *What vessels are used in modern Christian masses? What are the vessels typically made of?*

Another characteristic of ancient Near Eastern culture in the Old Testament is the existence of prophets. **Prophets** were not uncommon in the ancient Near East, and they were considered divine messengers who would either hear, see, or dream a message from God. In a shrine dating back to the eighth century B.C., we find a reference to the prophet Balaam. Balaam may have been a famous folk figure who is then described in Numbers as a charismatic prophet who spoke oracles from the God of the Israelites. In Numbers 22—24, Balaam refused to curse the Israelites.

**A Unique Culture** If characteristics of the Israelites were common among other peoples of the Near East, what made them so unique? The answer is found in the Israelites' beliefs about themselves and their relationship with God.

- The Israelite idea that God was a personal God, an autonomous creator, and not a part of a pantheon of gods was a radical belief that developed gradually. This was an expression of monotheism.

- Most ancient Near Eastern peoples believed in polytheism, with a few exceptions. One such exception was the Egyptian pharaoh, Akhenaton, who insisted that Aton, the sun god, was the only god to be worshiped. Akhenaton also outlawed **idolatry**, the honoring and revering of a creature in place of God.

It's important to remember that the biblical authors recorded the story of the Exodus long after the event itself. The understanding of God as the only God was much further developed than it was at the time of the event. Not until later was the God of the Israelites understood as the one and only God of all.

The Israelites also uniquely believed that God himself, rather than a leader guided by a divinity, issued justice in the form of covenants. In the ancient Near East, covenants were a common way for people to make agreements among themselves as well as between a powerful monarch, like Egypt, and a vassal, such as a city-state in Canaan. In contrast to the covenant with Abraham, which was an unconditional promise, the Israelites' deity now assured protection and favor, but the Israelites' obedience was required in return. In the covenant through Moses, God dictated laws that covered all relationships. For instance, in the Ten Commandments, the first three commandments are laws concerning the Israelites' relationship with God, while the other commandments dictate people-to-people concerns—such as how family life should be structured and what property rights people have.

**Faith Activity**

**Catholic Uniqueness**
Work with a partner. Make a list of the beliefs, practices, and rituals that identify Catholicism. Be sure to think of the cultural religious celebrations that remind us that the Church is universal.

# Work with the Chart

God's commands to Moses dealt with the relationship between God and his people and among his people. The Ten Commandments continue to guide the lives of Jews. These commandments play a role in Catholic morality, too.

*With a partner discuss each commandment and it's meaning. Make a list of ways society poses challenges to living the first five commandments.*

## The Ten Commandments

| Commandment | Meaning |
| --- | --- |
| I am the LORD your God: you shall not have strange gods before me. | Place one's faith in God alone.<br>Worship, praise, and thank God the Creator.<br>Believe in, trust, and love God. |
| You shall not take the name of the LORD your God in vain. | Speak God's name, and that of Jesus and the saints, with reverence.<br>Don't curse.<br>Don't call on God to witness to a lie. |
| Remember to keep holy the LORD'S DAY. | Gather to worship at the Eucharist.<br>Rest and avoid unnecessary work on Sunday. |
| Honor your father and your mother. | Respect and obey parents, guardians, and others who have proper authority. |
| You shall not kill. | Respect and protect your life and the lives of others. |
| You shall not commit adultery. | Be faithful and loyal to spouses, friends, and family.<br>Respect God's gift of sexuality and practice the virtue of chastity.<br>Learn to appreciate the gift of sexuality by practicing self-mastery. |
| You shall not steal. | Respect the things that belong to others.<br>Share what you have with those in need. |
| You shall not bear false witness against your neighbor. | Be honest and truthful.<br>Avoid bragging.<br>Don't say untruthful or negative things about others. |
| You shall not covet your neighbor's wife. | Practice modesty in thoughts, words, dress, and actions. |
| You shall not covet your neighbor's goods. | Rejoice in others' good fortune.<br>Don't be jealous of others' possessions.<br>Don't be greedy. |

**Wanderings** During their wanderings in the desert, the Israelites complain of food and hunger, stating that things were better in Egypt. The people rebel against Moses and lack faith: "Is the LORD among us or not?" (*Exodus 17:7*). God, hearing the Israelites, time and time again, provides food, water, and protection, again fulfilling his promise to be their God. The people at first did not recognize the manna from heaven as food. They asked, "What is it?" (In Hebrew this question is *man hu*.) Moses answers that it is "the bread which God has given to you to eat." The "bread" is a symbol of God providing for his people. Christians see the manna as a prefiguring of the Eucharist, the "Bread of Life."

The manna that God provided for the Israelites may have been similar to a substance that is considered a delicacy today by the Bedouin people, a nomadic group that roams the wilderness and desert areas of the Middle East. This delicacy is a sweet-tasting insect secretion that drops to the ground from the leaves of tamarisk thickets. The manna becomes firm in the cool night air and must be gathered early in the morning, or it will melt in the sun.

### Faith Activity

**There for You** When are some times that you have felt God was there for you, guiding you, listening to you, directing you to believe, giving you hope? How can you be like God to others, supporting and encouraging them and helping them to persevere?

### Interpret the Art

**Manna from Heaven** The Israelites Gathering Manna, Ercole de' Roberti. God set out very strict guidelines for how the Israelites were to use his gift of manna. Many of these guidelines were analogous to the Ten Commandments. *Which commandments did the Israelites fail to follow with regards to the manna?*

▲ The Golden Calf by the followers of James Jacques Joseph Tissot.

**At Sinai** After three months of wandering, the people arrive at the foot of Mount Sinai where God calls Moses to him. Amid flames and thunder, God delivers to Moses the Law, the requirements of the covenant, including the Ten Commandments. The Israelites become afraid to approach, so Moses assures them that it is their God who has come to them, instructing them how to be free of sin. Yet the people stay away. In Exodus 24, we read about the ratification of the covenant, which symbolized the union of God and his people.

## scripture

"Moses came and told the people all the words of the LORD and all the ordinances; and all the people answered with one voice, and said, 'All the words that the LORD has spoken we will do.' And Moses wrote down all the words of the LORD. He rose early in the morning, and built an altar at the foot of the mountain, and set up twelve pillars, corresponding to the twelve tribes of Israel. He sent young men of the people of Israel, who offered burnt offerings and sacrificed oxen as offerings of well-being to the LORD.

Moses took half of the blood and put it in basins, and half of the blood he dashed against the altar. Then he took the book of the covenant, and read it in the hearing of the people; and they said, 'All that the LORD has spoken we will do, and we will be obedient.' Moses took the blood and dashed it on the people, and said, 'See the blood of the covenant that the LORD has made with you in accordance with all these words.'"

*Exodus 24:3–8*

Moses returns to the mountain and stays for forty days. During this time, the Israelites demand that Aaron make a god for them because Moses has not yet returned. Aaron has an idol made, and the people worship it. Once again, like Cain, the son of the first humans, the chosen people rapidly turn away from God and choose to sin. Upon arriving at this scene, Moses is furious and throws the tablets with the commandments to the ground, breaking them. Moses asks those who are true followers of God to separate themselves from the idolaters. God threatens to destroy the Israelites, but Moses intercedes, and the Ten Commandments are written again by God. Interspersed into the end of Exodus, God explains further how he should be worshiped and who will be in charge of the worship.

**Covenant with a People** According to the epic, the Israelites become a people at Mount Sinai. This is the most significant event for the Israelites. Through Moses, God gives the Law and ratifies the covenant with sacrifice and a meal. This expression of the covenant, made with the nation rather than with an individual (Abraham), has requirements, and the Israelites must keep the moral and ceremonial laws as a condition or demand of the covenant. God, of course, will always be faithful; he will always be their God, and he will always call them back to the covenant when they fail.

The covenant made at Mount Sinai is not the first expression of the covenant that God made with his chosen people. Recall God's covenant with Abraham in Genesis.

| Compare the Covenants | |
|---|---|
| God promises a great nation and people to Abraham, but he does not place any requirements or obligations on his people. | At Mount Sinai, God fulfills the promise of a nation to the entire people—not just to one individual. |
| God does not include punishment as a consequence for failing to meet the covenant. | The covenant at Mount Sinai is the same covenant made with Abraham, but it establishes obligations and unifies the Israelites. |

# Leviticus

As a people, the Israelites represent a social unit or community. The priestly writers believed the Israelites as a community needed laws to live together and in relationship with God. This book contains cultic laws written by the Levites—the priests—during and after the return from exile. After Moses, the priests were all from the family of Levi (son of Jacob). The priests served as mediators between God and his people, performing sacrifices to make the people's gifts holy for God. The priests also served as teachers, oracles, and judges to settle disputes.

While the Book of Leviticus is a continuation of the listing of God's laws and commandments for the Israelites, it is basically a handbook for worship. The book portrays the priests as being instructed by God through Moses to tell the people of Israel all of God's statutes. For example, explanations are given for how relationships between people should be conducted and what to do when a sacrificial animal is slaughtered. The final section adds additional instruction about offerings and religious vows. Leviticus, as a whole, stresses the centrality of formal worship in the Israelites' spiritual and moral lives.

## Numbers

The Book of Numbers deals with the social organization of Israel based on the twelve tribes. In Chapter 2, you learned that the descendants of Abraham came to be organized into the twelve tribes. This is the book that sets up that definition of the people and contains "numbers" listing the numbers of Israelites.

The Book of Numbers also explores the journey of the Israelites from Mount Sinai to the Promised Land and explains how God sustains them on their journey. God gives instructions to Moses regarding what is expected of the people when they reach the Promised Land. When the Israelites continue to act rebelliously, God still continues to protect them in the wilderness. While wandering, they encounter enemies whom God helps them conquer. Numbers concludes with a summary of the laws.

## Deuteronomy

Deuteronomy means "second law." The theme or main message of the Book of Deuteronomy is that the people will succeed or fail depending on how they follow the Law. This book contains material repeated from other books, and Moses, called a prophet in this book, tells his story before he dies. He gives insight into the events of Exodus and explains why the Israelites did what they did. Moses is told that God will send another leader to the people to lead the people into Canaan; this man is Joshua.

In Deuteronomy, those who compiled the Law present Moses as telling the people of Israel all of God's statutes, ordinances, and codes, and then writing them down. Presented in this way, the Law gains great authority among the people. Moses, the prophet, is greater than any king. The Israelites would certainly become corrupt without these statutes. So, on the authority of Moses, God tells the people why he chose the Israelites—not because they were fewest in number, but because he loves them. The people are called to follow the laws not just out of duty, but out of love for God.

**BREAK OPEN** *the* **Word**

**Obligations** Read Exodus 34:4–11, in which the covenant is made, and Deuteronomy 30:15–20, in which the covenant is renewed. Compare the description of the covenant in each passage and the obligations it places upon the people of Israel.

# Immigration and Liberation

Immigrants to the United States often feel as if they are in a wilderness. The culture, language, and laws are all new. In the nineteenth and twentieth centuries, many immigrant groups coming to the United States established organizations to make their new home more like their old home. They set up their own banks and formed social clubs where they could meet and speak their primary language. Their churches were frequently their neighborhood centers for worship, social services, and social life. They found ways to assimilate, or become part of their new home, but they held onto the ideals from their country of origin that they felt were important to maintain.

Moses was an Israelite, but he was raised as an Egyptian. He was different from the people around him. He faced many trials as he tried to follow God's commands. Often his people complained and rebelled against him, not trusting him to be their leader. He found strength in God to carry out his mission.

Unfortunately, many people today experience isolation or oppression. Exodus represents the ultimate liberation from oppression. We have had many other examples of liberation from oppression in modern times. Martin Luther King Jr. was a model of liberation for African Americans in the United States. Nelson Mandela and Stephen Biko were leaders in South Africa. Daw Aung San Suu Kyi, a nurse, also liberated people from oppression. Her efforts for political reform in Myanmar (formerly Burma) resulted in her being awarded the Nobel Peace Prize in 1991.

The Catholic Church also has a continuing commitment to achieve racial justice worldwide. In July 1999, the National Catholic Gathering for Jubilee Justice met with 3,300 participants from around the world. In one workshop, groups met to address racism and its harmful effects. On a local level, the gathering called for the Church to address racism within Catholic institutions—including schools. In all schools (Catholic and non-Catholic), students face the challenges of treating one another with respect and dignity. The ideas of respect and dignity are simple: respect and treat others as you would like to be treated. However, putting these ideas into action takes genuine courage.

## Faith Activity

**Global and Local Justice** Everyone has a need to belong and feel a part of a community. Have you seen or experienced any racial tensions in your school? Why do you think they exist? What actions can your school take to become more accepting of other cultures and ethnic groups?

# Settling in the Promised Land

▲ This painting shows Moses parting from his friends before crossing the Jordan.

The Old Testament Books of Joshua, Judges, and Ruth follow immediately after the five books of the Law, or Pentateuch. Joshua is sometimes grouped with the Pentateuch, and this grouping is called the Hexateuch. The Book of Joshua is part of the ongoing story of God's chosen people and the covenant that they have with God. The promise of land made to Abraham is fulfilled in Joshua.

Many of the stories in Joshua and Judges were told over and over again. The stories in Joshua were popular war stories that the Deuteronomistic writers wrote down from the oral tradition to emphasize the conquest of Israel and how God fights for Israel. The God of Israel entered into the history of the people to once again fulfill his promise to be their God and to make them his people. The inspired accounts proclaim God's constant providence.

Joshua, Judges, and Ruth are usually listed as the first three Historical Books. Joshua and Judges are works of military history, dealing with the conquest and settlement of Canaan, the land promised to the Israelites by God. Thus, Joshua and Judges continue the story begun in the first five books of the Old Testament.

The Books of Joshua, Judges, and Ruth are set in the period of Israelite history between the death of Moses and the establishment of the Israelite monarchy. Joshua and Judges both deal with the conquest and settlement of Canaan.

## Faith Sharing

**Personality Traits** Over the next week, note personality traits of three people whom you admire. Note any similarities or differences between these people and the people in the Books of Joshua, Judges, and Ruth. Discuss these in your faith sharing group at the end of the week.

## Three Views

The Book of Joshua deals with the conquest and settlement of Canaan. Joshua describes a swift, successful military campaign in the central hill country of Canaan and the distributions of conquered territory among the tribes of Israel.

The Book of Judges also deals with the conquest and settlement of Canaan, but it presents another view—that the Israelite conquest and settlement of Canaan was less epic and only partially successful. Judges presents a long series of conflicts between the Israelites and the Canaanites.

The Book of Ruth turns away from accounts of warfare to tell a story of family affection and ethnic tolerance. The Book of Ruth ignores the larger history of the settlement to concentrate on the story of one family.

SICUT ADFUI MOYSI, ITA TIBI ADERO. *Iosua. C.1.*
*Mortuo Moyse, dominus incitat Iosue, ad Expeditionem in Chanaan. Iosua Cap I. 6v.*
*Gabriel Bodeneer fecit. Negotium Acad. Cos. Franc. excud. Aug. Vind. Cum Gratia et Priv. S.C.Mly.*

▲ Antique German print depicting
Joshua and his armies traveling
to the Promised Land, Gabriel
Bodeneer, 1500–1699.

## Break open *the Word*

**Crossing the
Jordan River** Read the
account of the Israelites
crossing the Jordan River
(Joshua 3:14–17; 4:4–7,
14–18) and compare it
to Moses leading the
Israelites across the
Red or Reed Sea
(Exodus 14:21–22, 26–31).

# The Role of Joshua

After the death of Moses, Joshua takes over in order to lead the Israelites into Canaan, the Promised Land.

Joshua's extraordinary heroism has two dimensions—moral and military. Joshua always seeks to follow God's lead; he is a man fully acceptable to God. Joshua is also a brilliant and ruthless soldier who conquers Canaan in a swift and brutal campaign. As with the story of Moses, Joshua's story is exaggerated in the style of an epic, and the actual events of the conquest were probably far less swift and far less brutal.

According to the story, Joshua himself is a heroic military leader of nearly the same stature as Moses, and Joshua's career often parallels the career of Moses. For example, before the siege of the city of Jericho, Joshua encounters a heavenly being who has come to aid the Israelites. Just as Moses was told by God in Exodus 3:5–10, Joshua is told, "Remove the sandals from your feet, for the place where you stand is holy" (*Joshua 5:13–15*).

The writers of Joshua present the stories in terms of previous events. Still other depictions of Joshua are similar to those of Moses. As Moses parts the Red or Reed Sea (See *Exodus 14:21–22.*), Joshua parts the Jordan River. (See *Joshua 3:7–17.*) God appears to Moses on Mount Sinai amid trumpet blasts (See *Exodus 19:16–19.*), and a series of trumpet blasts combined with the shouts of the people under Joshua's leadership cause the walls of Jericho to fall. (See *Joshua 6:20.*) Both Moses and Joshua meet God, and both send scouts ahead of them.

## Scripture

"After the death of Moses the servant of the LORD, the LORD spoke to Joshua son of Nun, Moses' assistant, saying, 'My servant Moses is dead. Now proceed to cross the Jordan, you and all this people, into the land that I am giving to them, to the Israelites. Every place that the sole of your foot will tread upon I have given to you, as I promised to Moses.'"

*Joshua 1:1–3*

"'No one shall be able to stand against you all the days of your life. As I was with Moses, so I will be with you; I will not fail you or forsake you. Be strong and courageous; for you shall put this people in possession of the land that I swore to their ancestors to give them. Only be strong and very courageous, being careful to act in accordance with all the law that my servant Moses commanded you; do not turn from it to the right hand or to the left, so that you may be successful wherever you go.'"

*Joshua 1:5–7*

# The Israelite Struggle

With whom did the Israelites struggle? The conflict between the Israelites and the Canaanites was, in a sense, "in the family" since these peoples were closely related. Both were part of peoples who had come from the desert regions east of Canaan; both spoke Semitic languages. Sometimes all the Israelites' enemies are grouped as *Canaanites*; sometimes they are referred to by specific names, such as the *Amorites* or *Jebusites*. At times the name *Canaanites* is also reserved for the peoples dwelling on the coast of the Mediterranean Sea. The word *Canaan* may refer to a red or purple dye from shellfish, a product for which the coastal Canaanites were well known.

Not all of the Israelites' enemies were former desert nomads, however. The Philistines were a notable exception. The Philistines had not reached Canaan from the desert but from the Mediterranean Sea. They were one of the Sea Peoples who ravaged the eastern Mediterranean world around 1200 B.C. After an unsuccessful attack on Egypt, the Philistines moved north and settled the coastal plain of Canaan. The Philistines brought with them the technology for smelting iron, which made their armor and weapons superior to the bronze armor and weapons of the Israelites. The Philistines eventually disappeared from history, but they are remembered in the name the Romans gave to this whole region, Palestine.

**Conquest and Settlement**  The Book of Joshua is divided into three parts. Chapters 1—12 narrate the conquest of Canaan; Chapters 13—22 detail the distribution of the land among the different tribes; Chapters 23—24 bring the book to a conclusion, reporting Joshua's last words, his death, and his burial.

In the Book of Joshua, the Israelites conquer the Canaanite cities in a rapid series of assaults. In the Book of Judges, the conquest is a gradual process which lasts several years. In fact, the Israelite occupation probably occurred in phases. Most of the infiltration was likely a relatively peaceful settlement of the sparsely populated hill regions, with occasional conflicts with the cities in the lowlands. Over time, many of the earlier groups most likely joined the ever stronger Israelites.

The Canaanite world pictured in the Book of Joshua is a fragmented society of small city-states. The Canaanites had no central government. This would explain the recorded swift success of Joshua's initial campaign of conquest, which occupies only five years. After crossing the Jordan River and entering Canaan, the Israelites first attacked and destroyed the city of Jericho, a trading center located a few miles north of the Dead Sea near the western wall of the Jordan Valley.

## Faith Activity

**The Canaanites and the Philistines**  In small groups, research the culture of the Canaanites or the Philistines. What is known about their religion, social and economic life, arts, and crafts? How does this information enrich your study of the Old Testament?

Jericho, whose name probably means "Moon City," is both the lowest (840 feet below sea level) and the oldest (8000 B.C.) known city in the world. Archaeological evidence indicates that Jericho was destroyed sometime in the middle of the late Bronze Age, which lasted from around 1500 to 1200 B.C., but this is too early to represent the Israelite attack described in Joshua. Perhaps the Israelites, in their success, appropriated the earlier destruction of Jericho into their glorified history.

Another important distinction is that the Canaanites worshiped fertility gods—named Baal and Anath. This difference is important because it is set in direct opposition to the God of the Israelites. The polytheistic religion of the Canaanites threatened Israel and God's plan for his people.

## War and Sacrifice

War was a religious activity for the Israelites. A pattern or code of war is evident in these stories. A standard of God always precedes them in the Ark of the Covenant. (See *Joshua 6:2–4, 6–7.*) The Ark was a box that contained the tablets of the commandments and perhaps some other items. It was highly decorated and topped with carvings of two cherubim. The box symbolized God's presence. The Israelites may have picked up the idea of a box from the Egyptians, who put their gods in a box.

▲ David Before the Ark of the Covenant, Giovanni Battista Pittoni the Younger, c.1725–1727.

Another part of this pattern is the sacrifice before war (See *1 Samuel 7:8–10.*) and the importance of ritual purity. The war camp was to be a holy place, free of anything that was designated unclean. (See *Deuteronomy 23:14.*) For instance, before the siege of Jericho, all of the soldiers were circumcised according to God's command. God explained to Joshua that circumcision removed the "disgrace of Egypt" from the men. (See *Joshua 5:9.*) They were then purified and able to celebrate the Passover. Warriors were also forbidden to have relations with their wives during war so as to retain a pure focus. (See *1 Samuel 21:4–5.*) Those who did not remain fully devoted to the conflict were discharged from war duty. (See *Deuteronomy 20:5–8.*)

# The Ark & The Synagogue

Jewish synagogues are community centers as well as places of study and worship. Many contain classrooms and libraries, and synagogues often serve as administrative offices for Jewish charities. The synagogue is structured to direct the focus of the congregation to a large cupboard that symbolizes the Ark of the Covenant. The Ark contains the parchment scrolls on which the Torah is written, and it is considered a great honor to open or close its doors or to read from the scolls. As a sign of respect, the congregation stands whenever the Ark is opened.

In Orthodox synagogues, men and women in the congregation sit apart so that the men will not be distracted by the women. In non-Orthodox synagogues, separate seating is not required; this enables families to sit together.

## Connect to the Past

**The Tabernacle** The Tabernacle is used for the reservation and worship of the Blessed Sacrament during Mass. The congregation kneels while its doors are open, showing worship to the Body of Christ. What special actions or words are used to reverence the Gospels prior to the Gospel reading during Mass?

## Holy War

Before the capture of the city of Jericho, Joshua tells the Israelites, "'Shout! For the LORD has given you the city. The city and all that is in it shall be devoted to the LORD for destruction'" (*Joshua 6:16–17*). Following this command, the Israelites killed every living thing in the city—"both men and women, young and old, oxen, sheep, and donkeys"— sparing only the family of Rahab, a woman of Jericho who had hidden Joshua's spies (*Joshua 6:21–23*).

The character of the warfare described in Joshua and Judges is extremely brutal. For example, the destruction of Jericho reflects the ancient Israelite custom known as the **ban**, in which everything in a captured city— the people, their livestock, and their possessions—is "devoted" to God, by being destroyed. Total destruction of the enemy would certainly ensure that there would be no intermarriage or weakening of the faith of the Israelites. Some of the livestock was unsuitable for consumption according to laws outlined in Leviticus, so the destruction of the livestock removed the problem.

To help understand this dreadful custom, it is important to remember that war for the Israelites was a religious act; it was "holy war." The background of holy war was the experience of the Israelites as desert nomads facing kings with trained, well-equipped armies, which included cavalry. The Israelites believed that they, literally, had God on their side to offset their significant military disadvantage. God was the Lord of hosts and was personally engaged when Israel fought. When Israel won, the victory was God's. Holy war was sometimes fought only by volunteers. The number of the Israelite warriors was considered less important than the spirit of the Lord that animated them. At the same time, we must remember that the concept of God presented is less developed than later concepts about God.

According to the rules for waging holy war set down in the Book of Deuteronomy, when the Israelites attacked a town, they were first to offer terms of peace. If the town surrendered peacefully, the inhabitants were to be spared (though they could be put to forced labor). However, if the town resisted, ". . . then you shall besiege it; and when the LORD your God gives it into your hand, you shall put all its males to the sword" (*Deuteronomy 20:12–13*).

**The God of History** Some people find it difficult to accept the way God is presented as a warrior in these stories. However, it is important to remember that God is the Lord of history. Israel's life is based on this idea—and so is our faith. Our particular circumstances influence how we understand God to be Lord of history. Remember that the Exodus is interpreted as God's defeat of the pharaoh. God is present in this event to bring Israel to freedom. As part of the covenant, God governs all parts of Israel's life—even war. God's love and concern is always present.

The land of Canaan represents the fulfillment of God's promise of a land. God's promise to Abraham is fulfilled in Joshua. The land is God's "gift."

The presence of God is very clearly reflected in the repeated moral pattern of the Book of Judges: The Israelites sin by worshiping other gods or marrying other groups' women; their enemies oppress them; the Israelites repent; God raises up a leader who delivers Israel; the land is at peace until the people again do what is evil.

**Faith Activity**

**God Acting Today**
Reflect on ways that you see God acting in the world today. What blessings and gifts do you see in your individual life and that of your family, school, and broader community? How do you see God's presence in the nation and in the world?

# JUST war

Throughout its history, one of the major efforts of the Christian Church has been to control warfare. The Christian theologian Saint Augustine of Hippo (A.D. 354–430) saw war as the result of sin, but he believed that warfare could be valid if the violence were used to restrain evil and protect the innocent. Augustine tried to define what constituted "just war," proposing that violence is acceptable if certain conditions are met—just cause, competent authority, comparitive justice, right intention, last resort, probability of success, and proportionality—all concepts that can be found to some degree in Israel's understanding of a holy war.

In their 1983 statement *The Challenge of Peace; God's Promise and Our Response,* the U.S. bishops enumerated the conditions of a modern "just war" doctrine.

**Just Cause** War may be waged only to confront "a real and certain danger"—to protect innocent life, to preserve conditions necessary for decent human existence, and to secure basic human rights.

**Competent Authority** War may be declared only by those with responsibility for public order, not by private groups or individuals.

**Comparative Justice** No state has "absolute justice" on its side. Even a "just cause" has limits: Do the rights and values involved justify the loss of others' lives?

**Right Intention** War can be legitimately intended only for the reasons set forth as a just cause. During the conflict, right intention means pursuit of peace and reconciliation, and the avoidance of unnecessary destructive acts or unreasonable conditions (such as unconditional surrender).

**Last Resort** For a resort to war to be justified, all peaceful alternatives must have been exhausted.

**Probability of Success** With a fair degree of certainty, intended results are likely to be achieved.

**Proportionality** The damage inflicted and the costs incurred by war must be proportionate to the good expected for a nation and the world community.

Conflict resolution and peacemaking are not tasks for nations only. Individuals and groups of every kind are constantly faced with situations of conflict that require the values and skills of nonviolent resolution. When the art of peacemaking is studied and practiced more than the science of war, the world will be renewed.

# Israel under the Judges

The Book of Judges collects the stories of men and women who deliver Israel from oppression. In ancient Israel, the title **judge** did not mean someone who presides over a trial; a judge was a brave, charismatic, resourceful military leader who was animated by the spirit of God.

Although the judges are heroic, they are definitely on a smaller scale than Joshua. Joshua is the successor of Moses as the leader of all those who entered the Promised Land; by contrast, the judges are associated with particular tribes of Israel. Unlike Joshua, who is both obedient to God and a brilliant soldier, some of the judges are morally flawed and even foolish. In general, the judges function as transitional figures between the heroic leaders of the past, Moses and Joshua, and the heroic leader to come, King David.

The Book of Judges covers the history of Israel from the time of settlement until just before the establishment of the kingship under Saul, a period of roughly 200 years. The Book of Judges narrates the careers of twelve charismatic leaders who fought various enemies of Israel during this time. In most cases, the Book of Judges indicates how long each judge "judged Israel." Adding up these periods—as well as the periods during which the Israelites were oppressed by various enemies—produces a far larger total than 200 years. Allowing for some exaggeration and some overlap of judges in different tribes may bring us to a more realistic time span.

The Book of Judges should not be viewed as chronological history of the era from the settlement to the kingship, but as a collection of tales of the ancient heroes of the various tribes of Israel. Although Judges presents each of these individuals as having led all of Israel, the individuals are also closely identified with specific tribes. For example, Ehud is of the tribe of Benjamin, Gideon of Manasseh, Tola of Issachar, Elon of Zebulon, and Samson of Dan.

| Judges of Israel | | | |
|---|---|---|---|
| **Name** | **Enemy** | **Term** | **Book of Judges** |
| Othniel | Aram | 40 years | 3:7–11 |
| Ehud | Moabites | 80 years | 3:12–30 |
| Shamgar | Philistines | Not given | 3:31 |
| Deborah/Barak | Canaanites | 40 years | 4—5 |
| Gideon | Midianites | 40 years | 6—8 |
| Tola | Not given | 23 years | 10:1–2 |
| Jair | Not given | 22 years | 10:3 |
| Jephthah | Ammonites | 6 years | 10:6—12:7 |
| Ibzan | Not given | 7 years | 12:8–10 |
| Elon | Not given | 10 years | 12:11–12 |
| Abdon | Not given | 8 years | 12:13–15 |
| Samson | Philistines | 20 years | 13—16 |

## Break Open the Word

**Moral Pattern** Read Judges 3:7–11 and examine how it displays the moral pattern. How does Israel do evil? What happens as a result? How does God rescue Israel?

## Break Open the Word

**The Battle** Read Judges 4 and 5. Did all the tribes of Israel participate in the battle? Who is given the glory for the Israelite victory over Sisera? Pay special attention to Judges 5:2–5.

# The Moral Pattern of Judges

The Books of Joshua and Judges offer many examples of standing up for one's beliefs. Joshua never loses his faith in God throughout the time he leads the Israelites, and at his death God renews the covenant between himself and his people. Deborah knew what God wanted for his people and did what was necessary to defeat the Canaanite army under Sisera. Samson, though a flawed leader, put his faith in God one last time and died a heroic death.

Some striking biblical examples of faith in God involve non-Israelites, such as Jael, the Kenite woman who killed the enemy general Sisera, and Rahab, the woman of Jericho who took the risk of hiding Joshua's spies.

An example of not standing up for one's beliefs can be found in the story of Achan in the Book of Joshua, which shows the consequences of an individual's lack of integrity, both to himself and to his community. After the capture of Jericho, Achan violates both God's command and Joshua's by stealing some of the city's treasure, all of which was to be destroyed. As a result of God's displeasure over this violation of the ban, the Israelites are defeated in their first battle with the men of Ai. When Achan's crime is revealed, he and his entire family are stoned to death.

**The Role of Women in Judges** Two women play major roles in the Book of Judges. The first is the judge, Deborah, who is described as a "prophetess" rather than a warrior. Deborah and her general, Barak, organize Israelite resistance against a Canaanite army led by a general named Sisera. Although Sisera has nine hundred chariots of iron, the Israelites, as is usual in these tales, utterly destroy the Canaanites: "All the army of Sisera fell by the sword; no one was left" (*Judges 4:16*).

Sisera flees following the battle, taking refuge in the tent of a non-Israelite woman named Jael. While Sisera sleeps, Jael takes his life. Deborah celebrates the Israelite victory and Jael's participation in a song that may be among the most ancient passages in the Old Testament.

## Scripture

"When locks are long in Israel,
    when the people offer themselves willingly—
    bless the LORD!
"Hear, O kings; give ear, O princes;
    to the LORD I will sing,
    I will make melody to the LORD, the God of Israel."
*Judges 5:1–3*

**Folklore and Myth in Samson** Samson, the strong man, is a famous figure in the Old Testament. However, his story often seems less like military history or moral fable than it does like a heroic myth, legend, or tall tale. For example,

- the episode of Samson killing a lion with his bare hands is similar to stories told about the Mesopotamian hero Gilgamesh and the Greek hero Hercules.

- the fact that Samson is vulnerable only if his hair is cut is reminiscent of the Greek hero Achilles, who could be wounded only in his heel.

- Samson does not seem inspired by religious or patriotic motives, but largely by a desire for revenge.

▲ Samson smiting the Philistines with a jawbone, Cubiculum F.

# The Narrative of Ruth

The Book of Ruth reflects a very different idea than the God of Joshua and Judges. Ruth presents a God of compassion and caring who sees both Israelites and non-Israelites equally as his people. The theme of tolerance and understanding is most clearly expressed in the character of Ruth herself, a virtuous Moabite who becomes an ancestor of both David and Jesus.

Although the Book of Ruth is set in the days when the judges ruled, it does not deal with military history. Rather, it deals with family affection and ethnic tolerance. It is a tender, engrossing short story with a skillfully structured narrative and vivid characters. The German poet Goethe praised it as the most beautiful "little whole" of the Old Testament.

▶ Ruth threshes her gleanings and brings the grain to Naomi (Ruth II:17–19); Naomi gives counsel to Ruth (Ruth III.1–5), France (probably Paris), c.1250.

## Faith Activity

**A Portrait** Select one of the three main characters in the Book of Ruth, and create an imaginary portrait of this individual. You may use any artistic medium you like. Before you begin, write down three or four personality traits that you think this character reflects, and then try to make your artwork embody these traits.

Each of the Book of Ruth's four chapters presents a single episode and concludes with verses that summarize the preceding action and forecast what is to come. Although the tale is very brief, each of its three main characters—Naomi, Ruth, and Boaz—emerges as a well-developed individual. The fact that Ruth, a Moabite, is presented as a virtuous woman and an ancestor of one of Israel's greatest heroes, David, helps establish one of the story's chief themes, the value of tolerance.

About two-thirds of the Book of Ruth is presented in the form of conversation. The dialogue ranges from sharply humorous wordplay to moving eloquence. For example, in a famous passage marked by beautiful parallelism, Ruth refuses to abandon her mother-in-law Naomi: "Where you go, I will go; Where you lodge, I will lodge; your people shall be my people, and your God, my God" (*Ruth 1:16*).

**Israelite Customs** The Book of Ruth was probably written after the exile, when many Jewish leaders were trying to restrict marriage and other interaction with outsiders. They were concerned that Judaism would not survive as a scattered people small in numbers. The Book of Ruth argues against these restrictions. It is also a valuable source of information about Israelite customs. For example, Ruth goes to glean in the fields of Naomi's wealthy kinsman, Boaz. Gleaning means gathering up the grain in the fields left behind by the reapers. According to Israelite law, people who were poor had the right to glean the fields, and farmers were required to leave part of the harvest for gleaning.

Another Israelite custom in Ruth is Levirate marriage. If a married man died without a son, the Levirate law required his nearest male relative to marry his widow and provide him with a male heir. Ruth's kinsman by marriage, Boaz, fulfills the requirement after first arranging for a nearer male relative to renounce his claim. The arrangement between this man and Boaz is sealed by the Israelite custom of handing over a sandal. Boaz's acceptance of the sandal is accepted by witnesses as binding the agreement.

In the end, Ruth becomes an ancestor of the great King David, so the restrictions on intermarriage are made to appear pointless.

**Peacemakers** The understanding of God that Jesus preached is similar to that found in the Book of Ruth—be compassionate and caring toward all people. Jesus himself was nonviolent. He chastised Peter for cutting off the soldier's ear in the garden. He went to the crucifixion without violence. The Beatitudes (See *Matthew 5:3–12.*) are clearly a call for nonviolence. In recent times, we have had calls for nonviolent conflict resolution from Christian activists such as Dr. Martin Luther King Jr. (1929–1968) and Dorothy Day (1897–1980). They not only rejected violence, but they also worked to resolve conflicts peacefully. As followers of Jesus, we can do no less.

The lessons of Ruth go beyond simple loyalty to one's own community. The lessons of Ruth go to a larger understanding of the needs of other people. Ruth's story is a tale about peacemakers. In our personal lives and as members of communities and nations, we need to abandon "enemy thinking" in viewing others and educate ourselves in the art of conflict resolution. We, too, need to become peacemakers.

### Faith Activity

**Modern Heroes** Name some twentieth-century American heroes. What distinguishes them as heroes? Do we regard peacemakers and activists as highly as warriors?

## Saint Joan of Arc (1412–1431)

One of the most famous warriors inspired by faith was Joan of Arc. Joan was a pious, illiterate peasant born in the village of Domremy in the French province of Lorraine. Three years after she was born, the French were defeated by the English at the battle of Agincourt. This was the last in a series of disastrous defeats for France in the long conflict with England known as the Hundred Years' War. Much of France was occupied by English forces, and in 1420 the French were forced to sign a treaty surrendering the crown of France to the English king when the reigning French king died.

In 1428, the French had little hope of regaining their homeland. Then, Joan appeared claiming that heavenly voices had given her a mission to rescue France from the English invaders and restore to the throne the French heir, Charles the Dauphin. She claimed that Saint Michael the Archangel, Saint Catherine of Alexandria, and Saint Margaret of Antioch spoke to her. The saints had told Joan she must rescue the city of Orleans—which had been besieged by the English for many months—and that she must see Charles crowned king at Reims.

Traveling across enemy territory to see Charles, Joan cut her hair short and wore men's clothing for safety. Her courage and conviction impressed Charles, who permitted her to lead troops against the English at Orleans. Inspired by her fearlessness, the French soldiers defeated their enemies and liberated the city. After this victory, Joan accompanied Charles to Reims, where he was crowned king of France on July 17, 1429. The following year, she was captured in battle and sold to the English. The English forces turned her over to the Church for trial.

Visionary experiences such as Joan's were not uncommon in the Middle Ages, but they were often associated with individuals who had physical disabilites or persons with a history of mental illness. The Middle Ages were also a period of widespread superstition. Many people believed in witchcraft, and a tree and fountain near Joan's village of Domremy were believed to be enchanted. Both Joan's claim to hear voices and the folklore of her village were used against her during the Church trial. Before and at her trial, she was questioned closely and for long periods of time; this led her to answer several leading questions in a way that damaged her case. Joan was condemned as a heretic and a witch, and she was burned at the stake in Rouen on May 30, 1431.

In 1455, Joan's mother and two brothers appealed to the pope to reopen her trial. The pope declared Joan innocent of all the charges against her. In 1920, the Church canonized her as a saint.

## Prayer

Begin by praying the Sign of the Cross.

**Leader:** Gracious God, we gather to celebrate our solidarity with our poor, hungry, or suffering brothers and sisters in the world. We have so much, and we pause to remember how we are called to share with others. Bless our class and help us to be one with your people…

**All:** Amen.

**Leader:** Let us read from Isaiah 58:9–10, that we may understand how living in solidarity with our less fortunate brothers and sisters in the world can bring light to our lives and their lives as well.

**All:** If you remove the yoke from
   among you,
the pointing of the finger, the
   speaking of evil,
if you offer your food to the
   hungry
   and satisfy the needs of the
   afflicted,
then your light shall rise in the
   darkness
   and your gloom be like the
   noonday.
Amen.

**Leader:** Jesus you brought light to the world…

**All:** through your actions of healing and miracles,
through your words of challenge and compassion,
through your humanity,
through your solidarity with those whom society abandoned.

**Leader:** Jesus help me to be light to the world…

**All:** through actions of healing and support, through words of love and caring, through my humanity, through solidarity with my brothers and sisters.
Amen.

End by praying the Sign of the Cross.

## Review

1. Who were some of the peoples who eventually became the Israelites?

2. What are some of the similarities and differences between the customs and culture of the ancient Near Eastern peoples?

3. Identify the differences between Orthodox, Hasidic, Conservative, Reconstructionist, Reform, and Humanistic Judaism.

4. In what ways can Moses be considered an epic hero?

5. How many times did Moses warn the pharaoh to let the Israelites go? How many plagues did God bring upon Egypt?

6. What key messages does the Book of Deuteronomy contain? How is Moses presented in this book?

7. Compare the books of Joshua, Judges, and Ruth. How do they address the same historical events in different ways?

8. What factors contribute to Joshua's heroic stature?

9. What is the Israelite concept of "holy war"? What condition, set in Deuteronomy, were the Israelites to offer towns they were going to attack?

10. In what form is two-thirds of the Book of Ruth presented?

11. What happens to Achan and the Israelites when it is discovered that Achan violated God's and Joshua's commands?

12. How does the Book of Ruth show the value of tolerance?

## Key Words

**ban (p. 83)**—Ancient custom of completely destroying everything in a defeated city.

**hapiru (p. 65)**—A class of people living in the countryside of Canaan, some of whom were former slaves; they may have been ancestors of the Hebrews.

**Hebrews (p. 65)**—Peoples enslaved in Egypt who eventually became the community known as Israel.

**idolatry (p. 69)**—False worship; honoring and revering a creature in place of God.

**Israelites (p. 65)**—A people who unified around 1050–1000 B.C. and included Canaanites, the hapiru, the shasu, Sea Peoples, and the original Hebrews.

**Jews (p. 66)**—Term originally used to describe the people who resettled in the area of Judah following the Babylonian Exile; most commonly used to refer to followers of Judaism.

**judge (p. 85)**—One of twelve charismatic military leaders of the Israelites during the period between the conquest of Canaan and the establishment of the monarchy who was animated by the spirit of God.

**Passover (p. 68)**—Refers to when the Israelites were "passed over" by the angel of death as dictated by the tenth plague; a holiday celebrated by Jews as a day of deliverance.

**prophets (p. 69)**—Persons who have a close relationship with God and communicate a divine message.

**rabbis (p. 67)**—Ordained Jewish teachers and spiritual leaders.

**Talmud (p. 67)**—A collection of Jewish oral law and commentary; a guide for conduct in particular circumstances.

## Teen to Teen

As a teen today in a world filled with strife and conflict, you are faced with many decisions on how to deal with conflict. Some world leaders choose violence as their response. How do you react when confronted with conflict? How would you like to see others in the world react when confronted with conflict?

*"I try to treat everyone with respect, first off. Second, I try to resolve conflict with teachings from the Church: turning the other cheek, loving unconditionally, and offering forgiveness without boundaries. I absolutely think that everyone should react with peace first instead of choosing war. I don't think that it is fair to the citizens of countries in war to suffer because of what a leader or what a government chooses."*

*Raymond J.*

## Personal Challenge—Solidarity

"Our culture is tempted to turn inward, becoming indifferent and sometimes isolationist in the face of international responsibilities. Catholic social teaching proclaims that we are our brothers' and sisters' keepers, wherever they live. We are one human family, whatever our national, racial, ethnic, economic, and ideological differences. Learning to practice the virtue of solidarity means learning that 'loving our neighbor' has global dimensions in an interdependent world."

(*Sharing Catholic Social Teaching: Challenges and Directions,* USCCB, 1998)

An increasingly difficult challenge we face in today's world is how to deal with anger, depression, and war, as well as other negatives that can tear apart our societal and religious bonds. As the U.S. Catholic Bishops acknowledge, a common response to many of these negatives around the world is to turn inward, to turn away from the problem. This is not an option, Jesus proclaimed the new commandment that all God's children may be loved as we love God himself. Proclaiming peace and assisting all those in need are first steps we all must take to achieve greater solidarity.

**BREAK OPEN** *the Word*

**Read Psalm 66:12,** the reading that opens the chapter. Consider for a moment all the trials, difficulties, challenges, wanderings, and other events that the Israelites endured before settling. Consider now all the challenges that exist for the modern state of Israel. What similarities are there between the ancient Israelites and modern Israel?

c. 1400–1200 B.C.
Hittites use iron
extracted from ore

1000–994 B.C.
David is king of Judah

961–922 B.C.
Solomon is king of Israel

922–587 B.C.
Divided Monarchy

1400 B.C.

1100 B.C.

1020–1000 B.C.
Saul rules the people of Israel

994–962 B.C.
David is king of all Israel

c. 960 B.C.
Solomon builds temple at Jerusalem

# Building the Kingdom

CHAPTER

4

"With upright heart he tended them,
and guided them with skillfull hand."

*Psalm 78:72*

## Chapter Goals

In this chapter, you will:

- consider the purpose and basic content of the Books of Samuel and the Books of Kings.

- learn about the monarchy and dynasty of the first kings of Israel.

- increase your knowledge of worship in the life of Jews, past and present.

- explore the importance of reverence for God.

- learn about Saint Thomas More.

**753** B.C.
Rome founded
on Tiber River

900 B.C.       700 B.C.       500 B.C.

**776** B.C.
First recorded Olympic Games
held in Greece

**587** B.C.
Temple at Jerusalem
destroyed by Babylonians

# The Books of Samuel and Kings

After the events recorded in the Book of Judges, the religious history of Israel continues to unfold to show the rise of a monarchy in Israel. In this chapter you will read parts of four historical books: 1 Samuel and 2 Samuel and 1 Kings and 2 Kings.

As with many other books in the Old Testament, the inspired writers of the Books of Samuel and Kings present religious truth within a historical framework. The Books of Samuel and Kings present the history of a monarchy. This history of the monarchy, in which God did wondrous deeds for his people, shows the blessings—given through obedience to the covenant—and the suffering—a result of disobedience—of God's people.

The main literary genre found in these four books is the narrative, which was discussed in Chapter 1. A literary form found in the Books of Samuel is the oracle. In 2 Samuel 7, Nathan gives us textual clues that he is to convey the word of God. Examples of such clues are: ". . .thus you shall say to my servant David: Thus says the LORD of hosts. . ." (*2 Samuel 7:8*). Some biblical oracles are *judgment speeches,* "bad news", and some are oracles of salvation, "good news". Both types of oracles are conditional. They depend on the action or inaction of the people in response to the oracle.

## Content of the Books

The writers of these four books present vivid accounts as eyewitness testimonies of certain historical events. The writers wrote and rewrote these stories many times—ending with a version written after 586 B.C. It was written for those Jews who remembered the destruction of the Temple and had gone into exile. These Scriptures were intended to encourage repentance and to give hope by reminding the Jews that God had remained faithful to his promise throughout a succession of disobedient kings. The readings of 1 and 2 Kings, when combined with the Books of Samuel, paint a portrait of admirable leadership.

A variety of opinions and traditions influenced the material finally included in the Books of Samuel and the Books of Kings. Those who wrote the Deuteronomic history after the exile in Babylon used many unknown sources. As a result, the books have inconsistent views of the kings. The kings, in the final analysis, sometimes led the people into living out their covenant responsibilities, and the kings sometimes led the people into evil ways.

**Samuel: Prophet and Judge** The role of Samuel is explained by two traditions, both found within 1 Samuel 1—12. In one tradition, Samuel, the seer and prophet, gives advice to Saul. From his "high place," he has the authority to appoint a king in the name of God. He secretly anoints Saul as "prince" of the people.

In the other tradition, Samuel is a judge who finds the idea of a monarchy displeasing. He appoints his own sons as judges, but the people continue to demand a king. They tell Samuel, "You are old and your sons do not follow in your ways; appoint for us, then, a king to govern us, like other nations" (*1 Samuel 8:5*).

These two traditions represent the struggle to form a unified nation under God. Samuel's remarks (*1 Samuel 7:3–17*) are important because he believes that the people are to be ruled by a **theocracy**—a nation ruled by God. Samuel believes that the formation of a kingdom with an earthly king is a violation of the covenant. The Israelites had to redefine monarchy to keep the proper order of command. To keep with the covenant, the Israelites understood power in this order: God, Law, King, People. This is distinct from the traditional understanding of monarchy: King, Law, People.

**Formula of Kingship** In the two Books of Kings, the writers present the reign of each king after Solomon by means of a formula.

- First, there is an introduction that has a time frame, forebearers, and accomplishments.
- Next come details of the king's death, descendants, and sometimes references to annals or other books, some since lost.

The report formula and a rough chronological order throughout 1 and 2 Kings makes it easy for readers to recognize the cycle of faithfulness and unfaithfulness to the covenant.

**Break open the Word**

**Compare Traditions**
Read 1 Samuel 1—12. In small groups make a list of scripture citations that refer to Samuel as prophet and those that reference his role as judge. Next to each citation, write one sentence to describe what the passage details. When all groups have completed the activity, compare your list with that of another group's.

*Faith* **Activity**

**Formula of Presidency**
Write a brief biography of a deceased U.S. president that follows the form given in the Old Testament for the kings of Israel and Judah. As a class, collect the biographies and put them in a chronological bulletin board display.

▶ Samuel anointing David.

# Anointed One

SAMUEL ANOINTS DAVID

You have read about oil being poured as part of a consecration ceremony. In the ancient world, perfumed or scented olive oil or ointment was cosmetic, often worn on festive occasions by women and men. Healing herbs and other ingredients were added to the oil and ointment to form a salve or medicine. In Israel and other Middle Eastern countries, special people and objects were set apart for political or religious service by a ritual of consecration during which someone poured oil over their heads.

Each king of Israel was a *mashiah* or "anointed one" singled out by God for leadership. From the Hebrew word *mashiah* we get **messiah**, also meaning "anointed one." **Messianism**—the belief in a messiah as the savior of the people—was a movement that developed centuries after King David. Believers expected a messiah in the here-and-now, although no one knew exactly when.

King David was perceived as having fulfilled the role of messiah-king in an earthly practical sense and was considered an anointed one. He met the kingly specifications by providing law and justice, securing God's blessing for his people, defeating enemies, and ruling on a large scale. The followers of Messianism hoped that one of David's descendants would establish his kingdom again.

**Jesus the Christ and Messiah** *Christos* is the Greek word for "anointed one." *Christ*, as applied to Jesus, means the same thing; it is not his surname. For Christians, the Messiah has come and will come again at the end of time. Jesus is the Messiah, the Christ. The prophet Isaiah spoke of the coming messiah with a sequence of honorific titles: "Wonderful Counselor, Mighty God, Everlasting Father, Prince of Peace" (*Isaiah 9:6*).

"Jesus went on with his disciples to the villages of Caesarea Philippi; and on the way he asked his disciples, 'Who do people say that I am?' And they answered him, 'John the Baptist; and others, Elijah; and still others, one of the prophets.' He asked them, 'But who do you say that I am?' Peter answered him, 'You are the Messiah.' And he sternly ordered them not to tell anyone about him."

*Mark 8:27–30*

Although in his answer, Peter correctly hailed Jesus as the Messiah, he did not understand the nature of Jesus' messiahship. Peter and the disciples were hoping for a hero-messiah, not a prophet-messiah. As Jesus began to prophecy his own death and Resurrection, Peter spoke up and rebuked Jesus. Jesus silenced Peter and compared him to Satan for worrying of human, rather than divine concerns. (See *Mark 8:31–33*.)

**An Unexpected Messiah** The rule that Jesus established was not what Jews of his time expected. He did not reestablish Israel as a political or military presence. His kingdom was not geographical or earthly, but a divine rule of justice, love, and peace. God's kingdom is his rule in our hearts and lives, and all are welcome to this kingdom, especially those who are poor or suffering.

The Church continues Jesus' work of preaching the Good News of his kingdom for all people. Christians are anointed with oil at Baptism to exemplify that they are called to share in the role of Jesus as priest, prophet, and king. They are consecrated to participate in Christian worship. The oil used for anointing is called *chrism* and is blessed by a bishop on Holy Thursday for use throughout the next year.

## Faith Sharing

**Anointed for Mission** The Church continues Jesus' work of preaching the Good News of the kingdom, healing and welcoming those in need. You share in this important work. What can you do at home and school to be welcoming and compassionate? How can you help others see the power of God's life and love in their lives? Discuss your thoughts with your faith sharing group and choose one thing you can do this week to live out your baptismal anointing.

# Monarchy and Dynasty

From about 1400 to 1200 B.C. the Hittites kept a great secret. They had extracted iron from ore and had made tools and weapons from this "new" metal. These iron instruments were superior to those made from bronze and copper. Around 1200 B.C. this secret spread to other peoples, and the Philistines mastered the technology.

The Philistines' control of this metal gave them an economic advantage over the Israelites, but the Israelites persisted in their struggle to build a strong nation. For the Israelites, creating a **monarchy** meant establishing a political and religious unit. To create this unit, they sought a king.

## Centralized Leadership

During the monarchy in Israel's history, many of the kings, though flawed, were wise, prudent, and strong.

- The kings brought about a centralization of leadership to unite the people, strengthen their faith, and build a holy city.
- They also worked to meet the expectations of God and of the people.

The prophets spoke of a king, a messiah, who would be a descendant of King David. A king's descendants who continue to rule in succession may be called a **dynasty**. Tracing the dynasty of David and the Davidic line—descendants of David—became an important factor in establishing a messiah's authenticity and authority.

The children of Israel had been a wandering people, a loose confederation of tribes, and it was natural that they would desire a king to unite them. The Israelites' desire for a monarchy developed gradually as they observed the nations around them. Some of Israel's judges were almost powerful enough to be considered kings. As the tribes became more prosperous, they wanted the trade and stability a central authority would provide. The threat from the Philistines convinced them that they needed a united defense.

### Faith Activity

**A New Material** With a partner, research to find out what products the Philistines made from iron and why this new material was such an improvement over what they had used previously.

### Break Open the Word

**Samuel's Cautions**
Read 1 Samuel 8:10–22 to understand why Samuel opposed the idea of appointing a king. Why do the people insist upon having a king despite Samuel's cautions?

# King Saul (c. 1020–1000 B.C.)

Saul, during his short, unsuccessful reign, had trouble forming a centralized nation. Saul died by his own sword after being wounded in a disastrous battle with the Philistines. He is a tragic figure in the history of Israel.

**Hannah's Song** Songs, which are another form of poetry, appear throughout the Scriptures. An example of this literary technique is found in 1 Samuel. Hannah, the wife of Elkanah the Ephraimite, was a devout woman. When she went to the shrine at Shiloh, she prayed, wept, and poured out her soul. Hannah prayed fervently for a son and made a **vow**, or solemn promise, to God. She promised to offer her son to the Lord as a consecrated person. Her son Samuel became the one who recognized and anointed Saul, the first king of Israel. After her son was born, Hannah thanked God in song for answering her prayer.

# King David (c. 1000–961 B.C.)

Many times during his reign, King Saul was troubled and restless. Some said God's spirit left him and an evil spirit came to dwell in him. According to one tradition, a servant sent for a shepherd boy named David who was known for his courage, strength, and ability to play the harp. The boy soothed Saul with music and was liked so well that he became the king's armor-bearer. The judge Samuel found David and anointed him as the Lord's chosen.

**Mary and Hannah** After reading Hannah's song, turn to the Magnificat (*Luke 1:46–55*), Mary's response to Elizabeth following the annunciation, when Mary learned that she would bear a child who was divine. Here are two women with remarkable pregnancies, for different reasons. Compare their thoughts and words.

◄ David Harping before Saul, English Psalter.

Saul and David had an on-again, off-again relationship, punctuated by jealousy and rivalry as indicated by the taunt in Scripture:

> **"Saul has killed his thousands,**
> **and David his ten thousands."**
> (*1 Samuel 18:7* )

Saul threatened David, and Saul considered Danid to be a threat, but they also admired one another greatly. David was close friends with Saul's son, Jonathan, and he married Saul's daughter, Michal. David was a courageous and faithful leader.

### King David's Accomplishments

At the age of thirty-seven David was anointed king, and he ruled and united Israel for forty years.

He brought the Ark of the Covenant in from the outlying territory.

His armies conquered the Philistines, the Moabites, and the Syrians.

Jerusalem came to be called the City of David.

David recognized God's favor to him and his people:

### scripture

". . . Is there another nation on earth whose God went to redeem it as a people, and to make a name for himself, doing great and awesome things for them, by driving out before his people nations and their gods? And you established your people Israel for yourself to be your people forever . . . ."

*2 Samuel 7:23–24*

▼ Book Illustration of a Georgian Fresco of King David the Builder Other Royalty. King David is depicted on the far right.

# King Solomon (c. 961–922 B.C.)

Solomon was a son of David and Bathsheba. Solomon consolidated his forces, drove out dissidents, and ordered the execution of Adonijah, his stepbrother and competitor to the throne. Early in his career Solomon prayed for understanding and the ability to discern between good and evil.

## scripture

"'And now, O LORD my God, you have made your servant king in place of my father David, although I am only a little child; I do not know how to go out or come in. And your servant is in the midst of the people whom you have chosen, a great people, so numerous they cannot be numbered or counted. Give your servant therefore an understanding mind to govern your people, able to discern between good and evil; for who can govern this your great people?'

It pleased the Lord that Solomon had asked this. God said to him, 'Because you have asked this, and have not asked for yourself long life or riches, or for the life of your enemies, but have asked for yourself understanding to discern what is right, I now do according to your word. Indeed I give you a wise and discerning mind; no one like you has been before you and no one like you shall arise after you. I give you also what you have not asked, both riches and honor all your life; no other king shall compare with you. If you will walk in my ways, keeping my statutes and my commandments, as your father David walked, then I will lengthen your life.'

Then Solomon awoke; it had been a dream. He came to Jerusalem where he stood before the ark of the covenant of the LORD. He offered up burnt offerings of well-being, and provided a feast for all his servants."

*1 Kings 3:7–15*

Solomon married a daughter of the Egyptian pharaoh and kept many women of other nations in his household. The Song of Songs (Song of Solomon), the Book of Wisdom (Wisdom of Solomon), Ecclesiastes, and Proverbs are attributed to this wise leader although he probably was not the actual author.

| The Splendor of Solomon's Reign |
| --- |
| Solomon appointed officers and established administrative districts with a prefect, or chief officer, in each. |
| He modernized the military by equipping his soldiers with horses and chariots. |
| He established a prosperous import-export business. |
| He launched an extensive building campaign—a palace, fortification walls, and a central temple—which he financed through the collection of taxes. |

**Solomon's Wisdom** Solomon was a man of many dreams and visions. The Queen of Sheba in Arabia brought trade goods to Solomon's court and challenged him with hard questions. She wanted to see for herself this king of wealth and wisdom, and she was properly impressed. When Solomon died— 1 Kings 11:43 expresses this with the words Solomon "slept with his ancestors and was buried"—his son, Rehoboam, succeeded him. During Rehoboam's rule, the kingdom split into north and south.

## Interpret the Art

**Solomon and the Queen of Sheba** A banquet given by Solomon in honor of the Queen of Sheba, Ethiopian miniature. The wisdom of Solomon was well renowned, but in a patriarchal world, we find that the Queen of Sheba was renowned as well for her wisdom. She visited Solomon and posed challenging questions that he answered for her with great honesty. *In this image, who do you think is Solomon? Who do you think is the Queen of Sheba? Why do you think they are positioned around the table as they are?*

## God Remains Faithful

When the leaders lose favor with God, they fail and fall away from right relationship with God. When Saul believes he is above the law, he falls. (See *1 Samuel 15*.) David commits adultery with Bathsheba and commits murder, and he too falls. (See *2 Samuel 11:1—12:14*.) Solomon worshiped other gods and failed. (See *1 Kings 11*.)

Despite the struggle in maintaining the correct relationship with God and others, the Saul-David succession culminated in the riches of Solomon's kingdom. After that time there was a division between Judah and Israel. Throughout these transitions, God remained faithful to his people even though his people and their leaders at times turned away from the covenant. As always, God was at work in the history of his people. He promised them a messiah, the ultimate leader. Christians interpret Old Testament prophecies to refer to Jesus, whom they believe is the anointed one sent to save God's people and all people. This salvation is of a spiritual nature, not a military conquest.

## Explore the Land
### Kingdoms of Saul, David, and Solomon

This map shows the extent of control that David, Solomon, and Saul before them had in the Middle East. Which regions and peoples remain noticeably unconquered through the rule of all three of these kings? What geographical features appear to be the northern and southern borders during Solomon's rule?

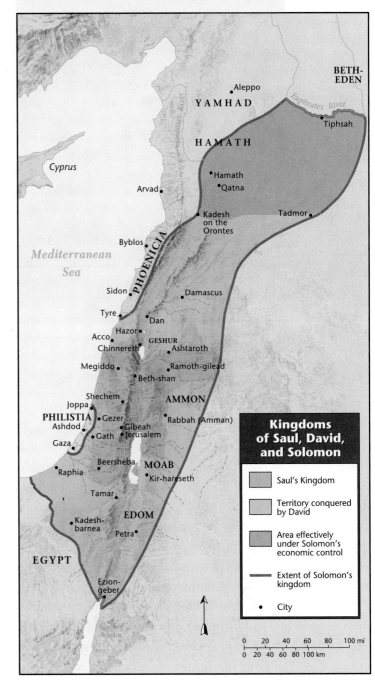

**Kingdoms of Saul, David, and Solomon**

- Saul's Kingdom
- Territory conquered by David
- Area effectively under Solomon's economic control
- Extent of Solomon's kingdom
- • City

# The Role of Worship in Judaism

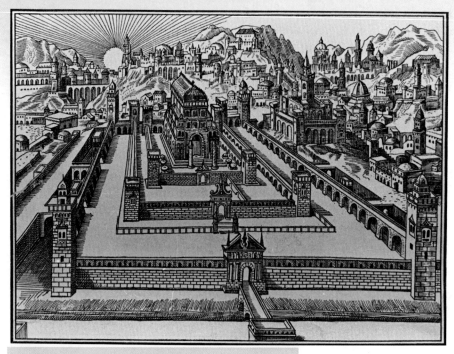

## Connect to the Past

**Temple Schematic** With a partner, list some of the temple furnishings mentioned in 1 Kings 6. Write about the function of each and the sense or senses to which they would appeal.

## Faith Activity

**Church Furnishings**
Work with a partner to make a list of all the furnishings and adornments found in Catholic churches. Also include vessels used in the celebration of the Eucharist. Once you have completed the list, discuss how these objects help the community to praise God.

God promised to build a house for David—a dynasty lasting forever. David wanted to build a house for the Lord. In 2 Samuel 7, the prophet Nathan receives a word from God for King David about building a house. God desired a house for his name and for the ark, a house where his magnificent deeds can be remembered. The people had been on the move, and it was time for them to be planted and to put down roots. God's house, too, had been temporary: a portable tent and tabernacle. As the leader of Israel, David felt a responsibility to begin construction of this temple.

The Temple was eventually built by David's son, Solomon. It took seven years to build and required the work of thousands of laborers. (See *1 Kings 9:20–23.*) The first commandment states that people are to worship God alone and not turn to idolatry. Religious practice could be more easily regulated in a central place. Priests brought the Ark of the Covenant and installed it in the innermost room. The ark contained the stone tablets on which the commandments were written. As a dark cloud filled the temple, Solomon blessed the assembly and presented lavish burnt offerings and grain offerings. The dedication ceremony and accompanying festivities lasted seven days.

## BREAK OPEN the Word

**Temple Worship** Psalms were used in Temple worship, just as we use them in our liturgy today. In pairs, read two of the following psalms and find references to the Temple and what took place there.

Psalm 11 (Song of Trust in God)

Psalm 24 (Entrance into the Temple)

Psalm 26 (Plea for Justice)

Psalm 122 (Song of Praise and Prayer for Jerusalem)

Psalm 134 (Praise in the Night)

# Ancient and Modern Holy Days

## Work with the Chart

**Observance** Research one of the holy days shown below to find out more about the significance of the occasion and how it is observed.

### Jewish Holy Days

On these holy days, Jews remember in a special way God's saving action on their behalf throughout history and the significant events that define them as a people.

| Holy Day | Description | Relevant Scripture |
|---|---|---|
| Rosh Hashanah (New Year) | New Year, start of Ten Days of Penitence | Leviticus, Numbers, Psalms, Ecclesiastes, Isaiah, Jonah |
| Yom Kippur (Day of Atonement) | Day of Atonement, concludes Rosh Hashanah | Genesis, Numbers, 1 Samuel, Jeremiah, Micah |
| Sukkoth (Tabernacles) | Harvest festival and reminder of wanderings in the wilderness | Leviticus |
| Chanukah (Lights) | Celebrating the victory of Maccabees | 1 and 2 Maccabees |
| Purim (Ester) | Commemorating the deliverance of Persian Jews by Jewish queen | Esther |
| Pesach (Passover) | Harvest festival and celebration of liberation from Egypt | Exodus |
| Shavu´ot (Weeks) | Also called Pentecost, celebrating the gift of the Torah | Exodus, Ruth |
| Tishah b´Av (Fast of the Ninth of Av) | Anniversary of the destruction of the first and second temples | Isaiah, Lamentations |

*In some cases, different sources indicate different spellings or titles for these holy days.

**The High Holy Days** The Jewish year begins on the first day of the autumn month of *Tishri. Rosh Hashanah,* literally "the head of the year," begins ten days of renewal and reflection ending with *Yom Kippur,* the Day of Atonement. The *Shofar,* a ram's horn that sounds beginning of the new year, is the symbol most associated with Rosh Hashanah. Yom Kippur is a day of fasting and repentance for wrongdoings of the previous year. It is the holiest day of the Jewish calendar. Even if Jews do not attend synagogue services on other days, they tend to participate in services during the High Holy Days.

**Sukkoth** If you live near a synagogue or a Jewish home, late in autumn you might notice on the property a hut-like structure covered with branches, fruits, and vegetables. This temporary dwelling is a *Sukah* and represents the Jewish harvest festival Sukkoth. In ancient Israel, during harvest-time it was more practical to stay out in the fields rather than to return home after the day's work. Jews found both historical and religious significance in this experience of the fragility of life and of dependency upon God, reminiscent of the time when their ancestors lived in temporary dwellings on their way to the Promised Land. The festival is also known as the "Feast of Booths" or the "Feast of Tents." Sukkoth ends with *Simchat Torah*, when the annual reading of Torah ends and a new cycle of reading Torah begins.

▲ Orthodox Jews making Sukkoth bundles.

**Pesach** *Pesach*, or Passover, is a springtime festival. It commemorates the Exodus from Egypt. The central event of Pesach is a ritualized meal, called a *seder*, celebrated in the home. The meal is solemn, festive, and elaborate. A seder is a meal of free people, celebrating Jewish freedom from slavery. In order to assure that the meaning of the meal is not lost, the youngest child present asks four questions focused on the one question: Why is this night different from all other nights? Seven weeks after Pesach Jews celebrate *Shavu'ot*, the festival of weeks. It marks both the end of spring and the receptionof the Ten Commandments.

**Chanukah** *Chanukah* is a minor Jewish holiday. However, especially in America, it has taken on increased significance simply because it falls about the same time as Christmas. It is the feast of the rededication of the Temple, when the Greek rulers who controlled ancient Israel were driven out and the Temple was repurified. Chanukah is celebrated mostly in the home where a nine-branched candelabrum, or menorah, is ritually lit each night for eight days. Chanukah, like Christmas, is associated with light during the darkest time of the year.

**Faith Activity**

**Passover and Easter**
The Catholic Church's celebration of Easter Triduum—Holy Thursday, Good Friday, Easter Saturday into Sunday evening—has its roots in the Jewish Passover. Jesus was celebrating the Passover when he had his Last Supper. What is celebrated in each? What religious rituals are involved in each? How long does each last? Research both online, through interviews, and at the library to complete your comparison.

**Faith Activity**

**Chanukah and Christmas** How are these holy days alike? How are they different? What is celebrated in each? What religious rituals are involved in each? How long does each last? Research both online, through interviews, and at the library to complete your comparison.

# Reverence for God

## Faith Activity

**Evaluate the Ruler**
Prepare a visual presentation about one of the early kings of Israel—Saul, David, or Solomon—showing their admirable qualities and deeds and their not-so-admirable qualities and deeds. Then prepare a list of your own admirable qualities and deeds.

A continued challenge to the leaders of Israel was the tendency of people to become impatient and anxious, to return to religious practices dating from before they believed in one God, or to borrow practices of their neighbors.

According to the Exodus epic, when Moses came down from Mount Sinai with the tablets on which the commandments were written, he found that the people had produced a golden calf as an idol to worship. The golden calf has been an example of false worship and idolatry for all time. The oracle of Nathan instructed the leaders of Israel to give the people a place to worship properly to prevent them from turning to idolatry.

## The First Two Commandments

When you read the first commandment in Exodus 20:2–5 or Deuteronomy 5:6–9, you may be surprised at the detail given on what the first commandment implies.

- The people are directed not to make images of heavenly things—such as God, angels, the pearly gates, or saints or common people who have died.

- The people are also directed not to make images of earthly things— plants, animals, and humans—or of things such as rock, water, or sea life.

The monotheistic religions of Judaism and Islam observe similar prohibitions to some degree. In Islam, artists do not make images of animals or humans. Important public places, especially mosques, are decorated with geometric or floral patterns and Arabic lettering.

Revering God and keeping his name holy are the first two of the Ten Commandments; otherwise, other objects or material things may become so important to us that God is shifted down from first place.

The first commandment teaches us to put God first in our lives, to place our hope and trust in him, and to believe in him and all that he has revealed. We must develop and grow in our faith, as well as nourish and protect it. The second commandment says that we should be careful about how we use the name of God. It is not right to swear and use God's name to condemn someone else. The first two commandments remind us that we owe respect and reverence to God. We are to worship, or adore, him alone. God is to be first in our lives—in our priorities, in our thoughts, in our words, in our actions, and in our hearts.

These commandments were not meant only for ancient peoples who worshiped many gods. They are quite relevant to people today. Our "false gods" are not necessarily the many gods of the Romans and the Greeks, gods like Apollo or Pluto. Instead, they can be any of the things we consider more important than God.

Finer and larger homes, cars, clothing, and gourmet food may tempt some and claim their devotion. Money, or misuse of money, can be a problem. Other entertainment, activities, or habits may become so important to us that we forget about God. Sports, hobbies, grades, games, and even health and physical fitness can claim too much of our attention. Some habits can resemble addictions. An insider seeing these behaviors might call them idolatry.

For high school students at the beginning of the twenty-first century, idolatry can have an extended meaning. It can be anything that gets in the way of their spiritual life. The possession of things and the need to participate in certain activities can cause students to get off track. Sports can claim students' energy and devotion. Activities intended for relaxation can become unhealthy competitions.

Our Church leaders provide teaching, guidance, and examples to help us live in relationship with God and according to God's commandments. One such example that helps guide us to live in relationship with God are virtues.

**Virtues** *Virtues* are good moral and spiritual habits that help us make good moral decisions and help us to avoid sin. There are two types of categories of virtues: *theological virtues* and *cardinal virtues*. The theological virtues are the pivotal virtues of faith, hope, and charity. The theological virtues are gifts from God. They are rooted in God, directed toward him, and reflect his presence in our lives. The theological virtues call for a response on our part. That is, by living faithfully, hopefully, and lovingly, we cooperate with God's gifts of faith, hope, and charity.

### Faith Activity

**Life Changes** Silently reflect on how you might change your lifestyle—through the choices you make, the activities in which you participate, perhaps even the friends with whom you spend time—to become less driven by other things and people and more driven by love of God and neighbor.

- *Faith* means believing in God and all that he has revealed to us and that the Church proposes for our belief.

- *Hope* is trust in God and the desire to do his will, achieve eternal life and the graces that make this desire come true.

- *Charity* means loving all of our neighbors as ourselves. It means that we love God above everything else.

The *cardinal virtues* are the principal moral virtues that help us lead a moral life by governing our actions, controlling our passions and emotions, and keeping our conduct on the right track. The cardinal virtues are prudence, fortitude, justice, and temperance. We develop the moral virtues by means of education, practice, and perseverance with the help of God's grace.

## Connect to the Past

**Church Decorations** The Iconostasis and arches of Saint Mark's Cathedral in Venice. Saint Mark's Cathedral is an example of Byzantine art, both inside and outside.
*Using this picture or other research tools, compare the detailed interior of Saint Mark's Cathedral to the interior of your church. What differences did you discover? What similarities did you discover?*

## Religious Art

What might we as Christians consider idolatry? Two interpretations will be mentioned here. Some religious groups have a conservative understanding of imagery in places of worship. Traditional Quaker and Amish meeting houses, Reformed and Evangelical communities, and some others place less emphasis on sculptures, paintings, or stained-glass windows. Eastern—Orthodox and Catholic—Christians treasure and honor their icons—stylized paintings of religious subjects, often saints. In the Church in the East, a historical challenge called the iconoclastic controversy was settled in A.D. 843 in favor of using icons. Catholics tend to favor colorful church buildings with two-dimensional and three-dimensional art, and some Catholic places of worship are filled with beautiful detailed decoration.

These forms of religious art are not idolatry, however. Such art points to, or symbolizes aspects of God or God's creation, starting with holy people; the art is not God. Representations of the Trinity, the Holy Family, and the saints remind us of God's love and faithfulness. Pictures and carvings show us scenes from the Old Testament and New Testament of the Bible. An outsider seeing someone praying in front of such representations might call this idolatry. These representations are not a replacement for God; rather, they are reminders of God and of our faith. The prayer before images of saints is a prayer of intercession, asking the saints to intercede with God the Father through Christ for the intentions of the one praying.

# saints

The Church is a community of believers striving to respond to God's grace and striving to live as faithful followers of Jesus. The Church consists of those living on earth and still striving to follow the Gospel, those who have already died and are in heaven, and those who have died and are in purgatory. We call the entire assembly of Church members the **communion of saints**.

The term *communion of saints* has two closely linked meanings: communion in holy things (*sancta*) and among holy persons (*sancti*). In one sense, all faithful members of the Church are called **saints** because Jesus has called us to be the holy people of God. In another sense, the term *saints* refers only to some deceased members of the Church, who have gone through the process of **canonization**—an official Church statement by which a person is declared a saint for having lived a holy life of heroic virtue. The Church applauds the witness of their lives and holds them up as role models for the way we should respond to God's grace. There are, however, many saints who have not been canonized, or officially recognized, by the Church. We celebrate these saints collectively on November 1, the feast of All Saints.

We believe that greatest among the saints in heaven is the Virgin Mary. Mary is not only the Mother of God—being the Mother of Jesus who is God incarnate—she is the Mother of the whole Church as well.

**Venerating the Saints** Many Catholic churches contain statues of Mary, Joseph, or other saints. Some Church members like to pray before these statues and ask for God's blessings. What is important to realize is that praying with a saint is much different from praying to God.

When someone prays to God, he or she gives adoration and praise to God, who alone is worthy of worship. When people pray with the saints, they are recognizing the saint's holiness and asking them to intercede with God on their behalf. This type of prayer is called intercession. The people honor or venerate the saint, but they do not worship the saint.

**Patron Saints** Patron Saints are saints that have lived holy lives, and many of them have done brave things to spread God's word. When a Catholic is baptized, he or she receives the name of one of the saints of God. This saint becomes the individual's patron saint and protects the individual. Not only are patron saints attributed to individuals, but also countries, dioceses, parishes, illnesses, occupations, causes, as well as many other things that we as Catholics consider to be important.

## Faith Activity

**Patron Saints** With a partner, research the patron saint of your parish or school, of a local hospital, or of a profession or activity in which you or your partner is interested. Discuss with your partner how you can follow the example of the saint.

## Saint Thomas More (1477–1535)

Thomas More was an English statesman and scholar born in London. He studied the classics and new humanistic learning at Oxford, then he attended law school. More was aware of the threat of material success to spiritual life. He discerned his vocation as a layperson and a married man, and he began practicing law.

As Plato's *Republic* and St. Augustine's *City of God* did, More's writing envisioned an ideal state, an island utopia with a just and equal society. More's book *Utopia*, published in 1516, is a social satire with a proposal for a commonwealth. In this work, More spoke against war, religious intolerance, and misuse of property. He advocated a kind of communalism in which "the father of every family or every householder fetcheth whatsoever he and his have need of, and carrieth it away with him without money, without exchange, without any gage, pawn, or pledge. For why should anything be denied unto him, seeing there is an abundance of all things . . . ?"

King Henry VIII took notice of More after *Utopia* was published, and More was appointed to several high-level positions within government. In 1520 he was knighted, so his name is often written with "Sir" before it. In 1529 More was appointed Lord High Chancellor, the highest position within the government that More would attain. Three short years later, More's faith and desire to serve the Lord would interfere with his ability to serve under King Henry VIII.

King Henry VIII sought from the pope an annulment of his marriage to Catherine of Aragon in order to marry Anne Boleyn. When the pope refused to grant an annulment, King Henry created a schism—a formal division—in the Catholic Church, ultimately forming the Church of England. Thomas More refused to side with the king in his revolt against the pope. To defend his beliefs and the Catholic faith, More subsequently resigned from his post. The king arrested More and put him in the Tower of London, at first with many of the amenities of home—including his books and writing materials. Later the king deprived More of most of these amenities. Finally, King Henry VIII set up a rigged trial in which More was convicted of treason. More was executed for rejecting the English king as head of the Church and as superior to all outside rulers, including the pope. More was canonized a saint in 1935.

The Catholic Social Teaching of Rights and Responsibilities maintains that the right to life and all things required for human decency are fundamental rights. Denial of the right to practice one's religion and one's right to life certainly violates this Social Teaching. Saint Thomas More greatly valued the practice of his faith and would not be held under the yoke of oppression. In the end he forfeited his life for what he valued.

## Prayer

Begin by praying the Sign of the Cross.

**Leader:** We pray today with the servants of God who have come before us, that we may learn to listen to and love God as they did, by sharing in their prayers and songs.

**All:** Amen.

**Leader:** Hannah, mother of Samuel, we pray for you to intervene on our behalf, teach us to rely upon the Lord and to thank him when good things happen in our lives.

**All:** My heart exults in the Lord; my strength is exalted in my God.

**Leader:** Solomon, great leader of the Israelites, we strive to have your wisdom. Teach us to pray to the Lord for the ability to choose what is right and follow the one, true God.

**All:** Lord, give your servant therefore an understanding mind...able to discern between good and evil.

**Leader:** We pray that Mary, the mother of our Lord, Jesus Christ, will teach us innocence and purity. Teach us to listen to God's word and to live faithfully and righteously all the days of our lives.

**All:** My soul proclaims the greatness of the Lord, my spirit rejoices in God, my Savior, for he has looked with favor upon his lowly servant.

**Leader:** We follow in the footsteps of Hannah, Solomon, and the Virgin Mary by praising the Lord and rejoicing in all things good. We, too, can rejoice when we follow in the way of the Lord. Pray for a moment in silence that you may have the strength to be like those who have come before us...

**All:** Amen.

**Leader:** We ask these and all blessings through the Father, Son, and Holy Spirit . . .

**All:** Amen.

End by praying the Sign of the Cross.

## Review

1. How do the Books of Kings present the reigns of the kings following Solomon? How is this presentation helpful?

2. What were two key uses of oil in biblical times? How is oil used today in the Church?

3. Through which means is 1 Kings and 2 Kings presented? How is it helpful to readers?

4. What is the difference between a monarchy and a dynasty? How would a monarchy aid the Israelites?

5. What was the Hittites secret?

6. What did Solomon ask of God? How was he rewarded? Name some accomplishments of Solomon's reign.

7. How did Solomon commemorate the completion of the Temple? What was contained within the Temple?

8. What are the High Holy Days of the Jewish year? What does each day mark in the year?

9. What is the symbol most associated with Rosh Hashanah? What does the symbol represent?

10. What does the golden calf symbolize?

11. How did the construction of the Temple help the Israelites honor the first and second commandments?

12. Explain the differences between veneration of saints and prayer to God, the Father.

## Key Words

**canonization (p. 113)**—An official Church statement by which a person is declared to have lived a holy life of heroic virtue; in the last stage of the process of canonization, the person is named a saint.

**communion of saints (p. 113)**—All faithful Church members on earth, in heaven, and in purgatory.

**dynasty (p. 100)**—A succession of rulers in the same family line, frequently father to son.

**messiah (p. 98)**—King or deliverer expected by the Jews; the "anointed one."

**messianism (p. 98)**—Belief in a messiah as the savior of the people.

**monarchy (p. 100)**—Rule by a single head of state, often a hereditary office.

**saints (p. 113)**—Deceased members of the Church, who have been canonized by the Church and are in heaven.

**theocracy (p. 97)**—A nation ruled by God.

**vow (p. 101)**—A solemn promise.

## Teen to Teen

The responsibilities that you have at home are tied to those you have in the greater community around you. Your responsibilities in the Church and to God are tied to everything and everyone around you. What responsibilities do you have at home to your parents? What rights are you granted because you fulfill those responsibilities? How do you think the responsibilities you have from your parents reflect responsibilities you have in the larger community of the world?

*"I think the simple things that I do as chores and house rules are a lot like things we need to do for our world. Taking out the garbage, cleaning the house, and treating each other with respect all come to mind. When I do everything that my parents expect of me, I make my parents proud, I gain a sense of accomplishment, and I feel good that I'm helping my parents."*

*Ethan F.*

## Catholic Social Teaching— Rights and Responsibilities

"In a world where some speak mostly of 'rights' and others mostly of 'responsibilities,' the Catholic tradition teaches that human dignity can be protected and a healthy community can be achieved only if human rights are protected and responsibilities are met. Therefore, every person has a fundamental right to life and a right to those things required for human decency. Corresponding to these rights are duties and responsibilities—to one another, to our families, and to the larger society. While public debate in our nation is often divided between those who focus on personal responsibility and those who focus on social responsibilities, our tradition insists that both are necessary."

(*Sharing Catholic Social Teaching: Challenges and Directions,* USCCB, 1998.)

The United States Declaration of Independence guarantees us certain "inalienable rights," among which are life, liberty, and the pursuit of happiness. What other rights are guaranteed us as citizens of the United States?

To guarantee these rights, we have certain responsibilities as citizens. Among these are the responsibility to vote, to pay taxes, and to obey laws. As the U.S. Catholic Bishops remind us, we have a duty to maintain both our rights and our responsibilities.

### BREAK OPEN the Word

**Read Psalm 78:72,** the reading that opens the chapter. Choose one verse from the Old Testament that prophesizes Jesus as the Good Shepherd and one from the New Testament that shows Jesus as the Good Shepherd. How do both David and Jesus accomplish their task of shepherding God's sheep?

**1020–587** B.C.
Age of Kings

1000 B.C.

**1000–500** B.C.
Vedic Period in India

**c. 922** B.C.
Division of
Hebrew Kingdom

**869–849** B.C.
The prophecy of Elijah

900 B.C.

**c. 900** B.C.
Chavín culture
established in Peru

**800–700** B.C.
Rise of Greek
city-states

# The Kingdom Divided and the Exile

CHAPTER
5

"Depart from evil, and do good;
so you shall abide forever.
"

*Psalm 37:27*

## Chapter Goals

In this chapter, you will:

- learn about the role and significance of the prophets.
- explore the message of the early prophets.
- consider the message of the prophets Isaiah and Micah.
- address the message of the prophets during the Exile.
- learn about Saint Rose Philippine Duchesne.

**c. 760** B.C.
Prophecy of Amos

**c. 730s–722** B.C.
Assyrian invasion
of northern Israel

**663** B.C.
Assyrians push
Nubians out of Egypt

**700 B.C.**

**600 B.C.**

**c. 755–732** B.C.
Prophecy of Hosea

**c. 716** B.C.
Nubian kings add
Egypt to their empire

# The Kingdom Divided and Prophetic Word

During the reigns of kings Saul, David, and Solomon, Israel remained unified. The kings ruled over the twelve tribes and their respective territories. When Solomon died, Israel split into two rival kingdoms—Israel to the north and Judah to the south. Israel and Judah existed side by side for several centuries. During the time of the **Divided Kingdom**, which divided Israel into two separate nations, Israel and Judah were each ruled by a succession of kings. Aside from fighting other invaders, such as the neighboring Arameans, many power struggles took place within the Divided Kingdom itself.

The time of the Divided Kingdom was a time of great upheaval. The people of Israel had many conflicts with the people of Judah and with surrounding kingdoms. Assyrian armies posed a strong threat to the political independence of the Israelites. The people turned from God and began to disregard his commandments. The Old Testament prophets reminded the people of Israel that God would hold them accountable for their actions; the decisions the people of Israel were making in their lives had repercussions. God worked through the prophets to bring the people back into right relationship with him.

Many prophets bore witness to and gave commentary on the political upheavals in the ancient world from the eighth to the sixth century B.C. During this time, the superpowers of the ancient world—Egypt and the great civilizations of the Tigris-Euphrates river valley—Assyria and Babylonia—struggled for control. The **Kingdom of Judea** was located geographically in the middle of these struggles, which directly impacted the kingdom.

## Explore the Land

**Kingdoms of Israel and Judah** This map shows the offshoot kingdom of Judah that broke off after Solomon died. This division created economic, military, and faith problems for each separate kingdom. Which kingdom do you think had the advantage in land? Why?

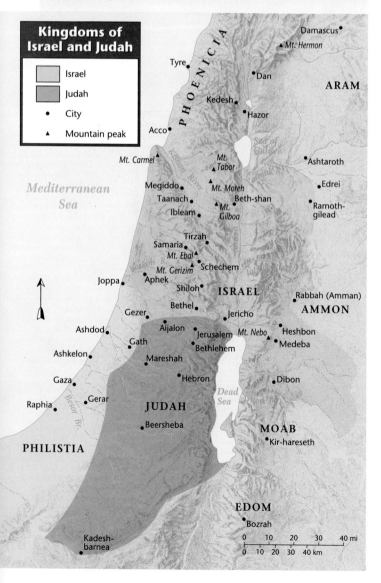

Kingdoms of Israel and Judah

Israel
Judah
• City
▲ Mountain peak

# The Prophets

Prophets in the Old Testament were called by God and given a divine message to convey to his people. Most were men, but some were women. The prophets came from many backgrounds, and some did not remain prophets permanently. When reading prophetic literature in the Old Testament, remember that the prophets were not like modern-day fortune-tellers. The prophets based their predictions on what God had revealed to him or her through religious and other life experiences. The prophets were authentic messengers of God. Conscious of God's authority, the prophets courageously communicated God's message to the people. The prophets' predictions were conditional, however. The predictions depended upon whether the people of Israel heeded God's warning. Israel was successful when it listened to the prophets.

The means by which the divine message, or **prophecy**, is expressed varies greatly from prophet to prophet. Although the message itself comes from God, each prophet has an individual speaking style and uses different types of literary devices to convey God's message.

**Prophetic Literature** Prophetic literature usually takes the form of anthologies of sayings and sermons delivered on different occasions and compiled later by followers of the prophets. The inspired prophetic books of the Old Testament anticipate the fulfillment of God's purposes. Through them, we see God at work in the lives and preaching of the prophets. Each book typically contains the story and speeches of the prophet for which it is named. Biblical scholars consider some prophets, such as Hosea and Amos, as minor prophets because of the brevity of the books named for them. These eighth-century B.C. prophets foretold the destruction of Israel at the hands of the Assyrian Empire and presented the people with some tough decisions.

**Judgment and Encouragement** The prophets of the Old Testament pronounced God's judgment upon Jerusalem, confronted leaders and false prophets, reproached the people of Israel, and gave oracles against Israel and other nations as well. Examples of this mode, or pattern of expression, of pronouncing judgment can be seen throughout the prophetic books. For instance, the prophet Isaiah delivers an oracle of judgment regarding Judah's religious superficiality:

## Faith Activity

**Receiving the Message**
Old Testament prophets lived unusual lives, often standing apart from the community as being "different." Do you think this helped or hindered their message? How would a modern prophet go about voicing his or her message? What effect would the person's way of life have on the public reception of his or her message?

## scripture

"Your new moons and your appointed festivals
 my soul hates;
they have become a burden to me,
 I am weary of bearing them.

When you stretch out your hands,
 I will hide my eyes from you;
even though you make many prayers,
 I will not listen;
 your hands are full of blood."

*Isaiah 1:14–15*

After warning people of impending doom, the prophets offered encouragement and consolation. They explained that if the people returned to God and persevered through the hard times ahead, they would see the eventual restoration of God's people. You will see examples of the mode of prophetic encouragement throughout the prophetic books. For example, the prophecy of Micah focuses on the future victory of God's people:

### scripture

"Do not rejoice over me, O my enemy;
   when I fall, I shall rise;
when I sit in darkness,
   the Lord will be a light to me.
I must bear the indignation of the Lord,
   because I have sinned against him,
until he takes my side
   and executes judgment for me.
He will bring me out to the light;
   I shall see his vindication."

*Micah 7:8–9*

*Faith*
**Sharing**

**Making Decisions**
Think about the following questions this week:

- What is required to make good decisions?
- What are some possible ramifications of making poor decisions?
- To whom am I accountable for the decisions I make?

**A Common Message** During the reigns of Uzziah of Judah and Jeroboam II of Israel, the oracles of the prophet Amos focused on Israel's domestic wrongdoings and predicted doom; however, Amos called for the people to reform. He stressed that they were once a united family. They shared the experience and history of the Exodus. Other prophets, such as Elijah and Hosea, warned of both cultural and political dangers to the chosen people in the Divided Kingdom. The prophets called upon the people of the Kingdom of Israel to make a decision and to act on it. They warned the people that they would be held accountable to God for their actions.

**Interpret the Art**
**Prophets of Old** The Transfiguration by Duccio di Buoninsegna, c. 1308–1311. In the Transfiguration, Jesus brought Peter, James, and John up a mountain and was revealed as God's only son to them.
*Which prophets were also present during the Transfiguration?*

# Prophets of a Just and Jealous God

The people of Israel and Judah had become less than enthusiastic in their commitment to the one true God, for they worshiped Baal alongside the one true God. Breaking the first commandment had become routine, and other sins—adultery, covetousness, and disregard for people who were poor—were widespread. The prophets Amos, Hosea, Elijah, and Elisha all preached God's call to justice. These prophets shared much in common.

| A Shared Vision |
| --- |
| The prophets answered to God as the sole authority. |
| They lived out a single-minded commitment to challenge the Israelites to live in right relationship with God. |
| They served a jealous God who called for justice. |
| They sought to guide the Israelites back to God, who awaited their return with open arms. |
| They modeled and publicly announced God's call to be faithful. |
| They sought God's compassion for themselves and for his people. |

Amos, Hosea, Elijah, and Elisha went to great lengths to explain to the Israelites the concept of a just and jealous God. Hosea depicted God as a jealous husband who demanded fidelity from his wife, Israel. God also called for justice and mercy. Fortunately for the Israelites, and also for us, God is compassionate and forgiving. He is always ready to reconcile with those who repent and return to him.

## scripture

"For the LORD will not forsake his people;
    he will not abandon his heritage;
for justice will return to the righteous,
    and all the upright in heart will follow it."

*Psalm 94:14–15*

The Prophet Amos from the Bible of Souvigny, France, late twelfth century.

## Break open the Word

**Meaning of the Plumb Line** Read Amos 7:7–9. What is the meaning of the plumb line in this prophecy? What other images could be used to get this message across today?

## Amos

The prophet Amos was not from northern Israel and used the word *you* instead of *we* when speaking to the Israelites. Amos was a shepherd before being called by God, and many of Amos' metaphors are drawn from that work.

Amos reiterates God's jealous nature and delivers God's judgment on Israel. He reminds the people of Israel that it is not for their own merit that God had chosen them as the people through whom all nations would come to know God. God's covenant with them brought responsibility, not merely privilege. Their pride and egotism had led to their repeated sin and departure from God's commandments.

The Lord judges the Israelites for their worship. Their worship of him contained the right elements, but they lacked the clean hearts necessary to truly honor God. Formal rituals were being substituted for social responsibility. Amos states, "But let justice roll down like waters, and righteousness like an ever-flowing stream" (*Amos 5:24*). This was God's assurance that in the end **divine justice** and righteousness would prevail. Divine justice is the moral standard by which God judges human conduct.

Many of the common people identified with Amos' work with sheep and cattle. They trusted his prophecy. The disparity between those who were rich and those who were poor was a focus of God's message through Amos. The rich were financially able to make extra sacrifice and to tithe, and seemed to do so as an atonement for their widespread abuse of the lower class. Amos recognized their complacency and in his prophecy pointed out that those who were rich were oblivious to the pain and strife they wrought on those who were poor. In Amos 6:7 we see God's warning: "Therefore they shall now be the first to go into exile, and the revelry of the loungers shall pass away." God holds the people accountable for their actions.

# Hosea

Hosea, an eighth-century prophet, delivered his prophecies to the northern kingdom of Israel as they were suffering through a war with Assyria. Hosea, as a member of the community to which he spoke, was able to identify with his listeners. He often used the word *we* when addressing the Israelites.

Hosea condemned Israel's worship of Baal. God, speaking through Hosea, states that, ". . . I will remove the names of the Baals from her mouth, and they shall be mentioned by name no more" (*Hosea 2:17*). In his prophecies, Hosea describes the political climate during the eighth century. Scholars believe that when Hosea mentions military activity in 5:8–12, he is either referring to an Assyrian invasion or a battle between Israel and Judah.

This prophet accuses both kingdoms of looking toward the two superpowers of the time—Egypt to the west and Assyria to the east—for security. Hosea prophesies that because of such infidelity to God, "They shall not remain in the land of the LORD; but Ephraim shall return to Egypt, and in Assyria they shall eat unclean food" (*Hosea 9:3*). This prophecy was realized when the Assyrians captured Samaria in 722 B.C. and annexed the land, placing about 27,000 Israelites in captivity.

## Break Open the Word

**Biblical Parallels** Read Hosea 2. The prophet Hosea used marital allegory to parallel his relationship with his wife, Gomer, and the relationship God had with his people. Read the four passages below. How might the relationship of Hosea and Gomer be compared to the relationship between God and his people?

Hosea 2:6

Hosea 2:7

Hosea 2:9

Hosea 2:12

## Interpret the Art

**Hosea and the People** The prophet Hosea, from the Missale Remense, c. 1285–1297. Hosea was a great prophet who spoke out against the many misdeeds and sins that the Israelites and Judeans committed.

*What do you think the words on the scroll he is holding says? What would you say to the Israelites and Judeans of his time?*

**Marital Allegory** The prophets often used an **allegory**, or symbolic characters or representations of religious truths, to explain God's covenant with Israel. The most common allegory used was one in which the covenant was compared to a marital commitment. Hosea uses the allegory of God's love and faithfulness to a betraying and adulterous people. The marital allegory includes an allusion to the divorce procedure of Mosaic law. The wording in Hosea 2:2— "she is not my wife, and I am not her husband"—closely resembles the declaration a husband was required to make upon putting his wife out of his house and thus divorcing her.

Hosea's personal life becomes an allegory of divine compassion and unconditional love. Gomer, Hosea's unfaithful wife, is representative of the unfaithful Israelites. Hosea's love for his sinful wife is an allegory of God's love for his sinful people. Hosea compares the Israelites' betrayal of God, through their idolatry and oppression of the poor, to the unfaithfulness of Gomer. This allegory is designed by God, as we can see in the following verse: "The LORD said to me again, 'Go, love a woman who has a lover and is an adulteress, just as the LORD loves the people of Israel, though they turn to other gods. . .'" (*Hosea 3:1*).

▲ Reading the Torah at the Western Wall.

## Faith Activity

**Make a Collage** Clip magazine photos or create your own illustrations of the images Amos and Hosea used to describe God. Make a collage of those images and include a scripture citation for each picture.

Gomer returns to the security of her husband after being unfaithful to him. The prophet calls the Israelites to return to God after being unfaithful to him—they had turned to idolatry and oppressed those who were poor. Gomer refused to see that all she owned was from Hosea, just as the Israelites refused to acknowledge that their very existence was due to God's goodness. The Israelites were instead giving credit to other gods for their vineyards and orchards. In the allegory, Hosea is told by God to restore his marriage. This mirrors God's love for the people of Israel despite their infidelity.

Hosea's message, given after the destruction began, was more gentle than that of Amos. Hosea's message was directed to everyone in Israelite society—ordinary people and priests alike. The priests of the day profited from the people's sins because of the contributions the priests received when people made sins offerings. The offerings were so numerous that some items were sold or given to relatives, thus increasing the priests' power and prestige in the community.

Hosea warned the southern kingdom, Judah, not to follow Israel's example. In his view, the sinfulness of the people of Judah was not as terrible as that of the Israelites, but they were equally chastised for their "adulterous" behavior. In Hosea 5:10, the princes of Judah are compared to people who move boundary markers, or landmarks. Moving territorial boundaries to increase one's property was obviously stealing, a serious crime in Mosaic law.

Hosea also was consistently opposed to paying tribute, a monetary payment to a stronger nation for protection. At this point in history, Israel was paying tribute to Assyria. However, God is a jealous God who insisted that tribute was owed to him alone—the monetary tribute being a symbol of the spiritual tribute due him. There was only one way for Israel to regain God's blessing—repentance. Hosea asked that Israel return to the wilderness to make a fresh start. Hosea spoke a message from the Lord, who did not give in to his wrath but subdued it by compassionately drawing his people to himself.

## Elijah

Elijah was a prophet in the northern kingdom of Israel during the reigns of Ahab and Ahaziah (869–849 B.C.). Ahab was a powerful king who expanded Samaria, Israel's capital city, and who fought many wars against Syria. According to Assyrian records, he also participated in battles against Assyria in an attempt to help the neighboring regions of Syria and Palestine. Ahab looked to Baal, the ancient Canaanite storm god, to replenish the land with rain (*1 Kings 16:30–33*). Baal's followers believed that he provided rain and insured fertility.

**Baal or the One True God?** The people of Israel were torn between worshiping Baal and worshiping the God of Israel. They could not make up their minds, nor could they decide upon their loyalty.

The belief in Baal and its various forms had so permeated ancient Near Eastern life that the Semitic word for Baal was synonymous with lord, owner, and husband. Elijah stressed that the God of Israel was universal in power and therefore the sole provider of rain and fertility.

*Faith*
**Activity**

**Figurative Language**
Old Testament prophets used metaphors and other figurative language to warn the people of Israel. Has a parent or teacher ever used a metaphor or an allegory in order to convey the potential consequences of an action you had done or were contemplating? Was the metaphor or allegory effective?

▲ Fresco of Elijah on Mount Carmel, Dura Europos, Syria

**The Showdown** Elijah orchestrated a very public showdown against Baal. The focus on fire at the showdown made a point of Baal's supposed strength. That Elijah chose a bull for the sacrifice on his altar to God is particularly telling of Elijah's personal devotion. When a priest chose a bull, it signified that the sacrifice was offered in atonement for the priest's personal sins. This underlined the fact that the power witnessed in this demonstration was the power of a pure and holy God, not that of the man offering the sacrifice. The twelve stones Elijah chose symbolized the twelve tribes of Israel prior to the division of the kingdom.

## scripture

"Elijah took twelve stones, according to the number of the tribes of the sons of Jacob, to whom the word of the LORD came, saying, 'Israel shall be your name'; with the stones he built an altar in the name of the LORD. Then he made a trench around the altar, large enough to contain two measures of seed. Next he put the wood in order, cut the bull in pieces, and laid it on the wood. He said, 'Fill four jars with water and pour it on the burnt offering and on the wood.' Then he said, 'Do it a second time'; and they did it a second time. Again he said, 'Do it a third time'; and they did it a third time, so that the water ran all around the altar, and filled the trench also with water.

At the time of the offering of the oblation, the prophet Elijah came near and said, 'O LORD, God of Abraham, Isaac, and Israel, let it be known this day that you are God in Israel, that I am your servant, and that I have done all these things at your bidding. Answer me, O LORD, answer me, so that this people may know that you, O LORD, are God, and that you have turned their hearts back.' Then the fire of the LORD fell and consumed the burnt offering, the wood, the stones, and the dust, and even licked up the water that was in the trench. When all the people saw it, they fell on their faces and said, 'The LORD indeed is God; the LORD indeed is God.'"

*1 Kings 18:31–39*

**Elijah's Credibility** Three times Elijah doused the altar with water to show his strong confidence and faith in God. Because the confrontation took place close to the Mediterranean Sea, the water used would have been salt water. Salt was an important element in Hebrew life. It preserved food, sustained livestock, was a universal medication, and was seen as a symbol of fidelity. To offer a sacrifice without salt was unsatisfactory. The salt symbolized the priest's own self being surrendered. It also made the smoke that was produced smell sweeter to those present as it rose to God.

The dramatic nature of this showdown convinced King Ahab of Elijah's credibility. Elijah experienced a holy fear of God's power. In telling his wife Jezebel about the events of the day, Ahab unleashed on Elijah a formidable enemy. Jezebel became furious when she learned that Elijah had killed the prophets of her god, Baal. Being quite human, Elijah ran away upon the threat of Jezebel even though he had just proven God's great power and invincibility. Ahab, however, saw how clearly Elijah spoke for God.

When Elijah was fearful, he was drawn to Mount Sinai, the place of Moses' meeting with God. God started tending to Elijah's needs immediately—first by angels and then through the word of God himself. Never did God condemn Elijah for his fear. Twice Elijah repeated a litany of his deeds and the Israelites' ignorant response. God spoke to Elijah in the sheer silence. Elijah's stay at Mount Sinai was brief, but it was sufficient time for him to shed his doubt and fear, reconnect with God, and grow in his understanding of God.

**Elijah's Works**  Elijah is one of the most memorable Old Testament prophets. Dramatic miracles occurred during his life and at his death.

| Miracles of Elijah |
| --- |
| Elijah received food from a raven, |
| He multiplied a poor widow's pantry, |
| He raised a child from the dead, |
| He caused a king's soldiers to be consumed by fire, |
| He parted the Jordan river, and |
| He rode to heaven in a flaming chariot. |

▼ Chariot of Elijah from the Verdun Altar by Nicolas of Verdun, 1181.

The miracles of Elijah focused on substances that Baal was credited for dominating: fire, rain, and farm crops. God worked through Elijah in dramatic ways in order to catch the attention of a nation lulled into complacency with a false god of convenience, Baal. The God of Israel is Lord of nature, as well as of history and of politics.

# Elisha

Elisha was the perfect replacement for Elijah. His youthful enthusiasm and dedication to learning is unmatched in the Old Testament. He walked as the apprentice to a great prophet, yet Elisha never changed his own character in the style of hero-worship. Elijah fought the powers of evil; Elisha kindled the powers of good. His last moments with Elijah were particularly telling of his character. When asked what he would like Elijah to do for him before he left, Elisha's response was one of pure wisdom coupled with respect for his teacher. He requested of Elijah, ". . . let me inherit a double share of your spirit" (2 Kings 2:9).

# Prophets in the Eighth to Sixth Century B.C.

## Faith Activity

**A Superpower?** The United States is often referred to as a superpower. Work with a small group to discuss what it means to be a superpower. Make a list of the characteristics of a superpower and then assess whether these characteristics apply to Assyria. You can reference Isaiah 5:26–30 and the Book of Nahum for specific characteristics.

▼ Guernica by Pablo Picasso, 1937.

Isaiah prophesied during the reigns of four kings of Judah from 783–687 B.C. He forewarned Judeans of Assyria's looming presence: "it will sweep on into Judah as a flood" (*Isaiah 8:8*). In response to this presence, Judah was pressured to rebel against Assyria, first by Israel and later by Egypt and Philistine. Isaiah warns of the folly of this later alliance. He tells the Judeans that they will be "dismayed and confounded" (*Isaiah 37:27*) because Egypt will be led away by the Assyrians. The Assyrians eventually did take control of the capitals of Israel and Samaria, and later of Judah.

The politics of Judah's powerful neighbors and its effect on Judah were not the only considerations of prophets at this time. While Micah was a contemporary of Isaiah, his prophecies addressed mainly the internal social evils present in Judah. Micah was originally a rural farmer, unlike the city-dweller Isaiah, and was a champion of those who were underprivileged. Micah, an advocate for social justice, preached against the evil policies of Jerusalem: "Its rulers give judgment for a bribe, its priests teach for a price, its prophets give oracles for money" (*Micah 3:11*). Micah's prophecies influenced King Hezekiah, who established social reforms.

Assyria, the superpower that Isaiah had feared, lost influence and control as Babylon's power began to strengthen. The prophet Nahum speaks directly of the events surrounding the fall of Assyria's most important city, Nineveh. In 612 B.C. Babylon captured and destroyed Nineveh. Nahum sees the fate of the Judeans at the hands of the Assyrians and the subsequent "Devastation, desolation, and destruction!" of Nineveh as an act of God's intent for his people (*Nahum 2:10*). He also reassures them: ". . . Though I have afflicted you, I will afflict you no more. And now I will break off his yoke from you and snap the bonds that bind you" (*Nahum 1:12–13*). He encourages the Judeans to celebrate their festivals, for ". . . never again shall the wicked invade you" (*Nahum 1:15*).

During the reign of Josiah in Judah (640–609 B.C.), a reform of Judaism took place. The reform was based on a book of the covenant found in the Temple. This book included the requirement of the elimination of the worship of other gods, the centralization of worship in Jerusalem, and a public recommitment of the nation to the covenant. Josiah is one of the few kings praised in the Deuteronomic History because he consulted a prophet before his reform. The "found" book may have been an early version of Deuteronomy.

## Isaiah

Isaiah is considered the greatest prophet of the Old Testament. He is quoted more than fifty times in the New Testament. His prophecy spanned the reign of four kings of Judah, and his ministry was strong despite his listeners' disregard for his message. Clearly seeing the great gulf between sinful people and God, Isaiah proclaimed his own uncleanness in a vision prompting the angels to touch his mouth with a live coal. Only then did he accept his call.

### Break Open the Word

**The Book of the Covenant** Read 2 Kings 22, the story of the finding of the book of the covenant during the reign of Josiah. Who is Huldah, and what is her role in the reform?

▼ Isaiah Visited by a Seraph by Giovanni Battista Tiepolo, 1726.

"In the year that King Uzziah died, I saw the Lord sitting on a throne, high and lofty; and the hem of his robe filled the Temple. Seraphs were in attendance above him; each had six wings: with two they covered their faces, and with two they covered their feet, and with two they flew. And one called to another and said:

'Holy, holy, holy is the LORD of hosts;
the whole earth is full of his glory.'

The pivots on the thresholds shook at the voices of those who called, and the house filled with smoke. And I said: 'Woe is me! I am lost, for I am a man of unclean lips, and I live among a people of unclean lips; yet my eyes have seen the King, the LORD of hosts!'

Then one of the seraphs flew to me, holding a live coal that had been taken from the altar with a pair of tongs. The seraph touched my mouth with it and said: 'Now that this has touched your lips, your guilt has departed and your sin is blotted out.' Then I heard the voice of the Lord saying, 'Whom shall I send, and who will go for us?' And I said, 'Here am I; send me!'"

*Isaiah 6:1–8*

In Isaiah's prophecy, we first read of the bridge to fill the gap between the sins of humans and the call of God. In Isaiah 6:5 the prophet cries out, ". . . yet my eyes have seen the King, the LORD of hosts!" This is the first instance of a prophet referring to a king other than the rulers of the day. In their message, Isaiah and the other prophets firmly establish that Israel will be punished, but God will provide salvation through a Davidic king.

Another message that Isaiah delivered involves his frequent reference to a *remnant*. The *remnant* refers to a portion of God's people who would be spared his punishment, because they alone had remained faithful to the covenant. Jeremiah and Ezekiel and some of the minor prophets include this concept, but Isaiah communicates the sense of salvation for a remnant rather than for the whole nation or people.

Clearly, national pride or solidarity will not guarantee being spared God's wrath. This leads Isaiah's listening audience, past and present, to the realization that personal faith and commitment are far more reliable as the means to salvation. In Isaiah's time, that was quite a novel idea. He develops this message further, giving guidance on how to develop that personal faith. A personal faith calls the individual to yearn for a relationship with his or her Creator and to live in obedience to God's will—to live justly.

# JESUS THE SUFFERING SERVANT

The Old Testament frequently pictured God as a warrior who at times, resorts to just force. But in the prophecies of Isaiah, God saves not by strength, force, or violence, but by suffering that of the Suffering Servant. Isaiah prophesied the coming of a suffering servant messiah, using graphic imagery and very distinct language. Isaiah tells the reader that the one who "by his bruises we are healed" will be "struck down by God and afflicted," "a man of suffering" and despised and rejected by others." (See *Isaiah 53:3–5*.)

In his public life, in his Passion, and in his death, Jesus took on the image of the Suffering Servant of Isaiah's prophecies. Even in the Infancy Narratives, suffering had already entered into the story of Jesus' birth:

- There was no room for him in the inn.
- Mary and Joseph had to wrap him in bands of cloth and lay him in a manger.
- Poor shepherds first recognize him.
- Herod the Great slaughtered the innocent children as he tried to kill Jesus after his birth. Mary and Joseph flee with Jesus into exile in Egypt.

At the Presentation in the Temple, Simeon said of Jesus, "This child is destined for the falling and the rising of many in Israel, and to be a sign that will be opposed . . . " and said to Mary, "and a sword will pierce your own soul too" (*Luke 2:34–35*).

Jesus is a suffering Messiah whose life—from the beginning—points to the cross. Jesus dies in order that his true identity be made known. Suffering and rejection are an inevitable part of Jesus' ministry and death. Jesus' death is as God wills it to be—a ransom—". . . the Son of Man came not to be served but to serve, and to give his life a ransom for many" (*Mark 10:45*).

But Jesus did not suffer in vain. He overcomes sin and death, and rises from the dead. He transforms suffering.

### Break Open the Word

**Servant of the Lord Oracles** The prophet Isaiah spoke of a servant who would bring about salvation through his suffering, most specifically in his four Servant of the Lord oracles. The New Testament and Christian Tradition identify Jesus as the fulfillment of these prophecies. Read the four passages below and describe how Jesus fulfills each.

Isaiah 42:1–4

Isaiah 49:1–7

Isaiah 50: 4–11

Isaiah 52:13—53:12

## Micah

The prophet Micah, a contemporary of Isaiah, had firsthand experience with the evils he attacked. A laborer from an obscure village in the foothills of Judea, Micah characteristically focused much attention on the capital cities—pinpointing them as centers for moral corruption. Micah vividly portrays the decay of the Israelite society and proclaims that God will use Assyria to punish the sins of Jerusalem. Although a native of the southern kingdom, Micah favored the Moses-Sinai tradition of Israel. But his prophecy of God's punishment is not limited to either the northern or southern kingdom.

Micah was particularly attuned to the socioeconomic injustices that abounded. He itemizes Israel's sins—from idolatry and covetousness to hate, dishonesty, and family discord. He laid out his argument like a lawyer, with God as the plaintiff. Each of the three sections—Micah 1—2: Trial of the Capitals; Micah 3—5: Trial of the Leaders; and Micah 6—7: Trial of the People—begins with the clear message of punishment and doom and concludes with a message of hope and salvation. The fulfillment of Micah's prophecies can be found in 2 Chronicles and Ezra.

Micah called his contemporaries to act with justice. His words continue to apply to all who hear them.

### Faith Activity

**Messages for Today**
If prophets who resembled those in the ancient world existed today, what do you think their message would be? How do you think the prophets and their message would be received?

### Faith Activity

**Social Action** With a small group, create a plan of social action about something that interests you. You might clean up a wilderness area or a neighborhood park. Or write a letter of protest to a U.S. corporation that employs child labor in another country.

### scripture

"He has told you, O mortal, what is good;
    and what does the LORD require of you
but to do justice, and to love kindness,
    and to walk humbly with your God?"

*Micah 6:8*

## Nahum

The prophecy of Nahum is full of nationalism. His message is that God would act exclusively on behalf of Judah in order to realize the hope of Israel. He had witnessed cruelties in Assyria and was overjoyed at the city's destruction. He portrayed God as the avenger, but with mercy.

# Prophets During the Babylonian Exile

Babylonia did turn out to be as wicked as Assyria. While Nahum did not prophesy this, Jeremiah did. Jeremiah states, "Even if you defeated the whole army of Chaldeans [Babylonians] who are fighting against you, and there remained of them only wounded men in their tents, they would rise up and burn this city with fire" (*Jeremiah 37:10*). The Babylonians forced many of the Jews from the southern kingdom into exile in 597 B.C. Ten years later the Babylonians forced another deportation of the Jews and destroyed the Temple in Jerusalem.

Ezekiel is the only prophet who came to his calling during the **Babylonian Exile**, the period of history when the Babylonians forced most of the inhabitants of Judah to migrate to Babylon. As God speaks through Ezekiel, he tells the **exiles**, or people banished from their home or land, that they are being punished for their infidelities and idolatry but will eventually be restored. He assures them that the national powers that have forced them into exile are under his control. In Ezekiel 29:20 he tells them, "I have given him [the Babylonian king Nebuchadnezzar] the land of Egypt as his payment for which he labored, because they worked for me, says the Lord GOD."

After the Babylonians had deported Jews a third time, in 582 B.C., the Jewish people's strength began to wane. Cyrus of Persia came into power. He was religiously tolerant and, beginning in 535 B.C. or maybe as early as 538 B.C., he allowed the Jews to return home and restore the Temple in Jerusalem. Chapters 40—55, called Second Isaiah, respectfully acknowledge Cyrus as an agent of God's plan for Israel. Second Isaiah refers to Cyrus as being anointed by God.

## Faith Activity

**Many Forms of Exile**
Think about a time when you have felt like an exile. In two to three paragraphs describe the circumstances. How did you cope? What were your feelings during and after your time of exile?

▼ The Tomb of Cyrus the Great stands in Pasargadae, Iran.

▲ Baskets of dried figs in the sunshine.

## Zephaniah

Zephaniah was influenced by Isaiah, although Zephaniah lived several decades after Isaiah. Zephaniah's message condemned practices common during the early part of Josiah's reign before the reforms, such as worshiping the sun, moon, and stars. His prophecy warned of judgment, but he allowed for the faithful remnant of Israel to be spared. He also protested against the sinful ways of the Assyrian court ministers.

## Jeremiah

Jeremiah does not preach of the renewal of the covenant made on Mount Sinai but of its replacement. As a priest, Jeremiah intercedes repeatedly for the people, but he also admonishes the Israelites for their reliance on formal religion as their only expression of faith. In fact, his vision of the baskets of figs in Jeremiah 24 clearly sets the Israelites in exile as the remnant that God will redeem.

### scripture

"Thus says the LORD, the God of Israel: Like these good figs, so I will regard as good the exiles from Judah, whom I have sent away from this place to the land of Chaldeans. I will set my eyes upon them for good, and I will bring them back to this land. I will build them up, and not tear them down; I will plant them, and not pluck them up. I will give them a heart to know that I am the LORD; and they shall be my people and I will be their God, for they shall return to me with their whole heart."

*Jeremiah 24:5–7*

The theme of justice appears in Jeremiah's prophecy, as it does with most prophets. In the Temple sermon (See *Jeremiah 7:1–15.*), Jeremiah condemns those who oppress refugees, orphans, and widows, and who think God will overlook their sins because they come to the Temple.

**Lessons Taught** Jeremiah's prophecy contains lessons he teaches by the use of objects. Probably the most recognized is that of the potter and the clay. (See *Jeremiah 18.*) Through this analogy and others, Jeremiah communicates God's plans for Israel. God could destroy Israel as easily as a potter can crumple a pot on the wheel. The people of Israel had become useless and ruined, like a spoiled linen belt. In Jeremiah 27:2–11 the prophet predicted destruction to any nation not submitting to Babylon's yoke of control. Even so, in Jeremiah 51:59–64 Babylon itself would sink and rise no more, like a sunken scroll.

Jeremiah was initially reluctant when called to be a prophet. He said, ". . . Truly I do not know how to speak, for I am only a boy" (*Jeremiah 1:6*). However, God reassured him with the promise of his presence and his rescue of Jeremiah. Jeremiah spent much time in exile, both physically and emotionally. Despite being criticized, rebuked, and exiled, Jeremiah remained faithful to God throughout his life.

### BREAK OPEN the *Word*

**Gospel** Read Jeremiah 31:31–34. These verses have been called the "gospel before the gospel." Why do you think these verses are referred to in such a way?

# vocation

The prophets were not the only ones to receive God's call. He also calls each of us to be a sign of life and hope for the world. God created each of us to be in his friendship and to share in his life. He continually calls all people to believe in him and to grow in his friendship. And, like the prophets, we rely on God for strength and direction.

Through Baptism, Christ calls each of us to holiness—to become more like him. We are called to take part in the Church's mission of spreading the Good News through our words and actions. This call is our baptismal or common vocation. The word *vocation* refers to one's calling or purpose. In religious terms a **vocation** is one's call to love and serve God and others. God calls us to live out this shared vocation in different ways.

**Single Life**   Through the single life, people profess to the mystery of the Incarnation and bring the message of the Good News to others through their work, civic involvement, and family life.

**Married Life**   In married life husband and wife affirm the image of God in one another and welcome children to share their lives. Like those in the single life, married people are called to be a witness to their faith in the world.

**Ordained Life**   Men receive the sacrament of Holy Orders to become deacons, priests, or bishops, and they minister to the Church through teaching, leading, and worship.

**Consecrated Life**   Some women and men are called by God to consecrate their lives publicly through vows of poverty, chastity, and obedience. These religious sisters, brothers, and priests live, pray, and work in community to stand together in opposition to the culture and values of the world that are not Gospel values.

## Faith Activity

**Called by God**   Quietly reflect on the ways God might be calling you to serve him and the Church. Ask yourself these questions:

- What gifts and talents can I share with the Church?
- When I really think about my life, where do I see myself in ten or fifteen years?
- Have I seriously considered what God's plan might be for me?

After reflecting on these questions, make a list of your own questions to ask people living out the different vocations. Your diocesan Web site probably has answers to some of these questions, and the ministers and religious men and women serving your parish or school might be able to help you, too.

**Acrostics of the Old Testament**  Biblical scholars attribute the Book of Lamentations to the prophet Jeremiah. It was written using a literary device called an **acrostic**. An acrostic is an ordered poem in which the first letters of the individual lines or verses, when combined in order, form their own pattern, phrase, or word. In the acrostics of the Old Testament, each line begins with a letter of the Hebrew alphabet. This method was probably used as a mnemonic device, or memory tool, to help people remember the verses. Very few English translations of the Old Testament have attempted to maintain this device, so the pattern is lost in translation. Lamentations 3 was originally an acrostic in which each letter of the twenty-two-character Hebrew alphabet was represented by a set of three verses. The other chapters of the book each have twenty-two verses.

Nahum 1:2–8 and several psalms (9, 10, 25, 34, 37, 111, 112, 145) were also written in the form of an acrostic. This very structured form of poetry works well in Lamentations because it provides a ritualized way of expressing grief, much like a funeral liturgy. Because the form is so commonly used, it provides familiarity at a time of great upheaval.

## Habakkuk and Ezekiel

Habakkuk is distinctive as a prophet because he is the first one to question God's ways of governing the world. The best part is that God answers willingly. He says that Babylon was the correcting rod, the Lord's avenging instrument.

As a prophet, Ezekiel's interest in the Temple and the liturgy is unequaled. Perhaps this is because he was both a priest and a prophet. His calling to the role of prophet was unique; he was the first to be called to go outside of Palestine—to Babylon. This singular experience reiterated to Ezekiel the message that God reaches the individual despite his or her lineage or his or her geographical location.

▼ Ezekiel and The Valley of Life Fresco, A.D. 239.

Ezekiel exhorted the individual to be alert for God and ready to repent. (See *Ezekiel 3:16–21*.) His commitment to priestly legislation has earned him the title of "The Father of Judaism." The absolute majesty of God is a strong undercurrent throughout Ezekiel's message. Historians believe that Ezekiel influenced the Law of Holiness, which is found in Leviticus 17—26. Portions of Ezekiel's prophecy were considered dangerous because of its strong images, prompting some groups to require that a reader be at least thirty years of age. Ezekiel makes a strong case for personal responsibility for sin and for goodness.

Ezekiel's view of salvation is one that begins with total obliteration. The Temple that was used in idolatry will be destroyed, as will the worshipers. Then a new Temple and restoration will occur. Ezekiel's prophecy comes to fruition with the new Temple that was built right after the exile about 520–515 B.C.

**Allegory and Imagery**  Like Hosea, Ezekiel offers a marital allegory. It can be found in Ezekiel 16. God chastises Israel, calling her, "Adulterous wife, who receives strangers instead of her husband!" (*Ezekiel 16:32*). Other allegories found in the Book of Ezekiel include the allegory of the vine (See *Isaiah 15.*), the allegory of the eagles (See *Isaiah 17:1–21.*), the allegory of the cedar (See *Isaiah 17:22–24* and *31:1–18.*), and the allegory of the pot. (See *Isaiah 24:1–14.*) Isaiah's vineyard song (See *Isaiah 5:1–10.*) illustrates a social justice theme: people who are rich, who build up large estates by taking land from those who are poor, are condemned.

Ezekiel used some powerful images to convey the need for, and experience of, new life. One of his most popular analogies is that of the dry bones in the desert.

## scripture

"Then he said to me, 'Prophesy to these bones, and say to them: O dry bones, hear the word of the LORD. Thus says the Lord GOD to these bones: I will cause breath to enter you, and you shall live; and you shall know that I am the LORD.'"

*Ezekiel 37:4–6*

**Use of Repetition**  The prophets of the Old Testament often used repetition to reinforce elements of their message. Scholars have pointed out that Ezekiel uses the word *mortal* in reference to himself as the prophet about a hundred times, and uses the phrase "and they/you will know that I am the LORD" about fifty times. Similarly, a line that recurs throughout a poem or song in such a way is called a *refrain*. Throughout the Book of Isaiah, key phrases and lines are often repeated or used as a refrain. Verses might begin with similar lines, such as Isaiah 51:9a: "Awake, awake, put on strength, O arm of the LORD!" and Isaiah 52:1a: "Awake, awake, put on your strength, O Zion!"

break open the *Word*

**Refrain**  In the Old Testament, verses are often repeated in different contexts. Read Jeremiah 49:19 and compare it to Jeremiah 50:44. Why do you think the verse is repeated?

# Second Isaiah

Second Isaiah or Deutero-Isaiah is the title given to chapters 40—55 of the Book of Isaiah. The distinction is based on the anonymous authorship of these chapters, which likely were composed and written down by disciples of the prophet Isaiah about 150 years after the first chapters. These chapters are characterized by consolation and peace. The "anointed one" to which the text refers is believed to have been Cyrus of Persia, consistent with the political times.

The author of Second Isaiah wrote that redemption was clearly coming and promises a deliverance based on the end of time—the end of the world. He distinguishes between the ages, then and now, "things of old" and "new things." The exile is God's judgment and will be followed by a time of eternal salvation. This clear time delineation furthered the Israelites' understanding of God as the *only* God. God was not only a practical choice for Israel, he was the only choice.

## Saint Rose Philippine Duchesne (1769–1852)

Rose Philippine Duchesne was born into a wealthy family in Grenoble, France. Early in life, she developed a concern for those who were poor. She loved to read books about missionaries and dreamed of helping Native Americans someday. By the time she was twelve, Rose knew she wanted to pursue the religious life. Much against her father's wishes, she entered the Visitation Order at the age of seventeen.

During the French Revolution, all religious orders in France were disbanded, yet young Rose continued her service to others. She cared for people who were sick or poor, sheltered fugitive priests, visited prisoners, and taught children. After the Revolution, Rose was frustrated by failed attempts to reestablish the Visitation Order at Grenoble. She joined the Society of the Sacred Heart.

In 1816 Bishop William DuBourg of St. Louis visited the Paris convent, seeking nuns to come to America to open schools in the new frontier. Rose enthusiastically volunteered, and, at the age of forty-eight, she and four other nuns embarked on a ten-week voyage across the Atlantic, followed by a forty-day trip up the Mississippi to St. Louis. Upon their arrival there, however, the bishop informed the weary nuns that he had chosen the town of St. Charles—some twenty miles further west—for their first mission. Rose obeyed the bishop and worked admirably in the midst of abject poverty.

The log cabin that had been rented for the nuns in St. Charles became the convent for five nuns, a boarding school for three young ladies from St. Louis, and a free school for local pioneer children. After one year of unstable enrollment, the decision was made to abandon St. Charles and open a school in Florissant. In 1828 the nuns were urged by the Jesuits to return to St. Charles to reopen the school near the newly established parish church built by the Jesuits.

Rose spent the next twenty years establishing schools in Missouri and Louisiana, some of which are still in use today. Her schools became models for educational excellence in the cities where they were built. The Society of the Sacred Heart spread around the world, in part due to Rose's missionary zeal.

Rose's childhood desire to work with Native Americans never faltered. In 1841, at the age of seventy-two, Rose was finally permitted to accompany other Sacred Heart nuns and Jesuit priests to a Potawatomi mission in Sugar Creek, Kansas. Although she considered herself a failure because of her inability to master the Potawatomi language, she deeply impressed the natives by her habit of constant prayer. They reverently named her Quah-kah-ka-num-ad, meaning, "Woman who prays always."

The Option for the Poor and Vulnerable is a difficult Catholic Social Teaching for many people today to act upon. We can look to Saint Rose for guidance and strength, for in her verve and zeal for caring for those who are poor, we see that she truly placed those with less ahead of those with more.

## Prayer

Begin by praying the Sign of the Cross.

**Leader:** Holy Spirit, grant that we may never be separated from the love of our Lord, as the Israelites were from their land, and at times, from the Lord. Show us ways to remain faithful, strong in our convictions, and never live in fear.

**All:** Amen.

**Leader:** Ahab ruled Israel and was worshiping Baal, a false god. Elijah knew the Lord was there for him and the Lord answered Elijah when he was most in need. Let us read together 1 Kings 18:22–23.

**All:** "I, even I only, am left a prophet of the LORD; but Baal's prophets number four hundred fifty. Let two bulls be given to us; let them choose one bull for themselves, cut it into pieces, and lay it on the wood, but put no fire to it; I will prepare the other bull and lay it on the wood, but put no fire on it. Then you call on the name of your god and I will call on the name of the LORD; the god who answers by fire is indeed God."

**Leader:** The Lord, of course, answered with fire and Baal did not. The Lord provides for those in need. Elijah experienced this and the Apostles experienced the fire of the Holy Spirit on Pentecost. Let us read together how the Lord helped the Apostles overcome their fear in Acts 2:2–4.

**All:** "And suddenly from heaven there came a sound like the rush of a violent wind, and it filled the entire house where they were sitting. Divided tongues, as of fire, appeared among them, and a tongue rested on each of them. All of them were filled with the Holy Spirit. . ."

**Leader:** God the Father and the Holy Spirit guided the prophets and the Apostles. We pray that God the Father and the Holy Spirit may guide us in our lives as well.

**All:** Amen.

End by praying the Sign of the Cross.

## Review

1. When did Israel divide into two kingdoms? What were the two kingdoms?

2. On what did the prophets base their predictions?

3. What is prophetic literature?

4. What was Amos before he was a prophet? What was the focus of God's message through Amos?

5. Name three images Hosea uses to describe God. Hosea's marriage to Gomer is an allegory for what concept?

6. During what reigns was Elijah a prophet? List three miracles that occurred during Elijah's life.

7. How does Nahum portray God?

8. What did the prophecies of Micah primarily address?

9. To what realization does Isaiah lead his audience? How many times is Isaiah quoted in the New Testament?

10. What literary device is used in the Book of Lamentations?

11. What is likely the most recognized lesson in the prophecy of Jeremiah? What is the lesson it teaches?

12. What are the vocations? How does each vocation call us to serve God?

## Key Words

**acrostic (p. 138)**—An ordered poem in which the first letters of individual lines or verses, when combined in order, form their own pattern, phrase, or word.

**allegory (p. 126)**—Symbolic characters that presents religious truths or generalizations about human nature.

**Babylonian Exile (p. 135)**—Period of history when the Babylonians forced most of the inhabitants of Judah to migrate to Babylon; the Exile.

**Divided Kingdom (p. 120)**—The result of the division of Israel into two separate nations: Israel and Judah.

**divine justice (p. 124)**—The moral standard by which God judges human conduct; the realization of that standard by God; an expression of God's righteousness, pity, love, and grace.

**exiles (p. 135)**—People banished from their home or land.

**Kingdom of Judea (p. 120)**—The kingdom south of Israel that existed from the time following Solomon's death in 925 B.C. until the destruction of the Temple in 586 B.C.

**prophecy (p. 121)**—The words of God, delivered through a spokesperson known as a prophet; generally calls for the Israelites to live justly and avoid idolatry.

**vocation (p. 137)**—One's call to love and serve God and others.

## Personal Journey

### Teen to Teen

Imagine for a moment that you have lost all of your money; you are alone, you are poor, and you have nothing. To whom would you turn in your time of despair? The Lord welcomes all, especially those who are in need or those who have less. What verses would remind you of God's loving plan for you and all others who suffer?

*"Luke 6:20–21 reminds me to help those who are poor and have less. It would be a strong, daily reminder of how the Lord promises care and eternal happiness especially to people who are hungry, sad, or poor."*

*Isabella M.*

## Catholic Social Teaching— Option for the Poor and Vulnerable

"In a world characterized by growing prosperity for some and pervasive poverty for others, Catholic teaching proclaims that a basic moral test is how our most vulnerable members are faring. In a society marred by deepening divisions between rich and poor, our tradition recalls the story of the Last Judgment (Matthew 25:31–46) and instructs us to put the needs of the poor and vulnerable first."

(*Sharing Catholic Social Teaching: Challenges and Directions,* USCCB, 1998.)

The prophets of the Old Testament spoke of a need for social justice. They warned that God will deal harshly with those who turn the other way when faced with the challenge of helping people in need.

We have a responsibility to care for people who are poor or oppressed in our community. We should stand up for social justice. One way that we can make a difference in our community is to volunteer with organizations that help people who are poor. We can also donate money to these organizations if we are not able to offer our time. Most of all, we must remember to treat people who are poor with respect.

Another way that we can demonstrate concern for social justice is to focus on groups within our society that are oppressed by others. Depending on the community in which you live, this might include people of a certain social class, ethnicity, or religious background.

**Break Open the Word**

**Read Psalm 37:27**
This verse is similar to the Beatitudes, in which God protects and blesses those who are faithful and righteous. Those who are wicked or evil are devoid of this blessing. Which rulers of the Old and New Testament show examples of not abiding by God's commands and thus not receiving his blessings?

**540–510** B.C.
Time period covered
by Third Isaiah

**522–486** B.C.
Persian king Darius I extends empire
from the Nile to the Indus River

**509** B.C.
Roman republic established

**550** B.C.

**500** B.C.

**539** B.C.
Cyrus conquers Babylonia;
Height of Etruscan expansion in Italy

**515** B.C.
Reconstruction of
Temple completed

# The Restoration and New Beginnings

"Create in me a clean heart, O God,
and put a new and right spirit within me."

*Psalm 51:10*

## Chapter Goals

In this chapter, you will:

- learn about the impact of the Persian empire on Israel's history.
- explore the ways Haggai, Zechariah, and Joel tried to preserve the religious tradition and the identity of their people.
- examine the time of renewal and reform called for by Malachi and third Isaiah.
- increase your knowledge of the books of Jonah and Esther.
- learn about Cesar Chavez.

**486–465 B.C.**
Xerxes I rules over Persia

**447–432 B.C.**
Parthenon built in Greece

450 B.C.      400 B.C.

**c. 450 B.C.**
Zenith of Greek drama

# The Persian Empire and Israel's History

## Faith Sharing

**Relationships** Think of a relationship you have—with a parent, sibling, relative, friend, or neighbor—that is strained.

- What can you do to improve the relationship?
- Make a list of actions and words you can use to restore the relationship.
- Can the actions and words you listed carry into your relationship with God?

## Break Open the Word

**Overlooking Shortcomings** Read 2 Samuel 1—4. With a small group, record the problems of David and Solomon's rule. Then discuss why you think the author of Chronicles did not include these issues.

The historical and postexilic prophetic books most likely were written between the sixth and fourth centuries B.C., when the ancient Middle East was part of the Persian empire. The Old Testament writers were active participants, but they also reinterpreted the events of previous times and of their time to portray Israel as one single community—a people intent on one place of worship in Jerusalem. The Book of Chronicles, for example, emphasizes David's role in establishing the nation's worship.

The two books of the Chronicles are grouped with the historical books of the Old Testament. They are a creative reinterpretation of history that presents a review of Israel's history in terms of God's unfolding plan rather than in a pristine chronology. The stories of the two books of the Chronicles are condensed or expanded to meet the needs of this theme.

A large emphasis is placed on the reigns of David and Solomon, but the personal shortcomings and difficulties these two men faced are omitted. For instance, none of the problems detailed in 2 Samuel 1—4 are mentioned by the authors of the Chronicles. David is placed on the throne quickly and easily: "So all the elders of Israel came to the king at Hebron, and David made a covenant with them at Hebron before the LORD. And they anointed David king over Israel, according to the word of the LORD by Samuel" (*1 Chronicles 11:3*). In addition, the Book of Chronicles uses a long genealogy from creation to King David (See *1 Chronicles 1—8.*) to give the impression that all the previous events were a preparation for David.

The people of Israel had been split apart and faced the challenges of reconstructing the Temple and restoring their way of life after returning from exile. At that time, worship became more important for defining Jewish identity since the people no longer had an independent nation.

# The Emperors

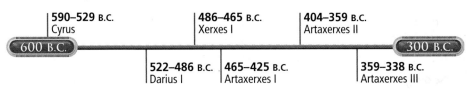

| 590–529 B.C. Cyrus | | 486–465 B.C. Xerxes I | 404–359 B.C. Artaxerxes II |
|---|---|---|---|
| 600 B.C. | | | 300 B.C. |
| | 522–486 B.C. Darius I | 465–425 B.C. Artaxerxes I | 359–338 B.C. Artaxerxes III |

The Persian empire's breadth was as great as its duration; it extended from Egypt in the west to the Indus River in the east. The founder of the empire, Cyrus the Great, was responsible for laying the cornerstones on which the empire thrived: military capability and efficient administrative systems. A characteristic of Cyrus the Great that affected the restoration, but did not extend to all of his successors, was his politically smart tolerance of other people's religious customs and practices.

**Cyrus the Great** Cyrus' mother was the daughter of the king of Medes, and his father was vassal prince. The historian Herodotus recounts that the king of Medes had a dream in which his infant grandson, Cyrus, would someday overthrow him. In a story that resembles the upbringing of Moses, the king orders Cyrus slain, but the king's chief adviser gives the infant to a shepherd who raises Cyrus. He lives and, as a young man, revolts against his grandfather. The king's army surrenders to Cyrus. With the surrender of the army, Cyrus inherits the empire of the Medes.

Cyrus' empire-building was the result of his military prowess and diplomatic skill. In 539 B.C. Cyrus conquered Babylonia. The rule of Syria and Palestine came with his conquest of Babylonia, the place where many Israelites of the former kingdom of Judah were prisoners—in exile—under Babylonian rule. Cyrus showed compassion to these exiles—Jews of the **Diaspora**. In one edict, he freed the exiled Jews and allowed them to return to Jerusalem to reconstruct the Temple after years of being scattered and of being exposed to idolatrous religious practices in Babylonia. Because this was such a significant event in Israelite history, Cyrus is referred to in Isaiah as being part of God's plan for Israel.

## Faith Activity

**Prayer and Worship**
In what ways do prayer and worship define Catholic identity? What forms of prayer, times or seasons, and types of worship help unite the universal Church? How do cultural or regional customs and practices play into Catholic identity? What activities does your parish have that set it apart? With a partner, discuss these questions. Share your thoughts with another group of partners.

▶ Engraving of Cyrus the Great.

Despite Cyrus' edict, the relationship the Jews had with the Samaritans adversely affected the reconstruction of the Temple. The Samaritans wanted to help reconstruct the Temple. The Jews, however, regarded the Samaritans as unholy, due to their intermarriage with peoples the Assyrian conquerors had placed in Judah. The Jews forbade the Samaritans to work on the Temple. As a result, the Samaritans did their best to interfere with its reconstruction, and they succeeded. As Ezra 4:4–5 states, "Then the people of the land discouraged the people of Judah, and made them afraid to build, and they bribed officials to frustrate their plan throughout the reign of King Cyrus of Persia and until the reign of King Darius of Persia."

**Darius I** Darius I, like Cyrus before him, was able to unify the diverse peoples of the Persian empires through administrative channels. The empire was divided into provinces called *satrapies*. Each **satrapy** was ruled by a governor, a satrap. The satrap was responsible for law and order, local military operations, and the collection of tribute. Zerubbabel, a descendant of David, became a satrap of Judah under Darius. Zerubbabel and the high priest Joshua were responsible for the completion of the Temple in 515 B.C.

Some historians attribute Darius' tolerance of the religious beliefs of others to the fact that he was a follower of a religion founded by Zoroaster. The religion, known as Zoroastrianism, centered around one god, known as the father of justice, but emphasized a dualism between good and evil. A follower of Zoroastrianism must think and say good thoughts and perform good deeds to reach paradise. Another example of Darius' religion affecting his politics was his order that the satrap in Egypt consult with the local priests when codifying laws.

**Artaxerxes I–III** Continuous rebellions threatened the stability of the empire after Darius' reign. Xerxes I succeeded Darius, followed by Artaxerxes I, another Persian emperor who directly affected the history of Israel.

Nehemiah, a treasured member of the royal court and a Jew, had been dismayed at reports of Jerusalem being in ruins. Either Artaxerxes I or Artaxerxes II sent Nehemiah to Jerusalem to help Jerusalem fortify its walls. Artaxerxes, however, may have had a political motive for sending Nehemiah. Artaxerxes' military had been fighting rebellions in Egypt. Perhaps it was in order to keep Egypt's nearest neighbor, Judah, pacified or under control that he sent Nehemiah to Jerusalem as governor. Artaxerxes also sent Ezra, a scribe, and others who were part of the **remnant**— exiles and former exiles who remained faithful to God—back to Jerusalem.

*Faith*
**Activity**

**A Great Leader** Discuss what it takes to be a great leader. Is it administrative skill, diplomatic skill, or military skill? If it is a combination of these attributes, which is the most important? Support your ideas with examples from the Persian emperors as well as from other political and spiritual leaders.

Whether Artaxerxes had political motives or compassion for the Jews, who were facing hostility from their neighbors in Jerusalem, the fact that Nehemiah and Ezra were allowed to return to Jerusalem greatly affected the history of Israel. Nehemiah's reforms as governor helped the Jews define who they were as a community; a member of the community needed to be of Jewish descent, and no intermarrying was allowed. Ezra reaffirmed that the Jewish community must live by the law of God. Indeed, this was decreed by Artaxerxes. Artaxerxes tells Ezra, "All who will not obey the law of your God and the law of the king, let judgment be strictly executed on them. . ." (*Ezra 7:26*). Both Ezra and Nehemiah worked to end mixed marriages and the influence of other cultures and languages, believing ending these was necessary in order for the scattered people to survive.

Keeping the Persian empire together proved to be difficult and constant work for the remaining Persian emperors.

- Artaxerxes II was able to keep the empire together through treacherous means. Sparta and Egypt were openly rebellious, and the emperor failed to keep Egypt as part of the empire. Later, many satraps, including those of Greece, Sparta, and Athens, rose in revolt, but they were quelled.

- Artaxerxes III was a cruel ruler who put most of his relatives to death to assure his throne. His initial failure to regain control of Egypt encouraged Phoenicia and the island of Cyprus to revolt. After quelling those revolts, Artaxerxes III again turned his sights toward Egypt, and he finally succeeded in defeating that nation. Egypt again became a Persian satrapy. Artaxerxes III and his elder sons were then killed by an influential eunuch in the court of Artaxerxes III.

# Preserving Tradition

The prophets worked to preserve the tradition of their people. The stories of Ezra, Nehemiah, Haggai, Zechariah, and Malachi helped to restore and to renew Israel as a religious community, not as a nation. The people had become scattered and had strayed from their traditions and commitment to God. Rebuilding the Temple was a significant event in attempting to restore the people's spirituality and fidelity to God.

In a sense, the return from exile and the movement to the Diaspora continue today. For Jews around the world, preserving their tradition comes through faithfulness to the covenant. Christians also strive together to maintain their faith and covenant with God. Each of us is given challenges and further chances in life to fulfill our roles and responsibilities to our families and communities—our world—and to God.

**Break open the Word**

**God's Command** Read Haggai 1:1–15. What command does God reiterate in these verses? How could these words apply to you in your own life today?

## Haggai

Haggai was the driving force behind the rebuilding of the Temple in Jerusalem. His call to finish the rebuilding overruled all the excuses made by the people. Fifteen years had passed since their return from exile, yet the people had done very little to reconstruct their house of worship. Preoccupied with the harassment by neighboring nations, they had instead become consumed with providing and protecting their own housing and material possessions.

Haggai was keenly aware of the importance of the Temple for strengthening the Israelites' faith and the re-establishment of religious symbols and rituals. He also knew the value of the community effort involved in the Temple reconstruction. Haggai's emphasis on rebuilding what the Babylonians had torn down served as a rallying cry. His prophecy had tremendous effect; the people began rebuilding just twenty-three days after Haggai's first message.

The Israelites had begun the Temple with zeal, but discouragement had stopped their enthusiasm. Their new focus became self-centered; God's house was left unfinished, abandoned while they toiled at other work. Once again God was directing the Israelites back onto his course. Haggai openly addressed the rumblings of the Israelites as they began the Temple reconstruction. In Haggai 2, Haggai delivers his message during the Feast of Tabernacles, targeting the older Israelites who remembered the glory of the Temple built by Solomon and who were discouraged by the limits of the new Temple. Haggai delivers the Lord's clear message that this Temple would see greater glory than the Temple built by Solomon.

## Faith Activity

**Feast of Tabernacles**
Research the celebration of this feast in the Jewish tradition. Find out what it is, how it started, and how it's celebrated today. Compare your findings with those of a classmate.

## scripture

"Yet now take courage, O Zerubbabel, says the LORD; take courage, O Joshua, son of Jehozadak, the high priest; take courage, all you people of the land, says the LORD; work, for I am with you, says the LORD of hosts, according to the promise that I made you when you came out of Egypt. My spirit abides among you; do not fear. For thus says the LORD of hosts: Once again, in a little while, I will shake the heavens and the earth and the sea and the dry land; and I will shake all the nations, so that the treasure of all nations shall come, and I will fill this house with splendor, says the LORD of hosts. The silver is mine, and the gold is mine, says the LORD of hosts. The latter splendor of this house shall be greater than the former, says the LORD of hosts; and in this place I will give prosperity, says the Lord of hosts."

*Haggai 2:4–9*

In Haggai 2:4, Haggai asks all the people to be courageous and to work. He emphasizes that they have been delivered from exile and that they are God's covenant people. They need to work—not just to be children of God, but to be working children of God. Haggai delivers God's call to make his house and his work a priority. Haggai declares God's willingness to bless us from our initial steps in obedience. The foundation alone is all that the Israelites have accomplished, yet the Lord declares it to be the beginning of his blessing. When God is given first place, he blesses his people richly.

## Faith Activity

**Priorities** We learn from Haggai that the Israelites lost focus on what was most important. List the five things that take top priority in your life. Where does God fit into the list? If he does not appear directly, do you see ways that he influences or is connected to any of the other items on the list?

# Zechariah

Like Haggai, Zechariah's message is one of encouragement of the Temple reconstruction project. In an apocalyptic style, Zechariah delivers encouragement to the Israelites as they rebuild and as they renew hope in a messianic kingdom to come. Zechariah directs the people to look ahead to the day of the Lord.

Zechariah, a priest as well as a prophet, delivers his first message from God two months after that of Haggai. In the first six chapters of Zechariah, Zechariah recounts eight visions he has experienced.

**Visions of the Apocalypse** An **apocalypse** is the presumed unveiling of future events, particularly the final struggle between the powers of evil and God, with God victorious and his kingdom established forever. When we hear the word *apocalypse* in the context of the Bible, we generally think of the New Testament Book of Revelation. What you may not know, however, is that the Book of Revelation draws upon apocalyptic literature found in the Old Testament.

This apocalyptic literature differs from prophecy in that it describes a divine intervention and the beginning of a new age, whereas prophecy interprets more ordinary historical events as actions of God. Moreover, apocalyptic literature is usually written in response to real or perceived persecution.

**Zechariah's Visions** The prophetic Book of Zechariah is an extremely visionary text, providing admonitions to repent, hope for a messiah, and revelations about a messianic community of the future that would be centered in Jerusalem. This book presents visions in the style of dialogues between God, the prophet Zechariah, and an angel who interprets the visions for Zechariah. Zechariah experiences a vision of the end of times, but after witnessing destruction, warfare, and suffering, he sees victory: "And the LORD will become king over all the earth . . . for never again shall [Israel] be doomed to destruction; Jerusalem shall abide in security" (*Zechariah 14:9, 11*). Zechariah's more hopeful visions and oracles speak of a time when enemies will become a thing of the past, when there will be peace between all people, and when the worship of God will be universal.

Zechariah's first vision is of "riders," or messengers, from other nations. (See *Zechariah 1:7–17*.) This vision is in response to the lament by the Israelites that sinful nations were prospering. The "riders" promise God's judgment on even the apparently prosperous nations.

The second vision is of horns. (See *Zechariah 1:18–21*.) The four horns symbolize the nations that had overpowered Israel. The horns are cast down, indicating that the oppressor nations would pay for their sinfulness as Israel had.

The third vision is of a measuring line. (See *Zechariah 2:1–13*.) As the Israelites continue to rebuild Jerusalem, God would remain as their protective wall; they would need no others.

Zechariah's fourth vision is of a heavenly court. (See *Zechariah 3:1–10*.) In this vision the high priest Joshua, who now leads the community, has his filthy clothes removed and clean garments placed on him. According to the vision, the accusations of Satan, a Hebrew word meaning "adversary" or "accuser," hold no sway over the people God chooses to restore. This is one of the earliest appearances in the Bible of the adversary Satan.

The fifth vision is of a lampstand. (See *Zechariah 4:1–14*.) The lamp holds an infinite reservoir of oil, symbolizing the infinite care God will show his people.

▶ The Angel Announces to Zechariah on the Baptistery of San Giovanni by Andrea Pisano, 1336.

"The angel who talked with me came again, and wakened me, as one is wakened from sleep. He said to me, 'What do you see?' And I said, 'I see a lampstand all of gold, with a bowl on the top of it; there are seven lamps on it, with seven lips on each of the lamps that are on the top of it. And by it there are two olive trees, one on the right of the bowl and the other on its left.' I said to the angel who talked with me, 'What are these, my lord?' Then the angel who talked with me answered me, 'Do you not know what these are?' I said, 'No, my lord.' He said to me, 'This is the word of the LORD to Zerubbabel: Not by might, nor by power, but by my spirit, says the LORD of hosts.'"

*Zechariah 4:1–6*

**Faith Activity**

**Modern Symbols** With a partner, choose five symbols that would convey God's message for today's society. Refer to Zechariah's visions, then choose symbols relevant to our culture. Make a poster to display your symbols and be ready to explain it.

The sixth vision is one of a flying scroll. The flying acroll represents God's curse (See *Zechariah 5:1–4*.) for those who go against God's Law. No one is exempt from God's punishment for sin. This reiterates that the individual—not just the nation—must live righteously.

The seventh vision is of a woman in a basket. (See *Zechariah 5:5–11*.) The woman in the basket represents the wickedness in all the land. In the vision, an angel packs the woman back into the basket and returns her to Babylon. This signifies God's removal of sin from society, both from the nation and from the individual.

The final vision is of four horses and chariots. (See *Zechariah 6:1–8*.) In this vision, the horses patrol the world in search of evil, especially in the north—the route from Babylon. This reassured the Israelites that all the world was now at rest and Judah could rise again in freedom.

These visions of Zechariah held an expansive message for the Israelites, proclaiming that they will not be his chosen people exclusively. Enemies will become a thing of the past.

Zechariah emphasized the importance of religious ritual just as Haggai did. In Zechariah 7, Zechariah answers a question as to the number of days for fasting. He responds by telling what is most important: ". . . Render true judgments, show kindness and mercy to one another" (*Zechariah 7:9*).

## Interpret the Art

**Zechariah and the Messiah** Entry into Jerusalem by Sassetta, c. fifteenth century. Jesus entered into Jerusalem on Palm Sunday on the back of a donkey, a very unassuming animal at that time. Jesus, as the suffering servant Messiah, instead fulfilled the prophecy of Zechariah.
*How do the reactions of the people in this image convey that Jesus is treated with great respect and honor?*

### Break Open the Word

**Influence on the New Testament** Work with a partner to analyze the influence of the Book of Zechariah on the Book of Revelation.

  Zechariah 4:10 and
    Revelation 5:6
  Zechariah 13:1 and
    Revelation 21:6, 22:1–2
  Zechariah 14:6–7 and
    Revelation 22:5
  Zechariah 14:9 and
    Revelation 11:15, 15:3–4

The second part of the Book of Zechariah (Chapters 9—14) was added to the original book and is more messianic. A messianic oracle in Zechariah 9 refers to the entry of Zion's king on the foal of a donkey. The symbolic significance of the donkey was in defiance of the then-current practice of a monarch arrogantly riding in horse and chariot. The donkey was a vehicle of nobility in the days of Genesis and Judges. Zechariah's message communicated that the king to come would be a humble and noble king. His vision of this messiah king is further elaborated in Zechariah 10:4–5. This king would be strong, trustworthy, stable, and victorious. In Zechariah 11, Zechariah explores the roles of an evil shepherd. His message is that the messiah will be a good shepherd.

**Joel** The prophet Joel calls the people to return to God. He uses the example of the plague of locusts that devastated the land as a warning of things to come. He presents apocalyptic prophecies of the day of the Lord, complete with judgments and blessings. He speaks of an apocalypse that will be an earthly disaster of cosmic proportions: "I will show portents in the heavens and on the earth, blood and fire and columns of smoke. The sun shall be turned to darkness, and the moon to blood, before the great and terrible day of the LORD comes" (*Joel 2:30–31*).

### Faith Activity

**The Apocalypse in Cinema** Many modern movies depict the destruction of the earth or the end of civilization as we know it. How do these portrayals relate to the apocalyptic literature found in the Old Testament?

# A Time of Reform and Renewal

The Promised Land of postexilic Israel splintered into many small enclaves. Jerusalem was in ruins, and the Jews were driven into poverty. The prophets Haggai, Zechariah, and Malachi focused on restoring a way of life and a religious community. With these challenges, the people of Israel struggled with a sense of the "absence" of God. It was difficult to remain focused on God's promise when it did not appear that he was watching over them any longer.

▼ Jewish sacrifice by Alessandro Franchi.

While Haggai and Zechariah encouraged the people during the restoration of the Temple, Malachi delivered his message more than eighty years after the completion of the Temple.

## Malachi

The actual name of this prophet is unclear because the Hebrew meaning of *malachi* is "my messenger." So the name Malachi was possibly a pen name. Even though the Temple had been completed, Malachi's message remains one of confrontation. The Israelites had once again placed their priorities on things other than God. They were neglecting the Temple and being willfully disobedient.

Prior to his argument, Malachi delivers God's message, "I have loved you, says the LORD" (*Malachi 1:2*). A good and wise father, God precedes his correction with an assurance of his love for his children. His instruction begins with the priests, saying that the sacrifices they offered were not satisfactory. They were presenting inferior animals, which was dishonoring to God.

In Malachi 2, Malachi addresses the ignorance of the priests about God's word, since the priests had caused many people to stumble. Next, Malachi directed his message to the people. They, too, were dishonoring God by divorcing their Jewish wives and marrying non-Jewish women. The Israelites were justifying their defiance of God's law by twisting God's word.

Finally, Malachi's message called for the people to reform their offerings. If they were to give the entire tithe, ten percent, of their harvest to God, he would open the floodgates of blessing. The current bad harvest from drought and pestilence was a result of the Israelites' withholding of tithes. Malachi concludes his prophecy with reference to the remnant; the faithful few who will be spared God's final judgment.

### Faith Activity

**Problem Solving**

Conduct research in newspapers, magazines, and on the Internet. Research at least three problems in the world and ways in which people are trying to solve them. Clip out all the articles and paste them on a poster board. Place the problems on the left and the solutions or efforts to resolve the problems to the right.

# Starting Over

When the exiled Jews were allowed to return to Jerusalem, the city was in ruins and needed to be restored. This period was a time of new beginnings. The restoration of this ancient city can provide an analogy for our lives. We have opportunities in our own daily lives to restore and to rebuild ourselves and our community.

For instance, the start of a new grading period at school is a time of restoration, another chance. We have the opportunity to start fresh and get things right. Whatever mistakes we may have made before that, whatever difficulties we may have had, can all be overturned when we start anew.

We may think that another chance is given to us only once in a while, or only if we're lucky. This is not true; we're given another chance daily. Have you had a difficult relationship with someone? Have you had a relationship that went sour? Have you had to deal with an adversary? All of these situations can be made better. Just as Ezra called for the people of Israel to renew their commitment to God, so, too, can you rebuild and restart your life.

The Book of Malachi describes dismal conditions: people who view worship of God as a burden, men who have divorced their Jewish wives to marry rich non-Jewish women. Similarly, in the Book of Haggai, poverty is widespread. The Jewish word **anawim** means "little ones" or "forgotten ones." It is used to refer to people in need, such as widows, orphans, and those who are poor. We read in Haggai that rich people care only about themselves. There is a clear need for reform.

## Faith Activity

**Modern Problems** In your opinion, what do you think is the most significant problem in the modern world? Why do you think so? What makes this problem worse than other problems? Discuss your thoughts with a partner.

## Break open the Word

**Jesus' Teaching** Read Isaiah 61 and the Sermon on the Mount in Matthew 5. How are these passages similar? In what ways are we as a society living in accordance with or in ignorance of these commands? What are some ways for us to more fully conform?

Our world today has its share of problems, such as poverty, hunger, war, disease, and prejudice. As in the time of the prophets, there is a need for reform. The Church's role is clear: to show love for all of God's people and to help them live in a just and peaceful society.

The Church strives to relieve suffering and to provide aid to people in difficult circumstances, such as those who are poor, homeless, lonely, or the victims of injustice. In many ways you, too, have the opportunity to do your part to serve others in God.

# Third Isaiah

Isaiah, as a book of the Old Testament, has three divisions, with each division being based on authorship. It is believed that Second and Third Isaiah were compilations of multiple authors, all disciples or members of the school of the prophet Isaiah. Third Isaiah comprises Chapters 56—66 and spans the time period 540 to 510 B.C. As with the message of his fellow prophets, the message of Third Isaiah is a lament for the falling away of the Israelites from God's plan and a call for renewal.

In particular, the message includes a radical concept for that time period: God's blessing of both people of other nations and of eunuchs, (See *Isaiah 56.*) and so to all who honor God. Justice is the theme of Third Isaiah. In the past neither people of other nations nor eunuchs were allowed into the Temple; nor were they even considered to be citizens. Third Isaiah ends with the certainty of God's justice with his people and the assurance of his salvation for them. A summary of the prophet's message can be found in Isaiah 66:2–3. There are two ways to live life: either in humble obedience or with arrogant disregard.

## Faith Activity

**Act It Out** In a small group, draft an outline for a skit based on a historical event in Israel's history, but one that is geared toward a particular theme. Perform your skit for the rest of the class.

# The Beatitudes

The Sermon on the Mount
by Fra Angelico
c.1436–1445.

The Sermon on the Mount is the first of Jesus' five major discourses recorded in the Gospel according to Matthew. As the Gospel verses begin, Jesus goes up to the mountain to teach the Beatitudes, just as Moses went to the mountain to receive the Ten Commandments. On the mountain Jesus—the "new" Moses—brought to light the value system of the *new* law.

"Blessed are the poor in spirit, for theirs is the kingdom of heaven.

"Blessed are those who mourn, for they will be comforted."

"Blessed are the meek, for they will inherit the earth.

"Blessed are those who hunger and thirst for righteousness, for they will be filled.

"Blessed are the merciful, for they will receive mercy.

"Blessed are the pure in heart, for they will see God.

"Blessed are the peacemakers, for they will be called children of God.

"Blessed are those who are persecuted for righteousness sake, for theirs is the kingdom of heaven.

"Blessed are you when people revile you and persecute you and utter all kinds of evil against you falsely on my account.

Rejoice and be glad, for your reward is great in heaven, for in the same way they persecuted the prophets who were before you."

*Matthew 5:1–12*

The **Beatitudes** express how God expects people to live in relationship with one another. The word *beatitude* means "blessed" or "happy." In the Beatitudes, Jesus teaches about the meaning and path to true happiness. The Beatitudes express the values of the kingdom of heaven, and they describe the way to attain eternal blessedness, or holiness, to which God calls all of us.

The Beatitudes do not negate the law of the Ten Commandments; rather, they are an expression of that law. Both the Beatitudes and the Ten Commandments offer guidance for living in faithfulness to God and his kingdom.

While the Ten Commandments express the fundamental duties of humans, the Beatitudes yield an understanding of the law of love that promotes attitudes of justice and of compassion.

 *Faith* **Activity**

**Put Into Today's Words** Imagine that Jesus is conveying his message of hope and blessedness today. What words do you think he would use to make an impact on his listeners? Where would he deliver the message? Work with a group to come up with some modern-day Beatitudes.

# Restoring a Religious Community

One theme that appears in the Books of Jonah, Chronicles, Ezra, and Nehemiah is the relationship between religion, culture, and nationalism. Jonah, for example, criticizes the people for wanting their prophets to be concerned only with their own nation. The other books try to define Jewish identity in a way that would survive the loss of the nation. The issue of tolerance or intolerance follows from this discussion.

## The Book of Jonah

The Book of Jonah is a prophetic book, but it is written in the form of a teaching story, or parable. Jonah is an **antihero**—his portrait is contrary to what we designate as being heroic. An antihero is usually presented as more of an ordinary person, complete with character flaws and human weaknesses.

In the Book of Jonah, **satirical humor** is used throughout to ridicule Jonah's weaknesses and expose his human frailties. This satire is really aimed at the people's expectations and demonstrates the futility of disobeying God; as Jonah learns from his mistakes, so must the chosen people, and so must we.

**Faith Activity**

**Jonah and the Whale**
What do you recall of this story of Jonah? Write down four things you remember, then read the story of Jonah. Compare and contrast what you remembered with what's in the Scriptures. What would you say is the moral in this story?

### scripture

"Then Jonah prayed to the LORD his God
from the belly of the fish, saying,
  'I called to the LORD out of my distress,
    and he answered me;
  out of the belly of Sheol I cried,
    and you heard my voice.
You cast me into the deep,
    into the heart of the seas,
    and the flood surrounded me;
all your waves and your billows
    passed over me.

Then I said, 'I am driven away
    from your sight;
how shall I look again
    upon your holy temple?'
The waters closed in over me;
    the deep surrounded me;
weeds were wrapped around my head
    at the roots of the mountains."

*Jonah 2:1–6*

◀ Jonah and the Whale by
Annie Lykes Lucas, 1985–1988.

# The Book of Esther

In the twentieth century, usage of the term **novella** grew to encompass any piece of fictional prose that was longer than a short story but not as long as a novel. However, earlier usage of the term referred to any tale that revolved around a specific situation. The term *novella* derives from the Latin term *novella narratio*, which means a "new kind of story."

Many novellas are full of suspense and drama—as is the Book of Esther. The hero or heroine of a novella must work out the resolution of a particular conflict. The Book of Esther models these characteristics, as Esther and Mordecai expose the evildoings of Haman. The suspense reaches its peak just before the people reveal Haman's sadistic plot to King Xerxes in time to save the Jews from persecution and death.

The Book of Esther is similar to a classic **fairy tale**. Esther, like Cinderella, comes from humble beginnings to become the wife of royalty. Haman is a caricature of evil, and the powerful are not really in control because the king is easily manipulated. This story of Esther goes beyond that happy ending, however, to show how her position as the queen of Persia benefits all the Jews. In her position of power, she is able to expose the evil Haman, who has issued an order that every Jew be put to death. An event of coincidence resolves the plot. (See *Esther 6:1–11.*) The book also uses irony. The events are set in motion when the first queen disobeys the king, but Esther, her supposedly obedient replacement, ends up controlling the events.

*Faith*
**Activity**

**Purim** The Jewish festival of Purim celebrates the story of Esther. Research this festival by using print materials or electronic resources, or, if possible, by speaking with members of the Jewish community. Present your findings to the class.

▼ The Feast of Esther by Jan Lievens, 1625–1626.

# RITES OF PASSAGE

The Jewish community has traditionally been a model of family values because the community nourishes strong bonds between generations. The family unit plays an important role in Jewish tradition. Tradition is handed down from generation to generation, so the home environment is a crucial training ground.

As members of the larger community, Jews are encouraged to support those in need and give generously to charitable organizations. They are called upon to observe the spirit of God's law as well as the letter of the law. A Jew is to be truthful and fair, kind and compassionate, and working toward peace at all times. Having been called upon to be "a light to the nations" (*Isaiah 42:6*), Jews maintain an ethical obligation to promote social justice.

**Birth** The birth of a child is a highly celebrated event within the Jewish community. It is customary for parents to visit the synagogue soon after the birth of a child to offer a prayer of gratitude to God.

Newborn boys are circumcised in a ritual ceremony, during which a professional circumciser, called a *mohel*, performs the surgery. Newborn girls receive a blessing in the synagogue.

Every Jewish child is given a Hebrew name, often during the circumcision service or blessing ceremony.

**Coming of Age** When a Jewish boy reaches the age of thirteen, his adulthood is celebrated in a rite of passage. A **Bar Mitzvah** ceremony is held in the synagogue, during which the boy reads from the Torah scroll. The term *bar mitzvah* means "son of the covenant," and the ceremony symbolizes the boy's duty to keep God's commandments. In non-Orthodox Jewish communities, girls are given a similar ceremony at the age of twelve or thirteen. It is called a **Bat Mitzvah**, meaning "daughter of the covenant." Among the Orthodox, girls are not allowed to read from the Torah in the synagogue, but they do receive recognition of having reached adulthood. This celebration is generally held in the home, rather than in the synagogue.

**Marriage** As young people reach a marriageable age, they are encouraged by the Jewish community to marry within their faith. The family members are highly involved in the courtship, often encouraging their child to marry a certain person. In a traditional Jewish wedding, the couple stands together under a marriage canopy, and a marriage contract is signed. A common marriage benediction is "Blessed art Thou, O Lord, who hast hallowed Thy people Israel by the rite of the wedding canopy and the sacred covenant of marriage." Wedding ceremonies vary among the different Jewish communities, but they are always joyous events involving the family and the couple.

# Cesar Chavez (1927–1993)

Cesar Chavez was born on a farm near Yuma, Arizona. During the Great Depression, Cesar's family was unable to pay their property taxes and lost their home. His family, including his five brothers and sisters, moved to Delano, California and worked as migrant farm workers. Cesar began to work in the fields when he was only ten years old.

Because the pay was minimal and shelter was scarce, Cesar and his family often lived in their car or joined other migrant families under a bridge. Although Cesar attended school when he could, he had little formal education. Because his family was always relocating to find work, Cesar attended 65 different schools, but he never actually graduated from high school. In spite of the fact that his family was poor, his mother always taught Cesar and his siblings to invite anyone who was hungry into their home to share whatever rice, beans, or tortillas were available.

As Cesar became an adult, he was distraught at the conditions the farm workers and their families were forced to live under. Often there was not enough work and many families went hungry and lived in conditions of filth and poverty. When there was work, the conditions were often very dangerous since the fields were sprayed with harmful pesticides. These chemicals caused the farm workers and their children to become very sick and sometimes to die. Cesar decided to change these unjust conditions.

Using the approach of non-violence taught and lived by Jesus, Gandhi, Martin Luther King, and others, Cesar organized the United Farm Workers, a union for farm workers. The union struggled to change laws and inform the public of the plight of farm workers. The United Farm Workers organized protest marches, hunger fasts, and boycotts. Eventually, the government passed laws that enabled farm workers to earn better wages and work under safer conditions.

Cesar managed to raise a family during this time with his wife, Helen. When asked how they were able to raise a family and accomplish all they had, their response was one of simple but profound faith. Both Cesar and Helen woke up at 4:30 every morning. Helen prayed and read Scripture, and Cesar meditated. Their commitment to a life of faith, prayer, Gospel-based justice, and their own experience of the poverty empowered them.

Cesar is an example of living out the Catholic Social Teaching of the Dignity of Work and the Rights of Workers. Cesar's own experiences with unjust working conditions led him to peacefully act out against them. By acting to preserve the Dignity of Work and the Rights of Workers, Cesar helped not only the migrant farm workers, but all other workers as well.

## Prayer

Begin by praying the Sign of the Cross.

**Leader:** We gather in prayer to celebrate our choices to be people of light.

**Reader 1:** For the times we have stepped forward in courage to speak out for the rights of others, we let our light shine.

**All:** Jesus, light the flame of love within my heart.

**Reader 2:** For the times we have defended the rights of someone being oppressed by another, we let our light shine.

**All:** Jesus, light the flame of love within my heart.

**Reader 3:** For the times we lived our responsibility to share our goods with others, we let our light shine.

**All:** Jesus, light the flame of love within my heart.

**Reader 4:** For the times we have enabled others to participate in decisions that affected their lives, we let our light shine.

**All:** Jesus, light the flame of love within my heart.

**Reader 5:** For the times we have used our power to influence a change for the promotion of the rights and dignity of others, we let our light shine.

**All:** Jesus, light the flame of love within my heart.

**Reader 6:** For the times we have said no to our desires for material things so that others could have what they needed, we let our light shine.

**All:** Jesus, light the flame of love within my heart.

**Leader:** Jesus, Lord of light, keep challenging us to be people of light in this world. Bless us with strength to stand strong, and have compassion to understand, and courage to believe and act in the transforming power of your love.

**All:** Amen.

End by praying the Sign of the Cross.

## Review

1. What is Zoroastrianism? Which king was a follower of Zoroastrianism?
2. Who was the founder of the Persian Empire?
3. Describe the relationship the Jews had with the Samaritans.
4. What was the effect of Haggai's first prophecy?
5. Define apocalyptic literature.
6. Which New Testament Book draws upon the apocalyptic literature of the Old Testament?
7. What is the theme of Third Isaiah?
8. Define *beatitude*. What do the Beatitudes express?
9. What is the Hebrew meaning of the word *malachi*?
10. What theme appears in the Books of Jonah, Chronicles, Ezra, and Nehemiah?
11. In what literary form is the Book of Jonah written?
12. Why is satire used in the Book of Jonah?

## Key Words

**anawim (p. 157)**—A Jewish term referring to people who are in need of assistance.

**antihero (p. 161)**—A character who is placed in the role of a traditional hero but is not idealized in any way.

**apocalypse (p. 152)**—A revelation of future events.

**Bar Mitzvah (p. 163)**—Jewish coming-of-age ceremony for thirteen-year-old boy.

**Bat Mitzvah (p. 163)**—Non-Orthodox Jewish coming-of-age ceremony for twelve-or thirteen-year-old-girl.

**Beatitudes (p. 160)**—Jesus' eight teachings about the meaning and path to true happiness; descriptions of the way to attain eternal blessedness, or holiness, to which God calls all of us.

**Diaspora (p. 147)**—The community of Jews in Babylonia after the Exile.

**fairy tale (p. 162)**—A myth with an earthly setting, human characters, and a happy ending.

**novella (p. 162)**—A suspenseful tale that revolves around a specific situation.

**remnant (p. 148)**—Exiles and former exiles who remained faithful to God.

**satirical humor (p. 161)**—Humor that exposes human frailties through a form of ridicule in order to achieve a moral purpose.

**satrapy (p. 148)**—An administrative province ruled by a governor called a *satrap*.

## Teen to Teen

The Dignity of Work and the Rights of Workers is not limited to the workplace; it can also affect schoolwork. How do the "bottom line" or other deadlines adversely affect your relationship with others? With God?

*"When I get an assignment, I sometimes procrastinate and wait until the last minute to finish. Often, that last minute falls on a Sunday, and all I can think about that day is the deadline and finishing the work, rather than having a day of rest. But I always take time out and go to church, and I take time to pray and reflect on my week. I've gotten better in the past few years about doing work at a reasonable pace, so I can enjoy mass on Sundays and actually take the day of rest fully."*

*Veronica S.*

## Catholic Social Teaching—The Dignity of Work and the Rights of Workers

"In a marketplace where too often the quarterly bottom line takes precedence over the rights of workers, we believe that the economy must serve people, not the other way around. Work is more than a way to make a living; it is a form of continuing participation in God's creation. If the dignity of work is to be protected, then the basic rights of workers must be respected—the right to productive work, to decent and fair wages, to organize and join unions, to private property, and to economic initiative. Respecting these rights promotes an economy that protects human life, defends human rights, and advances the well-being of all." (*Sharing Catholic Social Teaching: Challenges and Directions,* USCCB, 1998.)

The prophet Haggai emphasized to the Israelites the necessity of rebuilding the Temple and working at being children of God. While many of the issues covered in the Dignity of Work and Rights of Workers may not have been as relevant when the Temple was rebuilt, they are key issues in today's world. The rights of workers around the globe are frequently challenged, particularly in third world countries where working conditions are poor and wages are essentially cents a day.

How can people living in these conditions be helped? That is a very difficult situation to resolve quickly, but there are ways we can send aid. Your church or parish may have a sister church or parish in one of these areas in which working conditions are poor. You may want to organize a car wash or other fund-raiser to help missionaries in the area.

### Break open the Word

**Read James 5:4, 7–8.** James warns those who would oppress their workers that the Lord is watching and is aware of their actions. James goes on to remind sufferers to be patient and wait for the Lord to answer their prayers. Find two more examples in the Bible of warnings about the rights of workers.

597 B.C.
Nebuchadnezzar captures Jerusalem

600 B.C.

262 B.C.
Mauryan Emperor Asoka
reorganizes India

300 B.C.

336 B.C.
Alexander the Great becomes
the king of Macedon

# A Future Built on Promise

"With trumpets and the sound of the horn make a joyful noise before the King, the LORD."

*Psalm 98:6*

## Chapter Goals

In this chapter, you will:

- learn about the impact of Greek expansion and unification on Jewish life.

- explore the Books of Tobit and Daniel.

- examine the rebellion of the Jews as recorded in 1 and 2 Maccabees.

- consider how the Jewish people remained true to their faith.

- learn about Saint Francis Xavier.

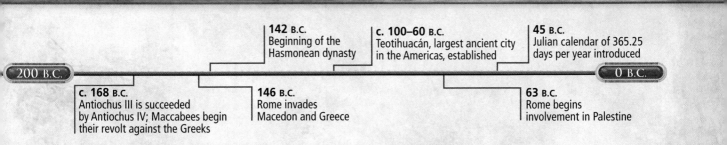

**142 B.C.**
Beginning of the Hasmonean dynasty

**c. 100–60 B.C.**
Teotihuacán, largest ancient city in the Americas, established

**45 B.C.**
Julian calendar of 365.25 days per year introduced

200 B.C.

0 B.C.

**c. 168 B.C.**
Antiochus III is succeeded by Antiochus IV; Maccabees begin their revolt against the Greeks

**146 B.C.**
Rome invades Macedon and Greece

**63 B.C.**
Rome begins involvement in Palestine

# The Impact of Greek Expansion

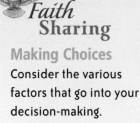
### Faith Sharing

**Making Choices**

Consider the various factors that go into your decision-making.

- Whose advice should you follow?
- How can you be certain that you are living according to what Jesus taught?
- What can you do to stay on the right path?

Discuss your thoughts with your faith sharing group.

As noted in preceding chapters, world events outside of Palestine often had a direct impact on the historical events of Jewish history. Jewish independence was a result of power struggles in the ancient Near East that came closer and closer to home for the Jews. Finally, the events literally came so close to the center of the Jews' religion, the Temple, that the only choice for some Jews was rebellion against the ruling power of the day. One story of rebellion is told in 1 and 2 Maccabees.

The stage was set for the rebellion in the fourth century B.C. by Alexander the Great who, as a lover of all things Greek, hellenized the ancient Near East. The Jews, as individuals and as a community, had to make difficult decisions when the rules of the governing powers were not in agreement with God's law.

## Alexander the Great

Philip of Macedon had unified the warring Greek city-states. This was quite an accomplishment since he was an outsider from Macedon, a less-civilized country north of Greece. Philip's son, Alexander, inherited his father's military skill and his mother's belief that, because he was a descendant of the Greek war hero, Achilles, he was destined for a divine mission. The Greek philosopher Aristotle was Alexander's tutor, and this instilled in him a greater appreciation of Greek, or Hellenic, thought and its way of life.

With the assassination of Philip of Macedon, Alexander inherited the throne in 336 B.C., at the age of twenty. Alexander, who had served in the field under his father, began his conquests with vengeance on his mind. He had 35,000 Macedonian and Greek soldiers and wanted to punish the Persians for their invasion of Greece almost a century and a half before he was born.

◄ Aristotle teaching Alexander the Great.

| Alexander's Accomplishments |
| --- |
| He defeated the Persian army in three major battles and quickly took hold of Syria, Palestine, Egypt, and Asia Minor—the lands dominated by the Persian empire. |
| He pushed his troops east beyond the Indus River and unified the East and West; trade was centered in the East. |
| He issued a standard coinage, which helped facilitate an easy flow of trade from East to West. |
| He created about seventy cities, settling them with his military and administrative personnel and their families, many of whom were Greek. In doing so, Alexander began the hellenization of the ancient world. |

**Faith Activity**

**Alexander's Influence**
Research one of Alexander's accomplishments. Report your findings to the class.

After Alexander died unexpectedly in 323 B.C., at the age of thirty-two, his heirs and generals fought for control of the empire. Eventually three of his generals divided it into three kingdoms.

## The Ptolemaic and Seleucid Empires

After Alexander's death, Ptolemy battled with other Greek generals for lands. He eventually won control of Egypt and with it the former Israelite kingdoms. Ptolemy allowed the Jews to pursue their religion without much interference. By this time, Egypt had become well populated with Jews, who began to use the Greek language politically and socially as well as commercially. The fact that during this time the Scriptures were translated into Greek (the translation referred to as the Septuagint), shows the predominance of the language. Some Jews, however, did not agree with this hellenization of the Scriptures, nor with the inclusion of books not in the existing Jewish canon.

**Faith Activity**

**A Common Language**
Through the spread of the Hellenistic empire, Greek became the common language of the ancient world. Discuss the advantages and disadvantages of people using another language other than their native tongue.

About 200 B.C. a Seleucid ruler, Antiochus III, turned his attention toward Egypt and Palestine. He won control of the region away from Ptolemy. Antiochus III treated Jews somewhat fairly.

| Actions of Antiochus III |
| --- |
| Antiochus gave the Temple a government subsidy. |
| He exempted the Temple's personnel from taxes. |
| He issued an edict that proclaimed that the Jews were allowed to live in accordance with their law. |

The books that come from this part of the Hellenistic period (Esther, Tobit, Daniel 1—6) often deal with problems that could occur under the rule of outsiders, with happy endings for Jews who stay faithful to their traditions.

Unfortunately for the Jews, Antiochus III attempted to take control of a part of Greece that was under Roman domination. At this time, Rome was emerging as a new superpower. The Romans chased Antiochus III back to Asia and forced him to yield all of Asia Minor to them, to provide hostages—including one of his sons (Antiochus IV *Epiphanes*)—and pay Rome a large sum of money. The sum was so large that Antiochus III raided Temples to pay the Romans. In 168 B.C. Antiochus III was succeeded by Antiochus IV *Epiphanes*, who came to play a major role in the religious crisis that led to Jewish rebellion.

## Connect to the Past

**A Lasting Legacy** Tetradrachm of Antiochus IV *Epiphanes*. The attempts by Antiochus IV ultimately led to the Maccabeean revolt. This coin represents part of a Hellenistic economic system he attempted to institute throughout Judea.
*What did Antiochus IV do to be placed on coins? Recall the presidents who are on American coins; what great deeds did they do to have their likenesses imprinted on millions of coins?*

# Suffering and Deliverance in the Books of Tobit and Daniel

The Book of Tobit is often classified as a fairy tale, due to the progression of events within the story and its happy ending. The book provides interesting information about life in ancient times. The story's characters are fully developed through monologues and dialogues, which give the reader insight into their thoughts and emotions throughout the narrative. In addition, the story often is classified as moralistic because it is filled with prayers and hymns, wisdom sayings, and concepts from angelology, or the study of angels.

The Book of Tobit describes two people who are faithful yet unjustly suffer through difficult life situations. Tobit and Sarah pray, fast, and give to people who are poor. Yet Tobit becomes blind while performing an act of mercy, and Sarah is widowed seven times.

The prayers of Tobit and Sarah were a final surrender to God. It is at this juncture that the solution to their struggles begins to manifest itself. The solution comes from God through another person, Tobias. Once they prayed, they saw who to ask for help.

According to the story, answers come to Tobit and Sarah through the intervention of an angel. On the other hand, Sarah's plight, her husbands' deaths, is the result of a demon. These images represent a clear conflict between good and evil. Raphael acts as the mediator at God's throne to bring about Sarah and Tobit's deliverance from persecution. They remain true to their faith and continue in obedience despite mistreatment.

Tobit's counsel to his son was the counsel of a Jew living in a hostile culture. His admonishment to marry only within the faith echoed the admonitions of many prophets before him. Tobit's message is a strong call to the community to maintain their faith. Tobit and Sarah prayed for protection, in praise and in thanksgiving, and their deliverance increased their dedication to God and their obedience to his covenant.

**BREAK OPEN the Word**

**Response to Suffering**
Read Tobit 3:1–6 and 3:10–15. How are the responses of Tobit and Sarah to their personal suffering similar?

**Secular Folktales** The Book of Tobit revolves around secular folktales. The first is the story of the Demon-Lover (also known as the Monster in the Bedchamber) and the Dangerous Bride. With this story, an evil creature is in love with a beautiful woman and kills her husband on their wedding night. A version of this folktale is also found in the Indian epic *Ramayana*. This epic tells the tale of a brave young man named Rama and his beautiful bride, Sita. Soon after their wedding, Sita is carried off by the demon-king Ravana, and the heroic Rama must rescue his beloved. The occurrence of this folktale across different cultures shows us that it was part of a secular oral tradition prior to being incorporated into various written works.

A second folktale within the Book of Tobit is the tale of the Grateful Dead: A man is first impoverished, then rewarded for burying an abused corpse. Using widely recognized, secular folktales helped the writers of Tobit capture the interest of their audience, thereby enabling them to deliver an important moral lesson.

### Interpret the Art

**Faith in the Lord** Shadrach, Meshach, and Abednego in the fiery furnace of Nebuchadnezzer, Byzantine Mosaic, eleventh century. The three youths thrown into the fiery furnace expressed their faith and refused to bow down before the king. They stood in support of the First Commandment.
*Research a martyr who refused to back down on his or her beliefs and respected the First Commandment.*

# Daniel

In Chapter 6 we looked at the apocalyptic visions in the Books of Zechariah and Joel. However, the Old Testament book best known for its apocalyptic symbolism is the Book of Daniel. The book is made up of six stories (Chapters 1—6), four dream-visions (Chapters 7—12), and a collection of short stories (Chapters 13—14). Revelations of the end times are received by Daniel and are explained to him by an angel. As we have learned, this is a common characteristic of the apocalyptic genre.

These narratives form a legend cycle, a pattern in which a religious figure is confronted with temptation but remains faithful to God and is delivered from danger. This cycle was most likely developed in an oral form before being written down. The stories tell of Daniel's legendary skill at interpreting dreams; Shadrach, Meshach, and Abednego in the fiery furnace; the writing on the wall; and Daniel in the lions' den. In the story of Susanna, the legend cycle is seen in the life of a devout woman who is saved by Daniel.

The **legends** in Daniel are presented to relay a spiritual message. Each is a depiction of the lifestyles of Jewish exiles in Babylon. Daniel's message was one of hope, with clear delineation of the boundaries necessary to live as a Jew in a non-Jewish world. Each story stresses the need to stay faithful to the Jewish traditions and law despite the demands of the Babylonian culture.

In Chapter 1 of the Book of Daniel, Daniel and his companions are servants to the Babylonian king, Nebuchadnezzar. Daniel and his three companions are trained in the Babylonian language and literature. ". . . They were to be educated for three years, so that at the end of that time they could be stationed in the king's court" (*Daniel 1:5*). They willingly participate and actively excel at these studies. Therefore they become ". . . stationed in the king's court" (*Daniel 1:19*), but also remain true to their faith without compromising.

In Chapter 3, Shadrach, Meshach, and Abednego stand together in their dedication to God and unequivocally refuse to bow down to Nebuchadnezzar's golden idol. The three heroes of the story clearly state in Daniel 3:17–18 that they are prepared to face a blazing furnace for their faith. "They disobeyed the king's command and yielded up their bodies rather than serve and worship any god except their own God" (*Daniel 3:28*). Through the power of God, Shadrach, Meschach, and Abednego are not touched by the flames. King Nebuchadnezzar is so impressed by the power of the almighty God that he promotes "Shadrach, Meshach, and Abednego in the province of Babylon" (*Daniel 3:30*).

Daniel's superior ability in interpreting dreams was a God-given gift. Daniel refused to take the many perks offered for his gift of interpretation, but he agreed to interpret the writing King Belshazzar saw on the wall. (See *Daniel 5:5, 17*.) Daniel did not compromise his integrity by being paid; this purity allowed him to tell the truth without qualms.

The story of Daniel's sojourn with the lions helps readers understand the political climate of the time. Because Daniel had many adversaries who wanted his position, King Darius was tricked into establishing an ordinance that anyone caught praying to ". . . anyone, divine or human" other than to the king be thrown into a den of lions (*Daniel 6:7*). Daniel defied the king's law by praying faithfully and openly three times a day. (See *Daniel 6:10–11*.) To have hidden his praying would have been showing fear.

## Faith Activity

**Take a Stand** Write about an instance when you took a stand for something despite the possible consequences. Did you have family or friends supporting you on this? If so, how did this help? If not, did it make your choice more difficult?

## Break Open the Word

**Detective Story?** Read Daniel 13:28, 51–62 and 14:10–22. How are these two stories similar to detective novels?

Clearly, the message of Daniel is obedience and courageous loyalty to God's law. In Daniel 6:16, King Darius' parting words to Daniel as he is lowered into the den are evidence of Daniel's strong impact on him: "May your God, whom you faithfully serve, deliver you!" (*Daniel 6:16*). Daniel's integrity had not gone unnoticed. The king's relief at finding Daniel still alive the following day shows the fondness King Darius held for Daniel, and the event also led to the king's decree, recorded in Daniel 6:26–27.

Daniel's daily life and actions were testimony to the power of God. Regardless of the governing political system, God is in control and all will resolve itself in his time. Believing this, we trust in his providence. The numerous visions that Daniel interprets for the king are symbols of God's justice and righteousness. Daniel and his friends give strong evidence to the power behind prayerful faithfulness to God's law.

A unique feature of Daniel is that it is the only book of the Hebrew Bible that clearly affirms resurrection for the individual. (See *Daniel 12:2–3.*) This belief is also found in 2 Maccabees 7, but this book is not included in the Hebrew Bible. Other books speak of restoration for the nation, but the Book of Daniel asserts that individuals will be resurrected.

# Antiochus IV *Epiphanes* Sets the Stage for Rebellion

Upon returning from his time as a hostage in Rome, Antiochus IV *Epiphanes* found that his kingdom was on shaky ground. The Ptolemaic king in Egypt was prepared to fight to regain control of Palestine and the coastal trade region of Phoenicia. The Romans were looming on the horizon in Greece, and Antiochus IV *Epiphanes* knew firsthand what the Romans were capable of doing. He decided it was time to unify his people as a preparation for facing these threats. The way to unify them was to enforce a more Hellenic way of life. Antiochus IV *Epiphanes* "sent an Athenian senator to compel the Jews to forsake the laws of their ancestors and no longer to live by the laws of God" (*2 Maccabees 6:1*).

The Hellenic way of life that Antiochus wanted the Jews to adopt differed greatly from their way of life. While the Jews were monotheistic, the Greeks were polytheistic. The Greeks believed their gods had good and bad human attributes. Statues and idols were created to represent them, and temples were built in the gods' and goddesses' names. Sacrifices were made in honor of the Greek gods and goddesses.

Central to the Greek way of life was the gymnasium, and a gymnasium was established in Jerusalem. In ancient Greece, the gymnasium was a center for intellectual learning. It was a public institution where the teaching of philosophy, literature, and music occurred as did training for public competitions. The gymnasium was dedicated to the Greek gods Hercules and Hermes. For Jewish men to participate in events held in the gymnasium was to openly admit to a belief in Hercules and Hermes. By this, they were calling into question the very thing that made them Jewish—their monotheistic belief. While some Jews did participate in the athletics in the gymnasium, many refused to do so.

▶ Ancient Roman Copy of *Discobolus* by Myron, second century B.C.

Antiochus IV *Epiphanes* went even further in his disrespect of the Jews. To further his cause of hellenization, he put into place a royal commissioner to help the high priest of the Greek religion. The commissioner treated Jerusalem as an adversary and built a citadel in the vicinity of the Jewish Temple. A colony of hellenized polytheists occupied the citadel, and, as a result, the Temple became a Greek shrine. Zeus, the major Greek god, was to be worshiped alongside the God of the Jews. While many Jews were deeply offended, many others went along with the edict. In 1 Maccabees 1:43 we are told: "All the Gentiles accepted the command of the king. Many even from Israel gladly adopted his religion; they sacrificed to idols and profaned the sabbath." As a result of Jewish resistance to this change, Antiochus IV *Epiphanes* annulled his father's earlier concessions to the Jews.

## The Fight for Independence

A Jewish family of priestly descent—a man named Mattathias and his sons—led a rebellion in response to Antiochus IV *Epiphanes'* decrees. They encouraged other Jews who believed in God and his law to join them. They waged guerrilla warfare against Antiochus IV's followers and the Jews who had joined them. After Mattathias' death, his third son, Judas Maccabeus, turned the rebellion into a full scale struggle for Jewish independence. With Judas' repeated successes against the Seleucid generals, more Jews joined the cause for independence.

Judas Maccabeus was the leader of the revolt against Antiochus IV. Judas was sometimes called *Maccabee*, which means "hammer." Both 1 and 2 Maccabees describe the military response to Seleucid persecution of the Jews. Three generations of the Maccabee family worked to free the Jews in God's name. However, Judas is presented as the ideal Jewish warrior, praying before and after battle and honoring Jewish rituals.

Antiochus' institution of an altar to Zeus within the Jewish Temple was unacceptable and blasphemous to the Maccabees. Again, they used guerrilla warfare against Antiochus, employing the gifts of wisdom and quick thinking. The sanctity of the Temple was fiercely defended, and Antiochus was ousted.

Judas eventually marched into Jerusalem, reclaimed, and cleansed the Temple, and restored the priests who had remained faithful. After the Temple was cleansed, it was rededicated. The feast of Chanukah is a celebration of this historic event.

**BREAK OPEN** *the Word*

**Judas as a Leader** Read 1 Maccabees 3—4. How would you describe Judas' leadership skills and style? Cite specific verses to support your answers.

**BREAK OPEN** *the Word*

**Chanukah** Read 1 Maccabees 4:52–59. Then read 2 Maccabees 1:2—2:18. This festival is known today as the Jewish feast of Chanukah. Why do you think it was important for the people to observe this feast?

**Use of Speeches in Maccabees**  The stories in 2 Maccabees affirm the role of martyrs in the restoration of Israel and include the incentive of resurrection for those who die for their faith. (See *Maccabees 7:9, 14, 23; 14:46.*) With the same spiritual fortitude as Daniel, the Maccabees died in protecting the Torah.

The two books of Maccabees are filled with elaborate speeches, persuasive arguments, and other types of commentary on events in Israel's history. Like the Deuteronomic History, Maccabees focuses on the theological significance of historical events. The books tell the story of a family and the role they played in bringing about Jewish independence.

An example of the elaborate speeches used in Maccabees can be found in the stirring speech Simon delivers.

### scripture

"[h]e encouraged them, saying to them, 'You yourselves know what great things my brothers and I and the house of my father have done for the laws and the sanctuary; you know also the wars and the difficulties that my brothers and I have seen. By reason of this all my brothers have perished for the sake of Israel, and I alone am left. And now, far be it from me to spare my life in any time of distress, for I am not better than my brothers. But I will avenge my nation and the sanctuary and your wives and children, for all the nations have gathered together out of hatred to destroy us.'"

*1 Maccabees 13:3–6*

▲ Franciscan martyr Saint Maximilian Kolbe.

Simon inspires the people to elect him as their ruler. He passionately reminds the people of his proven dedication to the laws and the sanctuary and that all his brothers have perished for the sake of Israel.

The author of 2 Maccabees places emphasis on holiness, on the fact that God defends his Temple, and on other religious matters. Because of this emphasis, 2 Maccabees is sometimes described as "Temple propaganda." It also tends to be less precise and less reliable for historical facts than 1 Maccabees; numbers tend to be inflated and events are exaggerated to have more of an emotional appeal. The second book also focuses more on individual stories of heroism rather than on the larger historical events.

▼ Tombs of the Maccabees in Modi'im.

# The Hasmonean Dynasty

The descendants of the Maccabee family came to be known as the Hasmonean dynasty. Its members began their rule in 142 B.C. The triumph by Judas allowed the Jews to be politically independent after centuries of subjection to Persian and then Greek rule. Judas' was the first in a long line of successes in which the people of the dynasty continually fought for and won the right to practice their ancestral religion. The Hasmoneans promoted devotion to the Torah and practiced fidelity to God. They believed that God justly rewarded those who were faithful to him. The Hasmoneans led other Jews to believe that their dynasty was rewarded by God and should thus follow God. As pragmatic leaders, the Hasmoneans compromised with people from other empires when necessary. This established them as the leaders of the Jewish people, and political leaders acknowledged the rule of the Hasmoneans. The result was an independent and influential Jewish Palestine that was recognized in treaties with Sparta and Rome.

The success came to an end, about 63 B.C., when the Romans started to intervene in Palestinian politics. Two branches of the Hasmonean dynasty quarreled, and the Romans put Herod, who was half Jewish, into office as governor of Palestine.

# HEROD
## IN THE NEW TESTAMENT

▲ Aqueduct built during the reign of King Herod.

When Jesus was born, Herod "the Great" was the handpicked Roman choice to govern Palestine. But Herod was not a "pure" Jew; his bloodline and social background were not completely Jewish because his mother was an Arabian princess. Also, Herod was an Idumaean Jew. Idumaeans were forced to accept Judaism when conquered by the Hasmonean ruler John Hyrcanus. Consequently, Herod was distrusted and hated by most Jews in the region.

Herod's own personality traits reinforced this distrust. Even though Herod was a genius at political and military maneuvers, he was also ambitious, ruthless, violent, and cruel. The Jews further despised him because he was a puppet of Rome and the visible symbol of the foreign rule and tyranny they were under.

Herod's violent and suspicious nature also affected his family. He is believed to have ordered the execution of a wife, three of his sons, a brother-in-law, and several other relatives.

The Gospel according to Matthew records that Herod attempted to kill the infant Jesus by massacring all the male infants in Bethlehem. He apparently feared competition for being "King of the Jews."

On the other hand, Herod prompted cultural and religious progress. One of Herod's accomplishments was in architecture. He reconstructed areas of Jerusalem, Jericho, and Caesarea. He built theaters, amphitheaters, and the hippodromes for Grecian games to honor Augustus. Most favorable in the eyes of the Jews were his efforts to reconstruct the Temple of Jerusalem. Yet these buildings were paid for at the expense of the people, who were taxed almost out of existence.

When Herod died in 4 B.C., three of his sons divided the territory. Herod Antipas (4 B.C. – A.D. 39) gained Galilee and Perea. He is the Herod mentioned most frequently in Scripture, and he was responsible for the execution of John the Baptist by beheading and for returning Jesus to Pilate.

# Remaining True to Faith

The Jews of the ancient Near East faced many challenges, but they tried to remain true to their faith in the promise of God. While under Persian and Greek control, the Jews endured great hardships. By living according to their faith and acting against the laws of the governing body that contradicted their religious laws, the Jews placed themselves in a position of potential martyrdom—they risked dying for their beliefs.

## Judith

Judith's heroism in saving Judah from the wrath of Nebuchadnezzar is another example of an individual using her wit and particular gifts to bring about God's victory. The name *Judith* means "Jewish woman," so the folktale of Judith commemorates all women of faith who are pivotal in carrying out the Lord's plan. Because she is a childless widow, Judith remains on the bottom rung of the ladder of Jewish social hierarchy. Yet she is God's chosen instrument for the rescue of his people. Her ironic weapons of wit, feminine wile, courage, and strength are clearly God's choice for this particular job at hand.

Judith's wisdom was readily acknowledged by Uzziah. Judith knew what her gifts were and prayed that God would bless her mission. In the male-dominated society portrayed in the Book of Judith, a woman's primary and strongest weapon was her beauty. In that sense, Judith put on her full armor, sparing neither perfume, nor jewelry, nor finery while she had her maid carry an extravagant meal along.

### scripture

"When Judith had stopped crying out to the God of Israel, and had ended all these words, she rose from where she lay prostrate. She called her maid and went down into the house where she lived on sabbaths and on her festal days. She removed the sackcloth she had been wearing, took off her widow's garments, bathed her body with water, and anointed herself with precious ointment. She combed her hair, put on a tiara, and dressed herself in the festive attire that she used to wear while her husband Manasseh was living. She put sandals on her feet, and put on her anklets, bracelets, rings, earrings, and all her other jewelry. Thus she made herself very beautiful, to entice the eyes of all the men who might see her. She gave her maid a skin of wine and a flask of oil, and filled a bag with roasted grain, dried fig cakes, and fine bread; then she wrapped up all her dishes and gave them to her to carry."

*Judith 10:1–5*

▲ Judith and Holofernes by Donatello, c. 1386–1466.

With these tools, and with the drunken state of Nebuchadnezzar's chief general, Judith successfully defeated him and preserved her chastity as well. God was clearly at work, proving that he will free his people if they obey him and rely on his covenant.

While the priests and elders were content to pray and surrender to Holofernes, Judith prayed and was led to action. Like Tobit and Sarah, Judith did more than admit powerlessness. And, like Daniel, she actively resisted the assault on her faith.

**Irony** There is a great deal of situational irony in the Book of Judith. The story of Judith is the tale of an unlikely heroine who overcomes her fears and defeats a powerful enemy of her people.

- One example of irony in the story is that a woman, rather than a man, saves Judah. This was ironic within the patriarchal and sexist society of Judah. Judith is a particularly unlikely heroine in that she is a childless widow and, therefore, has low standing.

- It is also ironic that Judith defeats Holofernes not with military prowess, as would be expected, but with her beauty and charm. She wields her beauty as a weapon and destroys the enemy.

## *Faith* Activity

**Family Victories**
Write a gratitude list of all the accomplishments or victories you and your family have experienced. Include stories of success and God's providence that your ancestors, as well as your immediate family, have encountered. Title your list "Great Things God Has Done," and use it as a prayer of praise to God.

## *Faith* Activity

**Irony** Have you ever been in a situation that struck you as ironic? Describe the situation and explain its irony.

Judith by Pordenone.

# Communicating Faith

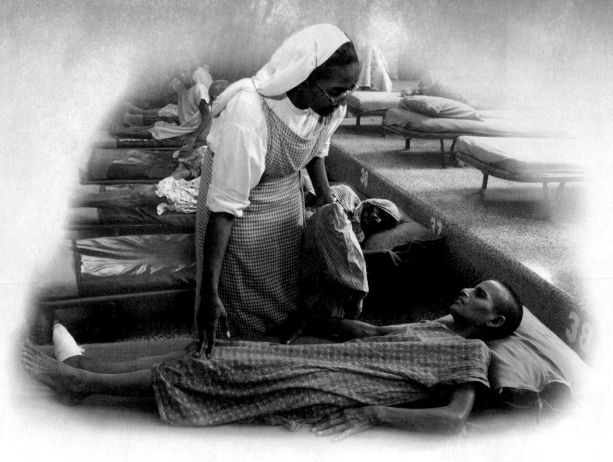

The community of Jews scattered outside Israel came to be known as the Diaspora. The Jews of the Diaspora had very limited methods of communication or mutual support. It was difficult for them to stay united and remain in contact with each other.

Today modern technology allows us to communicate quickly and easily. With telephones, teleconferencing, faxes, and the Internet, people across the world can stay connected. With so much technology available, you can easily communicate and provide support for one another. Communications technology can be a powerful resource within the Christian community worldwide.

 **Faith**
**Activity**

**Spread Good News** How can you utilize modern communications technology to help others? In what ways can you use it to help spread God's word?

**Missionary Work** A missionary is a person who devotes his or her life to **evangelization**, proclaiming the Good News of Jesus Christ to the world through words and actions, and service. Missionaries work in home missions or missions in other lands. In addition to evangelization, missionaries work to improve education, medical care, employment, and agricultural methods, and to provide help during natural disasters such as earthquakes, floods, famines, and storms.

Christian missionary activity began nearly 2,000 years ago. Enthusiastic missionary work by Saint Peter, Saint Paul, and others led to the rapid spread of Christianity. By A.D. 300, the faith had spread throughout the Roman Empire and to North Africa. By the Middle Ages, most of the people of Europe were Christian. The next far-flung missionary work occurred in the 1500s, when Catholic missionaries began to travel with European soldiers and explorers to Africa, Asia, and the Americas.

Catholicism in the United States would not have developed so quickly and so well without the work of missionaries. Many Catholic missionaries in the world today come from the United States and travel to Asia, Africa, Latin America, and many Pacific Islands. Missionaries share their faith, but do not impose it. They use modern technology and scientific knowledge to help the people they serve, and they cooperate with the local church.

Missionaries work in our own country, too. People of all ages can get involved in supporting or taking part in missionary work, both at home and in other countries.

### *Faith* Activity

**Missionaries in Action** Request information from your local parish about missionaries who travel to other countries. What problems do they attempt to help solve? What obstacles do missionaries encounter? What are the statistics on individuals converted to Catholicism through missionary work?

# Saint Francis Xavier (1506–1552)

Saint Francis Xavier was born at the castle of Xavier in Navarre, Spain. In the early 1530s, while studying at the University of Paris, he met Ignatius of Loyola. Francis became one of the original six young men who joined with Ignatius to form the Society of Jesus, the Jesuits, in 1534. Francis was ordained a priest in 1537.

In 1541, Francis was named the Apostolic Nuncio to Asia, giving him the freedom and responsibility to do missionary work there. At the request of Portugal's king, Francis immediately set off for Goa, a section of India controlled by Portugal. He arrived after a perilous thirteen-month voyage. Francis thus became the first Jesuit missionary. Christianity had already been established in Goa, but the Church was poorly run and in bad shape. With Goa as his base, Francis traveled down the coast of India and to islands in southern Asia, immersing himself in the local language. He converted many individuals through his preaching, mostly people from the lower castes.

As he continued his missionary work, Francis heard many reports of the highly advanced kingdom of Japan. However, he was determined to continue his missionary service in Japan. He arrived in Japan in 1549. As he settled in, Francis was impressed with the sophistication of the Japanese culture. Francis' work with the Japanese helped him develop a new approach to missionary work. He realized the need to understand the local culture, comprehend its inherent strengths and virtues, and find ways to make connections to the Gospel message. By being a cultural observer and tapping into, rather than subjugating, the practices of other peoples, Francis can be considered a prophet of cross-culturalism.

After Japan, Francis set his sights on an even more challenging frontier, China, which at the time was closed to people from other nations. Francis was eager to minister in this virtually unknown land. In 1552, after numerous attempts to travel there, Francis finally found a ship willing to transport him to China. With his dream about to be realized, he became seriously ill. He was taken off the ship and was placed on an island off the coast of China. There Francis' health deteriorated, and he died at the age of forty-six. Francis Xavier was canonized a saint in 1622, and in 1927 he was named patron of missions to other countries.

Francis challenged the European standards of his time by seeking to understand other cultures and not subjugating people and using force to teach the Gospel. Many others throughout history have attempted to subjugate people and have completely disregarded the Life and Dignity of the Human Person. Saint Francis ardently believed fair treatment of all people, regardless of race, religion, or economic status was an essential part of being Catholic.

## Prayer

Begin by praying the Sign of the Cross.

**Leader:** We pray to you, Lord Jesus Christ, seeking the ability and wisdom to respect all people's inherent dignity.

**All:** Jesus, teach us to treat all people fairly.

**Leader:** When Jesus invited Zacchaeus to dine with him and the Apostles, even Zacchaeus was shocked. Jesus treated the tax collector with kindness and dignity.

**All:** Jesus, teach us to treat all people fairly.

**Leader:** When Jesus spoke with the Samaritan at the well, he told her of everlasting life if she drank of the living water. The Apostles were surprised that Jesus spoke with the woman, particularly a Samaritan.

**All:** Jesus, teach us to treat all people fairly.

**Leader:** When Jesus was upon the cross, he blessed those who crucified him, for they knew not what they did.

**All:** Jesus, teach us to treat all people fairly.

**Leader:** Lord Jesus, your life is an example of how to treat others fairly and with respect. Grant us the peace and love in our hearts to follow you and all the saints who have followed, as well. We ask this in your name, Amen.

**All:** Amen.

End by praying the Sign of the Cross.

## Review

1. In what ways was Antiochus III a fair ruler over the Jews?
2. What action by Alexander the Great significantly simplified trade between the East and West?
3. What were the Scriptures called when translated into Greek?
4. How does the Book of Daniel present a spiritual message? What is the main purpose of this message?
5. Name two folktales that are incorporated within the Book of Tobit. What happens in each?
6. Which concept is unique to the Book of Daniel in the Hebrew Bible? In which other book of the Old Testament does this concept appear?
7. Describe the personality traits of Herod that made him both a hated and respected leader.
8. What actions of Antiochus IV inflamed Judas Maccabeus into action?
9. Why did Jews not participate in events held in the gymnasium? What would participation have implied about them?
10. How does the story of Judith represent irony? How is similar irony repeated in the life of Jesus?
11. Briefly describe the history of Christian missionary activity.
12. What aided in the spread of Catholicism to the United States?

## Key Words

**evangelization (p. 185)**—Giving witness to one's faith by proclaiming the Good News of Jesus Christ to the world through words and actions.

**legends (p. 175)**—Unverifiable stories that are passed down from generation to generation and accepted as true or partly true.

### Teen to Teen

Think of a time when you received the full forgiveness of your parents, in spite of how bad your actions seemed at the time. How did you feel when your parents forgave you?

*"I had cheated on a test, and then lied about it to my teacher and principal. I finally admitted to it once they called my mom and dad. My teacher, principal, and parents all sat me down and talked to me about what I did and the consequences of cheating in life. I then went to church and said my penance. When I got home, my mom and dad hugged me and told me how proud they were of me for accepting God's forgiveness. They forgave me as well, and I was relieved and strengthened by God's love and the love of my parents."*

*Jack A.*

## Catholic Social Teaching—Life and Dignity of the Human Person

"In a world warped by materialism and declining respect for human life, the Catholic Church proclaims that human life is sacred and that the dignity of the human person is the foundation of a moral vision for society. Our belief in the sanctity of human life and the inherent dignity of the human person is the foundation of all the principles of our social teaching. In our society, human life is under direct attack from abortion and assisted suicide . . . . We believe that every person is precious, that people are more important than things, and that the measure of every institution is whether it threatens or enhances the life and dignity of the human person."

(*Sharing Catholic Social Teaching: Challenges and Directions,* USCCB, 1998.)

The actions of King Herod the Great directly echo the opposite of what this Catholic Social Teaching stands for. King Herod sought only the crown, and the title "King of the Jews"—a title meant for Jesus. He slaughtered infants in his quest for glory. Several rulers of the Old Testament slaughtered people for their belief in the Lord, and not in a golden idol.

As Catholics, we are called to speak out against modern acts of needless violence such as the killing of unborn children and assisted suicide. Organize a meeting with your pastor to see what your class can do to spread God's word and remind the world of the Life and Dignity of the Human person.

**break open** *the Word*

**Read Luke 15:11–32.**
The Parable of the Prodigal and His Brother presents a son who demanded his inheritance then proceeds to squander all the riches he gained. The prodigal son returns to find great rejoicing, for his life alone is worth more to the father than the lost riches. Find two more verses that support the belief that people are worth much more than things, especially in the eyes of God.

**2000–1000 B.C.**
Egyptian and Mesopotamian wisdom literature flourishes,
including Babylonian poem resembling Book of Job

**c. 1000–961 B.C.**
Reign of King David

2000 B.C.

1500 B.C.

**c. 1290–1250 B.C.**
The Exodus

**1000–600 B.C.**
Egyptian Instruction of
Amen-em-opet written

# The Wisdom of Israel

## CHAPTER 8

"Let my cry come before you, O LORD;
give me understanding according to your word."

*Psalm 119:169*

## Chapter Goals

In this chapter, you will:

- learn about wisdom literature in the Old Testament.
- examine the teachings and advice found in Job and Proverbs.
- explore the beauty of the Book of Psalms and wise instructions found in the Old Testament.
- deepen your understanding of the Liturgy of the Hours.
- learn about Venerable Pierre Toussaint.

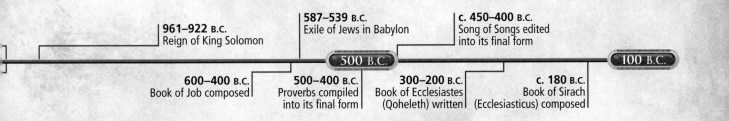

**961–922 B.C.**
Reign of King Solomon

**587–539 B.C.**
Exile of Jews in Babylon

**c. 450–400 B.C.**
Song of Songs edited
into its final form

500 B.C.

100 B.C.

**600–400 B.C.**
Book of Job composed

**500–400 B.C.**
Proverbs compiled
into its final form

**300–200 B.C.**
Book of Ecclesiastes
(Qoheleth) written

**c. 180 B.C.**
Book of Sirach
(Ecclesiasticus) composed

# Wisdom Literature

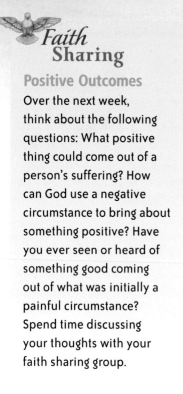

## Faith Sharing

### Positive Outcomes

Over the next week, think about the following questions: What positive thing could come out of a person's suffering? How can God use a negative circumstance to bring about something positive? Have you ever seen or heard of something good coming out of what was initially a painful circumstance? Spend time discussing your thoughts with your faith sharing group.

The wisdom literature of the Old Testament provides a commentary on the faith of Israel. Wisdom literature generally asserts that wisdom leads to prosperity, and folly leads to destruction. This type of literature uses examples from daily life and teaches readers how to cope with everyday struggles. While wisdom instruction appears throughout the Old Testament, it is more highly concentrated in those texts classified as wisdom literature.

Much of the wisdom literature is attributed to King Solomon. Many of the psalms, however, are attributed to King David. Attributing writings to these great leaders in Israel's history was a way of honoring them. Most of the literature was most likely produced by scribes and intellectuals in Israelite society, often in the style and usually in the spirit of the person to whom the writing is attributed.

| Wisdom Books |
| --- |
| Job |
| Psalms |
| Proverbs |
| Ecclesiastes |
| Song of Songs (Song of Solomon) |
| Wisdom (Wisdom of Solomon) |
| Sirach (Ecclesiasticus) |

▼ King David playing the Psalms from the Bible.

# Advice for Living

The Books of Job, Proverbs, and Sirach differ from other books in the Old Testament in a very distinct way. While other books focus on the twists and turns of Israel's history and on Israel's unique relationship with God, these books deal with universal human experiences of any time or any place and are not tied specifically to events in Israelite history.

These books were compiled in postexilic times when Israel was most concerned with being a community that worshiped the God of Israel, yet this is never mentioned. Instead, these books offer advice on living a meaningful life and dealing with the perplexing problems of being human. Similar advice, or wisdom, was a part of life in the ancient Near East. The wisdom tradition probably started orally and eventually came to be recorded and used in royal courts and schools. This process is referred to as the wisdom movement, and evidence of this movement is found in the wisdom literature of the Old Testament.

**Personification of Wisdom** **Personification** is the literary technique by which something nonhuman, such as an object or abstract quality, is described by using human characteristics. For example, justice, good luck, bad luck, death, and time have all been personified in literature. Wisdom is often personified as a female with positive characteristics, thereby emphasizing the desirability and elusive nature of wisdom. The use of the words *her* and *she* in reference to wisdom, or knowledge, signify personification. The personification of wisdom appears in Proverbs 1—9, the Book of Wisdom, and in the Book of Baruch.

**Faith Activity**

**Modern Sayings**
Write down three wisdom statements that have meaning to today's society. Indicate whether these statements have meaning to you and if they support or contradict Christ's teachings. Discuss your statements in small groups.

**Humanizing Wisdom**
Read Baruch 3:9—4:4,
Wisdom 7, and Proverbs 8.
Create a list of similar con-
cepts and terms used in these
personifications of wisdom.

Some biblical scholars believe that the female personification of wisdom in these books of the Old Testament was a way to counteract the ancient Near Eastern practices of goddess worship. Wisdom bears a striking resemblance to the Egyptian goddess *Maat*, meaning "truth," and to the Canaanite fertility goddess Asherah. While the biblical writers condemn worship of the goddess, archaeological evidence suggests that some Israelites were devoted to Asherah, perhaps worshiping her as a female counterpart to the God of Israel. The wisdom books in the Old Testament preserve the qualities of the goddess, but they apply them to the wisdom of the one true God.

**Wisdom in the Ancient Near East**  Ancient texts provide insight into the wisdom movement and its place in ancient Near East society. One such text is the *Counsels of Wisdom*, a Mesopotamian text of a reflective nature that resembles the Book of Proverbs. About 2450 B.C. in Egypt, a collection of sayings from a vizier, or adviser to a pharaoh, was compiled. This collection provided instruction regarding the path to material and political success and recommended hard work and strict discipline. Other Egyptian texts—labeled *seboyet* (meaning "instruction")—counseled the court of the pharaoh. Reflective literature also existed in Egypt, as in the text *Dispute with His Soul of One Who Is Tired of Life.*

▲ Detail of wall painting of Tutankhamon with Anubis and Nephthys.

**The Wisdom Movement in Ancient Israel**  In preexilic times, wisdom was important to the king. According to 2 Samuel 16:23, David listened to the advice of a counselor and took his advice very seriously: "Now in those days the counsel that Ahithophel gave was as if one consulted the oracle of God; so all the counsel of Ahithophel was esteemed, both by David and by Absalom." During Absalom's rebellion, David receives advice from a wise woman of Tekoa. The fact that she is sought after by Joab indicates that she had a professional standing as a wise person and that such a class of people existed. (See *2 Samuel 14:2.*)

The wisdom movement in Israel was prominent enough for the prophet Jeremiah to acknowledge it. Jeremiah 18:18 states that ". . . instruction shall not perish from the priest, nor counsel from the wise, nor the word from the prophet." The sages who represented the movement had enough of a presence in Israelite society to be compared to priests and prophets. The sages even had enough sway to influence events.

*Faith*
**Activity**

**Cultural Sayings**
Research the proverbs or
wisdom sayings of another
culture. Create your own
"book" of wisdom by
compiling and illustrating a
collection of these sayings.

# Moral and Righteous Living

Why do bad things happen to good people? This question appears in many forms throughout wisdom literature as people try to understand events in their lives. The writers of wisdom literature question the necessity of suffering, and they sometimes cannot find an answer. But they also place their faith in the providence and wisdom of God and praise him for his deliverance and guidance.

## Job

While little is known about the origins of the Book of Job, the author may have been influenced by other ancient Near Eastern wisdom literature. A Mesopotamian text has a central character who is wealthy and well, but then is suddenly subjected to illness and trouble. The character complains that the will of a god is beyond understanding. At the end of the story, as in the Book of Job, the god returns him to his previous healthy condition.

A Babylonian text comes even closer to matching the Book of Job, not only in content but in form. In the *Dialogue about Human Misery*, the main character, who questions the justice of the gods, is joined by a friend. The dialogue between the main character and his friend resembles Job's dialogue with his friends.

▼ Engraving of Job and his friends by Gustave Dore, 1866.

BREAK OPEN
the Word

**Hymn** In a small group, read aloud Job 28 and discuss the meaning of this hymn.

**The Inspired Text** The inspired writers of the Book of Job were able to take the form of these writings and refashion them into a testament to God's impact on human life. Questioning one of the tenets of conventional wisdom—that God rewards the righteous—is one of the things that sets the Book of Job apart from most of the wisdom literature.

The story line within the Book of Job follows a pattern of tests of faith and subsequent suffering. The book is structured in such a way that prose narratives in the **prologue** and the **epilogue** frame an internal poetic debate. This literary structure highlights the pattern of thematic content within the story line.

| Structure of Job | |
|---|---|
| **Job 1—2** | In the prose prologue God gives Satan permission to test the righteous Job. |
| **Job 3—31** | Job discusses with his friends the reason for suffering in this world. These discussions are in the form of poetic dialogue. |
| **Job 32—37** | A monologue by another person, Elihu, follows the dialogues. |
| **Job 38—42:6** | Two speeches are made by God and two subsequent submissions by Job. |
| **Job 42:7—17** | In the prose epilogue, we read about Job's restoration. |

Through this structure, we follow the story's protagonist, Job. When we first meet Job, he is a successful, righteous chieftain. He is portrayed as having wealth of money and heart, prospering at work and at home. Then a sudden change of events, or a reversal of fortune takes place. Job loses his land and his children. He contracts a disease that racks his body, and a deep sadness overtakes his soul. Job does not blame God, but he does curse the day he was born.

SCRIPTURE

"Let the day perish in which I was born,
  and the night that said,
   'A man-child is conceived.'
Let that day be darkness!
  May God above not seek it,
  or light shine on it.
Let gloom and deep darkness claim it.
  Let clouds settle upon it;
  let the blackness of the day terrify it.
That night—let thick darkness seize it!
  let it not rejoice among the days of the year;
  let it not come into the number of
   the months.

Yes, let that night be barren;
  let no joyful cry be heard in it.
Let those curse it who curse the Sea,
  those who are skilled to rouse up
   Leviathan.
Let the stars of its dawn be dark;
  let it hope for light, but have none;
  may it not see the eyelids of the morning—
because it did not shut the doors of my
   mother's womb,
  and hide trouble from my eyes."

*Job 3:3–10*

Job does not know why he has been thus afflicted, and his friends believe his situation can only be punishment for wrongdoing as well as the chance to repent. Job maintains his innocence and wants to speak to God himself about the cause of his suffering.

## scripture

"If I have rejoiced at the ruin of those who
    hated me,
    or exulted when evil overtook them—
I have not let my mouth sin
    by asking for their lives with a curse—
if those of my tent ever said,
    'O that we might be sated with his flesh!' —
the stranger has not lodged in the street;
    I have opened my doors to the traveler—
if I have concealed my transgressions as
    others do,
    by hiding my iniquity in my bosom,

because I stood in great fear of the multitude,
    and the contempt of families terrified me,
    so that I kept silence, and did not go out
        of doors—
O that I had one to hear me!
    (Here is my signature! Let the Almighty
        answer me!)
    O, that I had the indictment written by
        my adversary!
Surely I would carry it on my shoulder;
    I would bind it on me like a crown;
I would give him an account of all my steps;
    like a prince I would approach him."

*Job 31:29–37*

### Break open the Word

**God's Response**  Read Job 38. What is the Lord telling Job in this part of his speech? What is the point of the Lord's words?

God speaks to Job, but he does not explain or justify his actions. God speaks of his being all knowing and all powerful, and Job accepts this response. Job returns to being humble and trusting of the Lord, his faith and trust being strengthened by his experience of suffering.

## scripture

"Then Job answered the LORD:
'I know that you can do all things,
    and that no purpose of yours can be thwarted.
"Who is this that hides counsel without
    knowledge?"
Therefore I have uttered what I did
        not understand,
    things too wonderful for me, which I did
        not know.

"Hear, and I will speak;
    I will question you, and you declare to me."
I had heard of you by the hearing of the ear,
    but now my eye sees you;
therefore I despise myself, and repent in
        dust and ashes.'"

*Job 42:1–6*

## Proverbs

Much of the wisdom literature in the Old Testament is attributed to Solomon. Solomon's wisdom was renowned, and scribes in his court may have written down some of his sayings. Solomon was recognized as a ruler who welcomed regional influences and had many diplomatic ties, which also may have influenced the collections in Proverbs.

▲ "Anyone who tills the land will have plenty of bread . . ." (*Proverbs 28:19*)

The Book of Proverbs is a collection of moral and religious sayings, poems, and warnings, many of which are attributed to King Solomon. **Proverbs** establish strict dichotomies of good and evil, wise and foolish—there are no "gray" areas. Proverbs are usually two lines of parallel thought that offer wisdom, often in a style similar to that of a riddle. These sayings of folk wisdom are of such universal appeal that many have become accepted as figures of speech. You may even recognize some of them. The proverb form is also used in the Books of Sirach and Wisdom and occasionally in the Book of Ecclesiastes.

The Book of Proverbs as we know it was probably compiled in the fifth century B.C. to help the people live in harmony with God.

**Break Open the Word**

**Motherly Advice**

Read Proverbs 31:1–9, wise sayings attributed to the mother of King Lemuel (a non-Israelite). Compare the advice given to the advice you receive from your mother or other important women in your life.

### The Writers of Proverbs

Some of the proverbs are attributed to Solomon as a tribute to him as a wise leader.

Some sayings are attributed to a professional class of sages and are labeled "The Words of the Wise." (See *Proverbs 22:17—24:34*.)

There is also a record of proverbs compiled by royal advisers: "These are other proverbs of Solomon that the officials of King Hezekiah of Judah copied." (See *Proverbs 25—29*.)

In keeping with Solomon's diplomatic stature, some proverbs are attributed to foreign kings: "The words of Agur son of Jakeh." (See *Proverbs 30*.)

Some proverbs, such as Proverbs 22:17—24:34, closely resemble the Egyptian *Instruction of Amen-em-opet*, which was written for a pharaoh about 1000 B.C. The writers of Proverbs recognized the universal human experience and truth found within these writings, adapted it, and incorporated the wisdom within the Book of Proverbs.

## Work with the Chart

**Find a Proverb** Choose two types of proverbs described below. Then, find an example of each from the Book of Proverbs. As a class, discuss your selections and create a chart listing them.

| Types of Proverbs | |
|---|---|
| **Type** | **Example** |
| Proverbs of comparison | Proverbs 11:18 |
| Proverbs of command | Proverbs 14:7 |
| Proverbs of fact | Proverbs 20:12 |
| Proverbs of condemnation | Proverbs 24:20 |
| Proverbs of similes | Proverbs 26:14 |
| Proverbs of encouragement | Proverbs 29:25 |
| Proverbs of numerical sayings | Proverbs 30:15 |

### scripture

"The name of the LORD is a strong tower;
  the righteous run into it and are safe."
                    *Proverbs 18:10*

"Do not love sleep, or else you will come to poverty;
  open your eyes, and you will have plenty of bread."
                    *Proverbs 20:13*

"Those who are generous are blessed,
  for they share their bread with the poor."
                    *Proverbs 22:9*

"Just as water reflects the face,
  so one human heart reflects another."
                    *Proverbs 27:19*

# Songs of Praise and Wise Instruction

The relationship between God and the Israelites is dynamic and active. The relationship traverses through cycles: The covenant is made, the covenant is broken, Israel is punished, a savior overcomes suppressors, the Israelites return to right relationship with God. Throughout this cycle, the Israelites (and later the Jews) found ways to preserve their religious community. Laws and rituals were formulated into religious practices, and the temple provided a place for worship. Prayer came to embody the individual and communal experience of God.

## Psalms

The psalm is a literary form that occurs throughout the Old Testament. See, for example, Hannah's prayer in 1 Samuel 2:1–10. The Book of Psalms is a collection of 150 songs and poems that were used in Israelite worship and continue to be used in religious services today. The word *psalm* is derived from the ancient Greek word *psalmoi*, which designates the instrumental music that originally accompanied the lyrics. The psalms are divided into five books, as was the Law of Moses in the Pentateuch. The typical structure of a psalm includes:

- an invocation or praise of God.

- a description of a particular situation.

- an affirmation of God's power.

The longest psalm, Psalm 119, is a 176-verse meditation on God's law and commandments.

You are probably familiar with psalms because they are incorporated into the prayer life of the Church. The Book of Psalms, or Psalter, is a group of religious songs that address a wide range of topics. You may have noted this variety in the opening psalms of each chapter in this text.

break open
the *Word*

**Songs** The psalms were originally written to be sung. With that in mind, look at Psalms 4—8, 65—68, and 148—150. How do these psalms resemble songs?

## Work with the Chart

**Compare Psalms** Choose one of the types of psalms described below, and select two psalms from the list of examples provided. Read both psalms, and identify the invocation or praise of God, the particular situation being described, and the affirmation of God's power. *How are the psalms alike? How are they different? Present your findings to the class.*

| Psalms | | |
|---|---|---|
| **Type of Psalm** | **Description** | **Examples** |
| Hymns | songs of praise | Psalms 46, 48, 76, 84, 87, 122 |
| Songs of Thanksgiving | celebrating deliverance, recognizing God as the rescuer | Psalms 18, 30, 40, 66, 116, 118 |
| Laments | prayers for help | Psalms 6, 7, 22, 38, 41—43, 51, 69 |
| Royal Psalms | celebrating a coronation or other royal occasion | Psalms 2, 18, 45, 72, 101 |
| Wisdom Psalms | wisdom sayings | Psalms 1, 33, 37, 49, 73 |
| Question and Answer | question and answer format | Psalms 15, 24, 50, 82 |

### Faith Activity

**Poetry Connection** In a small group, read aloud Gerard Manley Hopkins' poem, "God's Grandeur." Discuss how the poem is similar to a psalm.

### Break Open the Word

**God as Shepherd**
Read Psalm 23, the psalm that compares God to a shepherd. Why do you think this psalm is so loved? What images might be used to express the same sentiments today?

The subject matter varies, as does the speaker—from the most intimate and personal expression to the voice of a large group or community. Some psalms are hymns of thanksgiving and of praise—pleas for help. In the Book of Psalms you may find an individual crying to God, a community lamenting some distress, or great crisis or crying for help.

In individual laments, the psalms often speak against enemies and ask God to intervene. An individual voice in the psalms may also ask for a personal rescue from wickedness or sickness. Like some of the stories in the Old Testament, many psalms contain a cycle or a structure that includes a complaint or an appeal to God, a plea for God to intervene, and God's answer, response, or acknowledgment. Another psalm form is one of praise and then thanksgiving to God as king.

Some of the psalms were created for the ritual life of the temple. The psalms also were part of great festivals held for celebrating the renewal of the covenant. (See *Psalm 24.*) Singers, trumpeters, dances, and shouts for those festival days contributed to the psalms we have today. (See *Psalms 68, 89, 149.*) These festivals also included gifts and feasts that are the subject matter of some psalms.

The psalms express how the Israelites experienced God in liturgy. The word *liturgy* is based on a Greek word for "public" and originally meant a "service in the name of or on behalf of the people" or a "public work." The liturgy is designed to bring people together into a common experience of worship.

# THE IMAGE OF SHEPHERD

 s a faithful Jew, Jesus would have been familiar with the image of God as a shepherd. The imagery of the Lord as shepherd can be found in several places in the Old Testament. Psalm 23 is perhaps the most well-known reference. However, Isaiah speaks of God's actions in Israel's liberation, and Jeremiah used this image as well.

This image reminds listeners of God's care and providence. He provides for his people, guides them, and protects them throughout their journey.

"He will feed his flock like a
    shepherd;
  he will gather the lambs in his
    arms,
and carry them in his bosom,
    and gently lead the mother
    sheep."

*Isaiah 40:11*

"Hear the word of the LORD,
    O nations,
  and declare it in the coastlands
    far away;
  say, 'He who scattered Israel will
    gather him,
  and will keep him as a shepherd
    a flock.'"

*Jeremiah 31:10*

## Interpret the Art

**A Personal Image** The Good Shepherd by Bartolome Esteban Murillo, seventeenth century. The biblical image of the Messiah—Jesus—as the Good Shepherd is common to both the Old and New Testaments. Murillo chose to depict Jesus as a child-shepherd in this image.

*How does the image of Jesus as a child and shepherd affect your personal image of the Good Shepherd? Find other examples of the Good Shepherd image on the Internet or in the library and compare them with your personal image.*

**New Testament** Jesus referred to himself as the Good Shepherd (See *John 10:1–6, 11–18*), and he told parables of the Lost Sheep (See *Luke 15:1–7*) to show God's love and care for all, even for those who strayed.

After his Resurrection, Jesus gave Peter the authority to tend Jesus' flock and feed his sheep. In this the Church sees Peter, and thus all subsequent popes, receiving responsibility of the universal Church—shepherd over the whole flock of his Church.

### Break Open the Word

**The Good Shepherd** Read Ezekiel 34:11–16 and John 10:1–6, 11–18. List the similarities and the differences between the two passages.

## BREAK OPEN the Word

### A Time for Everything

Read Ecclesiastes 3:1–15. Discuss with a partner the message being conveyed in this passage. What meaning do these words have for you in your life right now? How can these words give meaning to events or situations taking place in your home, in your family, in your community, and in the nation right now?

## Unique Wisdom Literatures

**Sirach** The Book of Sirach is a unique work among wisdom literature in that the entire book was probably written by the person to whom it is ascribed (c.180 B.C.). Sirach was a scribe who traveled widely and acquired "much cleverness" (*Sirach 34:11*). He states that he has written his book—which is a collection of diverse sayings, psalms of praise and lament, and moral maxims— ". . . for all who seek instruction" (*Sirach 33:18*). He probably had a school or an academy for young men from wealthy families. These students would probably, like Sirach himself, become scribes.

**Ecclesiastes** The author of Ecclesiastes is referred to as "The Teacher," and the book was written in the third or fourth century B.C. Because of its wisdom focus, the book was often incorrectly attributed to Solomon. This book addresses the purpose of human life and the value that comes from it. The wisdom in the book is contrary to popular wisdom. Hard work and righteousness do not always lead to reward in this life. (See *Ecclesiastes 1:2–11; 9:1–3, 11–12.*) And coming to know God does not happen in the way people have come to expect. (See *Ecclesiastes 3:10–15; 5:1.*) But "Wisdom makes one's face shine . . ." (*Ecclesiastes 8:1*).

# Song of Songs

The Song of Songs (also called the Song of Solomon or the Canticle of Canticles) is a collection of love poems and is often grouped with the wisdom literature, even though it has a different character and purpose. One reason for this is its presumed connection with Solomon. Each song is an independent work of deliberate artistry, perhaps composed by a professional singer. Although the songs were written by multiple unknown authors, similarities in vocabulary, imagery, form, and content unify the text as a whole.

The songs alternate points of view as the lovers take turns describing one another and their relationship. The lovers describe each other using natural and **sensory images**. What develops through the dialogue of these lovers is a description of an ideal form of love—free of restraint, direct, honest, and mutual. The love portrayed is a communion of souls, and the man and woman are portrayed as equals. As an allegory, the Song of Songs can be understood as the love story between God and Israel or, from a Christian viewpoint, the love story between Jesus and the Church.

# Worship

Much of the wisdom literature can be found in the prayers of Christians and Jews today. Words and ceremonial acts that developed in early Judaism and Christianity have been incorporated into the sacraments, hymns, and the Liturgy of the Hours. We are invited to participate in all of these forms of prayer and worship.

## The Liturgy of the Hours

Christian prayers today include significant elements taken from Old Testament wisdom literature. Words and ceremonial acts, flowing from early Judaism and Christianity, are incorporated into the celebration of the Liturgy of the Hours.

The Liturgy of the Hours is a prayer of the entire Church, not something private. It aims at consecrating and making holy the whole day and night. Praying at definite times of the day (the canonical hours) originated in Jewish practice. The canonical hours are the Church's cycle of daily prayer consisting of prayers, readings, hymns, and psalms.

The entire Liturgy of the Hours developed from the practice of praying and singing communally at set times each day, especially at a vigil, prior to a holy day. In the early Church, a prayer service often was held in three parts on the night before a feast day. These hours were called Vespers, Matins, and Lauds. The present canonical hours of Evening Prayer, Office of Readings, and Morning Prayer correspond to these hours. When monasteries developed, the monks prayed Vespers as an evening prayer, Matins in the middle of the night, and Lauds in the early dawn. Later, the monks added a second Morning Prayer, called Prime, and a second night prayer, called Compline—the last canonical hour they prayed before retiring. Since monks wanted to pray throughout the day, they added prayer at three-hour intervals during the day. These were called *Terce*, *Sext*, and *None*, Latin words for the "third" (9 AM), "sixth," (Noon) and "ninth" (3 PM) hours of the day. Over time, the canonical hours were modified, especially for clerics, religious, and member of the lay faithful.

Although the Liturgy of the Hours is primarily a communal prayer, it also can be prayed individually. The clergy, religious, and laity pray it today in parishes, monastic communities, religious houses, and retreat settings. It is a special obligation of the ordained clergy.

**Faith Activity**

**Community of Prayer**
Imagine what it would be like to live in a monastery of monks or nuns. How would you feel at dawn in this environment? What sights or sounds might you experience? How might such an environment facilitate prayer for you?

| The Liturgy of the Hours | |
|---|---|
| **Term** | **Definition** |
| Office of Readings | Hymn, psalms, readings from Scripture/Church fathers/other readings, and various prayers |
| Morning Prayer | Hymn, psalms, short reading, Gospel canticle (canticle of Zachary), prayer of intercession, and other prayers |
| Daytime Prayer | Hymn, psalms, short reading, and other prayers |
| Evening Prayer | Hymn, psalms, short reading, Gospel canticle (canticle of Mary), prayer of intercession, and other prayers |
| Night Prayer | Prayer, examination of conscience, hymn, psalms, short reading, responses, other prayers, and antiphon to honor the Blessed Virgin |

**Morning and Evening Prayer** are the principal Hours of the Liturgy of the Hours. Morning Prayer sanctifies the morning, and Evening Prayer gives thanks for the day. The Liturgy of the Hours also includes other canonical hours that are prayed through the day.

**The Office of Readings** originated in what once was called Matins. Monks prayed it around three o'clock in the morning. The Office of Readings still is prayed during the night in some monasteries, but other monasteries pray it later in the day. Besides an invitatory, psalms, and other prayers, it includes a first reading from Scripture and a second reading from an early century writer, a saint, a Church document, or other pertinent source.

**Morning Prayer** relates to what was called Lauds. It is a celebratory canonical hour. Symbols of this hour include creation, light, dawn, the awakening of nature, and the Resurrection. These connect symbolically to our rising from slumber and awakening the human spirit. Morning Prayer recalls Jesus' Resurrection and aims at making holy the morning. The psalms include songs of praise.

*Faith*
**Activity**

**Meaningful Psalm**
Find a psalm that relates to a current situation in your life. Describe how your emotions are similar to those expressed in the psalm.

**Break Open the Word**

**Which Hour?** Read
Psalm 6. Identify a canonical
hour that might include this
psalm.

**Faith Activity**

**Illustrated Hours**
Research illustrated ver-
sions of books of hours or
the Book of Psalms (Psalter)
from medieval Europe.
Write an essay describing
the importance of these
works and the time devoted
to creating them. How
does the beauty of these
books express reverence
for wisdom literature?

**Daytime Prayer** is prayed in the Midmorning, at Midday, and in Midafternoon, and was once was known as the "Little Hours." These short pauses during the day help us raise our minds and hearts to God. Hymns and psalms of Daytime Prayer relate to themes at the hour they are prayed. As the day proceeds, these prayers remind us of the end of our life and the end of time.

**Evening Prayer** was formerly called Vespers. The prayer thanks God for what we have received and accomplished during the day. It focuses on the themes of thanksgiving, praise, redemption, and salvation. Along with Morning Prayer, Evening Prayer has a position of highest importance in the Church.

**Night Prayer** takes its origin from Compline. It, too, recalls the end of our life. During Night Prayer we commend ourselves to God, ask for divine protection and peace. Finally, we pray for a restful sleep and happy death. This prayer sums up the day's events and turns our lives over to God.

The Liturgy of the Hours is a rich weaving of prayer and praise on behalf of the entire Church. The psalms used for the Liturgy of the Hours are universal in their themes and sentiments. Our lives often contain themes that are reflected in the psalms. We, like the ancient Israelites, also experience moments of defeat, victory, failure, grace, and love. Such experiences are intrinsic to being human. We can apply the themes of the psalms to our lives and use them to face our challenges and crises. As such, they are timeless.

# Finding Meaning

The wisdom books of the Old Testament show us how to pray, love the Law, and live a good life. For the Israelites, these books might read like a sort of self-help book. You have probably come across self-help titles in bookstores; there are books to improve health, to take college entrance exams, and to overcome shyness. However, the purpose of the wisdom books is to show people how to find integrity in living a good life. In a broader sense, the entire collection of Scriptures is a guide for living.

What is a good life? How do you recognize wisdom? Part of the challenge in reading the Old Testament (including the wisdom books) is to apply it to your experience today. How can you keep the word alive in yourself? How are your actions a response to what you have read and learned?

Wisdom can come in the form of instruction about moral conduct. Every day you are confronted with choices big and small, and each choice is an exercise of the strength of your character. Some of the choices may not present much of a challenge: If your friend approaches you in a time of trouble, you would extend yourself and help.

You might not come to a decision so easily for other choices: If you find a $100 bill on the sidewalk outside of a home, would you knock on the door of the home and return it? If someone starts an argument with you over something small, would you walk away? Wisdom comes from experience, which the sages expressed in sayings, observations, and psalms.

Remember that prayer can bring peace to a troubled mind and heart. Prayer with a community brings even greater strength. A community of faith seeks religious expression. You have read about the Israelites and how they shared a need to express their understanding of God. Some of these expressions dealt with love of God, God's love for them, and their commitment to live in justice and peace—in right relationship with God. Many of these ideas have been passed from one generation to the next, all the way to your generation.

The Church's religious expression can be seen in the liturgy and in the sacraments. Understanding these expressions helps you experience the Church and understand the Scriptures, which were written thousands of years ago. You are living in the mystery of God as your ancestors lived in God in their day. The messages still hold true, and they are carried forth in the worshiping community. You are the believers of today. In community, you share, encourage each other, and celebrate your experience of God. The community challenges you to live in right relationship with God and with others.

## Venerable Pierre Toussaint

(1766–1853)

Venerable Pierre Toussaint is one of the few Haitians to be recognized for holiness by the Church. He was born into a Haitian slave family in 1766, and soon after he became a house slave to the Jean Berard family. Jean Berard taught Pierre how to read and write, and had Pierre baptized and brought up in the Catholic faith. In 1787 the Berard family relocated to New York City, due to the slave revolts taking place in Haiti.

Upon arriving in New York City, Pierre was apprenticed out to a hairdresser. Soon after, Pierre found himself in great demand by some of the city's most elite clients. His clients found him charming both in hairdressing skills and in social skills. All of Pierre's clients were comfortable in talking with and confiding in Pierre. Though Pierre was very devoted to his profession, his true devotion was to God, his family, and local community.

In 1807 Madame Berard granted Pierre his freedom, and shortly after he married a Haitian woman named Juliette. Pierre and Juliette took in many orphans, including Pierre's niece. Pierre and Juliette also opened their home to many impoverished people and slaves. As a former slave, Pierre recognized the importance of freedom, and he helped many slaves to purchase their freedom.

Pierre was devoted to the Church and exhibited a charitable relationship with the needy. Pierre always helped those around him and those in his community. He joined Elizabeth Ann Seton in building one of New York's first orphanages. He aided in funding the building of Saint Patrick's Cathedral in Manhattan, and he gave donations to black schools and religious orders.

Venerable Pierre Toussaint's actions illustrated many of the Catholic Social Teaching's major themes, including the call to family, community, and participation. Pierre participated in his community, and he made a conscious effort to focus on working for the common good of all people. Consider how you can answer the call to family, friends, and participation with the same generous and loving actions.

## Prayer

Begin by praying the Sign of the Cross.

**Leader:** Eternal father, grant that we may always look to you for guidance, but that we may also remember to seek the right guidance of our own parents, grandparents, and other persons in positions of authority.

**All:** Amen.

**Reader 1:** Father, guide our hands that we may work with our community and build strong relationships.

**All:** Amen.

**Reader 2:** Father, guide our eyes that we may see injustice in our community and work to eliminate it.

**All:** Amen.

**Reader 3:** Father, guide our feet that we may travel outside of our community to the world and spread our knowledge and love.

**All:** Amen.

**Reader 4:** Father, guide our hearts that we may love our community and all communities around the world.

**All:** Amen.

**Reader 5:** Father, guide our lips that we may spread the message of your Son, and his message of peace and togetherness.

**All:** Amen.

**Reader 6:** Father, guide our actions that we may protect our community, our family, and our loved ones from anything that may harm us.

**Leader:** We ask these blessings through Christ, our Lord . . .

**All:** Amen.

End by praying the Sign of the Cross.

## Review

1. What is the focus of the Books of Proverbs, Job, and Sirach?

2. To whom are many of the psalms attributed?

3. Name three objects that are often personified in literature? What object is personified in the Book of Baruch, the Book of Wisdom, and in Proverbs 1—9?

4. To whom is much of the wisdom literature in the Old Testament attributed?

5. What events took place in Job's life, which made him curse the day he was born?

6. Proverbs are attributed to which four different people or groups of people?

7. How should love be, ideally, according to the Song of Songs?

8. What is the typical structure of individual psalms? What purposes did they have in the Old Testament?

9. In which books of the Old Testament can allusions to the Messiah as the Good Shepherd be found?

10. What are the names of the prayer times within the Liturgy of the Hours? When are they all prayed?

11. What is the purpose of the "little hours"?

12. How can the wisdom books help direct you in life?

## Key Words

**epilogue (p. 196)**—The conclusion to a literary work.

**personification (p. 193)**—Something nonhuman is described with human characteristics.

**prologue (p. 196)**—The introduction preceding a literary work that gives information to help the audience understand the story that follows.

**proverbs (p. 199)**—Brief statements that convey a general truth or rule of conduct.

**sensory images (p. 205)**—Images that appeal to any of the five senses.

## Personal Journey

### Teen to Teen

In the larger community of the United States, we have the judicial system to resolve conflicts that boil over from simple conversation and open discourse. How do you resolve conflicts that arise within your family?

*We all sit down at the kitchen table, all of us: my mom, my dad, my brothers, and I. Then we present our sides of the story. Usually it stays pretty calm, but sometimes in trying to resolve the problem we just throw kindling on the fire. But my parents always find a way to bring the arguments back down to conversations, keeping the lines of communication open. In the end, my brothers and sometimes my parents and I see each other's way of thinking, why the problem came up to begin with, and how to avoid it in the future.*

*Kathryn P.*

## Catholic Social Teaching—Call to Family, Community, and Participation

The family is the central social institution that must be supported and strengthened, not undermined. While our society often exalts individualism, the Catholic tradition teaches that human beings grow and achieve fulfillment in community. We believe people have a right and a duty to participate in society, seeking together the common good and well-being of all, especially the poor and vulnerable. Our Church teaches that the role of government and other institutions is to protect human life and human dignity and promote the common good."

(*Sharing Catholic Social Teaching: Challenges and Directions*, USCCB, 1998.)

We live in an age when both outside forces and forces from within challenge the bonds that hold families together. Instead of talking about problems, some families or members of families choose to internalize their feelings. By participating in family meetings or discussions about problems we can strengthen the bonds that may have been weakened.

Learning to move into society at large and use what we learn with our families is a challenge as well. Maintaining an open discourse between community leaders and others in positions of authority and those who are being led can help prevent unjust situations.

### Break Open the Word

**Read 1 Kings 3:16–28.** Solomon wisely discerns who the real mother of the child is. He uses deductive reasoning and the righteous wisdom God granted him. Think of a time you made a decision that relied upon your logic and God-given abilities. How did your decision affect the situation? How do you think Solomon would have dealt with the situation?

# Catholic Source Book

## Scripture & Liturgy

Catholics gather to praise and worship God in liturgy, the official public prayer of the Church. The original meaning of the word *liturgy* was a public work, or a service in the name of or on behalf of the people. In Christian terms, the word *liturgy* describes the participation of the whole People of God in the work of God. The liturgy consists of the celebration of the sacraments, first and foremost the Eucharist, and the Liturgy of the Hours.

Scripture is integral to how we pray and worship. The celebration of each sacrament includes a Liturgy of the Word. This proclamation of Scripture expresses the meaning of the sacrament and calls those who receive the sacrament to respond in faith.

**Liturgy of the Hours** The Liturgy of the Hours is a prayer that includes psalms and readings and is prayed several times a day as a way to mark time as holy and recall God's saving work in creation. The psalms are an integral part to the Liturgy of the Hours.

## The Seven Sacraments

In the sacraments Jesus continues his saving work. During his life Jesus welcomed, fed, healed, and forgave people. Through the sacraments he continues to share God's life and love with his followers. Because the sacraments are founded on the ministry of Jesus and witnessed to in the early Church, we can find Biblical roots for the sacraments.

**Sacraments of Initiation** Three sacraments together complete initiation into the Church: Baptism, which begins new life in Christ; Confirmation, which strengthens that life; and, Eucharist, which nourishes that life and transforms the recipient to become more Christ-like.

- Baptism—John 3:5; Matthew 28:19–20; Romans 6:3–11
- Confirmation—Acts 8:14–17, 9:17–19, 19:5; Titus 3:4–8
- Eucharist—John 6:1–15, 25–71; Matthew 26:26–28; Mark 14:22–25; Luke 22:7–20

**Sacraments of Healing**  In the Sacraments of Healing God's forgiveness of sins and healing are given to those suffering physical and spiritual sickness.

- Reconciliation (also called the Sacrament of Penance, the Sacrament of Conversion, and the Sacrament of Confession)—John 20:19, 22–23; Mark 1:15, 2:5, 10; Luke 7:48, 15:18

- Anointing of the Sick—Mark 6:12–13, 16:17–18; Matthew 10:8; James 5:14–15

**Sacraments at the Service of Communion**  In these sacraments Catholics receive the grace to commit to and serve God and the community.

- Holy Orders—John 10:36; Acts 1:8, 2:4; 1 Timothy 4:14; 2 Timothy 1:6–7

- Matrimony—Matthew 19:6; John 2:1–11; 1 Corinthians 7:39; Ephesians 5:31–32

# The Mass

Several ritual books are used in the celebration of the Eucharist. The lectionary is the collection of readings assigned by the Church for liturgical proclamation. The Church promulgated the current lectionary for use in 1970, and it was revised in 1998. The lectionary is comprised of:

1. A three-year cycle of Sunday readings (first and second readings)

2. A two-year weekday cycle

3. A one-year sanctoral cycle

4. A variety of other readings for various occasions

5. Responsorial psalms and alleluia verses

The Book of Gospels is used for the proclamation of the Gospels during Mass. The Church released the most recent revision in 1999. The bishop presents a Book of Gospels to new deacons upon their ordination; the book is also raised over the heads of new bishops during their ordination ceremonies.

# The Liturgical Year

The liturgical year is the Church's annual cycle of seasons and feasts that celebrates the Paschal mystery. It begins on the First Sunday of Advent and ends on the feast of Christ the King. Throughout all the season, the Church celebrates some aspect of Christ's Paschal Mystery.

**Holy Days of Obligation in the United States**  The Vatican has listed ten holy days of obligation, but each conference of bishops determines which holy days will be locally observed. In the United States we celebrate six. Catholics are required to participate in Mass on all Sundays and on these holy days.

Mary the Mother of God (January 1)

The Ascension of the Lord (40 days after Easter or the Sunday nearest the end of the 40-day period)

The Assumption of Mary (August 15)

All Saints' Day (November 1)

The Immaculate Conception of Mary (December 8)

Christmas (December 25)

**Fast, Abstinence, and Days of Penance**  All Christians are obliged to live in a spirit of penance whereby their exterior act of prayer, self-denial, and charity bear witness to the inner values of their faith.

Fasting is the limitation to one full meal and two lighter meals a day, with no food between meals. In the United States the obligation to fast binds those from eighteen years of age to the beginning of the sixtieth year.

The Eucharistic fast requires that a person fast from food and drink for one hour before receiving Communion. This does not include water and medicine. The fast for those who are elderly or sick is fifteen minutes.

■ Grave circumstances—sickness, dietary needs, social obligations— excuse a person from the obligations to fast and abstain, but not from seeking out other forms of penance.

■ Abstinence generally refers to refraining from eating meat on certain days. The obligation to abstain from meat binds Catholics from the age of fourteen throughout life.

Ash Wednesday and Good Friday are days of fast and abstinence, as are all Fridays during Lent. All Fridays during the year and the entire Season of Lent are days of penance. Works of penance include voluntary abstinence, fasting, prayer, works of charity, and other acts of self-denial.

# Vocations

The Resurrection of Jesus is one of the defining mysteries of the Catholic faith. All of us are called to live in light of the risen Jesus and be a sign of life and hope for the world. God created each of us to be in his friendship and to share in his life. He continually calls all people to believe in him and to grow in his friendship.

Through Baptism, Christ calls each of us to holiness—to become more like him. We are called to take part in the Church's mission of spreading the good news through our words and actions. This call is our baptismal or common vocation. The word *vocation* refers to one's calling or purpose. In religious terms a vocation is one's call to love and serve God and others. God calls us to live out this shared vocation in different ways.

**Single life:** Through the single life, people profess to the mystery of the Incarnation and bring the message of the Good News to others through their work, civic involvement, and family life.

**Married life:** In married life husband and wife affirm the image of God in one another and welcome children to share in their lives. Like those in the single life, married people are called to be a witness to their faith in the world.

**Ordained life:** Men receive the Sacrament of Holy Orders to become deacons, priests, or bishops and minister to the Church through teaching, leading, and worship.

**Consecrated life:** Religious sisters, brothers, and priests live, pray, and work in community to stand together in opposition to the culture and the values in the world that are not Gospel values.

As Christians, we are called to make the world holy. Which vocation will you choose to bring holiness and wholeness, or resurrection, to the world?

# Scripture & Morality

## The Ten Commandments

**1.** I am the Lord your God: you shall not have strange gods before me.
- Place one's faith in God alone.
- Believe in, trust, and love God.

**2.** You shall not take the name of the Lord your God in vain.
- Speak God's name, and that of Jesus and the saints, with reverence.
- Don't curse or call on God to witness to a lie.

**3.** Remember to keep holy the Lord's day.
- Gather to worship at the Eucharist.
- Rest and avoid unnecessary work on Sunday.

**4.** Honor your father and your mother.
- Respect and obey parents, guardians, and others who have proper authority.

**5.** You shall not kill.
- Respect and protect your life and the lives of others.

**6.** You shall not commit adultery.
- Be faithful and loyal to spouses, friends, and family.
- Respect God's gift of sexuality, and practice the virtue of chastity.
- Learn to appreciate the gift of sexuality by practicing self-mastery.

**7.** You shall not steal.
- Respect the things that belong to others.
- Share what you have with those in need.

**8.** You shall not bear false witness against your neighbor.
- Be honest, truthful, and avoid bragging.
- Don't say untruthful or negative things about others.

**9.** You shall not covet your neighbor's wife.
- Practice modesty in thoughts, words, dress, and actions.

**10.** You shall not covet your neighbor's goods.

- Rejoice in others' good fortune.
- Don't be jealous of others' possessions and don't be greedy.

# The Great Commandment

"You shall love the Lord your God with all your heart, and with all your soul, and with all your strength, and with all your mind; and your neighbor as yourself."

*Luke 10:27*

# The New Commandment

"I give you a new commandment, that you love one another. Just as I have loved you, you also should love one another."

*John 13:34*

# The Beatitudes

Blessed are the poor in spirit,
  for theirs is the kingdom of heaven.
Blessed are they who mourn,
  for they will be comforted.
Blessed are the meek,
  for they will inherit the earth.
Blessed are they who hunger and thirst for righteousness,
  for they will be filled.
Blessed are the merciful,
  for they will receive mercy.
Blessed are the pure in heart,
  for they will see God.
Blessed are the peacemakers,
  for they will be called children of God.
Blessed are they who are persecuted for the righteousness sake,
  for theirs is the kingdom of heaven.

*Matthew 5:3–10*

# Works of Mercy

Matthew 25:31–46 lays the foundation for the Works of Mercy, particularly the Corporal Works of Mercy.

| Spiritual Works of Mercy | Corporal Works of Mercy |
| --- | --- |
| Teach the ignorant. | Feed the hungry. |
| Counsel the doubtful. | Give drink to the thirsty. |
| Comfort the sorrowful. | Shelter the homeless. |
| Bear wrongs patiently. | Clothe the naked. |
| Forgive injuries. | Visit the sick. |
| Warn the sinner. | Visit the imprisoned. |
| Pray for the living and the dead. | Bury the dead. |

# Virtues

**Theological Virtues**  The theological virtues are gifts from God. They are called the theological virtues because they are rooted in God, directed toward him, and reflect his presence in our lives. (In Greek *theos* means "god.")

- Faith means believing in him and all that he has revealed to us and that the Church proposes for our belief.

- Hope is the desire, bolstered by trust, to do God's will and achieve eternal life.

- Through charity, we love God above all else, and our neighbors as ourselves.

**Cardinal Virtues**  The cardinal virtues are the principal moral virtues that help us lead a moral life by governing our actions, controlling our passions and emotions, and keeping our conduct on the right tract.

- prudence (careful judgment)

- fortitude (courage)

- justice (giving God and people their due)

- temperance (moderation, balance)

# Precepts of the Church

The precepts of the Church are laws that name specific actions that all Catholics are obligated to carry out. According to the *National Catechetical Directory*, the following precepts apply to Catholics in the United States.

1. To keep holy the day of the Lord's Resurrection: to worship God by participating in Mass every Sunday and holy day of obligation; to avoid those activities that would hinder renewal of soul and body on the Sabbath (e.g., needless work and business activities, unnecessary shopping, etc.).

2. To lead a sacramental life; to receive Holy Communion frequently and the Sacrament of Reconciliation regularly—minimally, to receive the Sacrament of Reconciliation at least once a year (annual confession is obligatory only if serious sin is involved); minimally also, to receive Holy Communion at least once a year, between the First Sunday of Lent and Trinity Sunday.

3. To study Catholic teaching in preparation for the Sacrament of Confirmation, to be confirmed, and then to continue to study and advance the cause of Christ.

4. To observe the marriage laws of the Church; to give religious training, by example and word, to one's children; to use parish schools and catechetical programs.

5. To strengthen and support the Church—one's own parish community and parish priests, the worldwide Church and the pope.

6. To do penance, including abstaining from meat and fasting from food on the appointed days.

7. To join in the missionary spirit and apostolate of the Church.

# Catholic Social Teaching

Strengthened by the grace of God the Father and the power of the Holy Spirit, the Church reaches out to the entire world with the saving message of Christ's Passion, death, and Resurrection. The Church defends those who are poor and impoverished—those whom the world has cast aside. The Church protects life in all its forms and in all its stages. The Church struggles for justice where there is hatred and prejudice.

In these ways the Church lives out Jesus' message of just action and living. Over the past century, popes and bishops have appealed to the Church to honor the dignity of all people and to work to ensure that the rights of all are protected and upheld. This is the core of Catholic Social Teaching. The U.S. Bishops have identified the following seven themes or principles of Catholic Social Teaching:

- The Life and Dignity of the Human Person
- Call to Family, Community, and Participation
- Rights and Responsibilities of the Human Person
- Option for the Poor and Vulnerable
- The Dignity of Work and the Rights of Workers
- The Solidarity of the Human Family
- Care for God's Creation

The mission of the Church to bring the saving love and forgiveness of Jesus "to all the world" begins with loving God and loving our neighbors. We are called to be "good Samaritans," to be people of forgiveness, to heal and invite, to convert and reconcile, to be the loving, healing, forgiving presence of Christ in the world.

# Catholic Prayers and Practices

## The Lord's Prayer
Matthew 6:9–13, Luke 11:2–4

Our Father, who art in heaven,
hallowed be thy name.
Thy kingdom come;
thy will be done on earth as it is in heaven.
Give us this day our daily bread
and forgive us our trespasses
as we forgive those who trespass against us.
And lead us not into temptation,
but deliver us from evil. Amen.

## Hail Mary
Luke 1:28 and Luke 1:42

Hail, Mary, full of grace!
The Lord is with you.
Blessed are you among women
and blessed is the fruit of your womb, Jesus.
Holy Mary, Mother of God,
pray for us sinners,
now and at the hour of our death. Amen.

# Magnificat

## Luke 1:46–55

My soul proclaims the greatness of the Lord,
my spirit rejoices in God my Savior
for he has looked with favor on his lowly servant.
From this day all generations will call me blessed:
the Almighty has done great things for me,
and holy is his Name.
He has mercy on those who fear him
in every generation.
He has shown the strength of his arm,
he has scattered the proud in their conceit.
He has cast down the mighty from their thrones,
and has lifted up the lowly.
He has filled the hungry with good things,
and the rich he has sent away empty.
He has come to the help of his servant Israel
for he has remembered his promise of mercy,
the promise he made to our fathers,
to Abraham and his children for ever.

The title of this prayer—*Magnificat*—is the Latin word for "proclaim."
It is derived from Mary's response to Elizabeth's greeting during the
Visitation. The Church sings Mary's song during Evening Prayer, also
known as Vespers.

# The Rosary

Early Christians used beads or knotted strings to keep count of prayers. As devotion to Mary increased, it became popular to create psalters or books dedicated to Jesus or Mary, using biblical scenes. The Rosary we know today developed from both of these practices. As you pray each decade of beads, you think of one mystery in the life of Jesus or Mary.

**Praying the Rosary** The rosary begins at the cross with the Sign of the Cross and then the Apostles' Creed. Then at the first bead, the Lord's Prayer followed by three Hail Mary's—one for each bead. After moving past the third Hail Mary bead, pray a Glory to the Father. At the last bead, announce the first mystery of the Rosary, and then pray the Lord's Prayer again.

After passing the medallion, move to the right on the rosary and pray ten Hail Mary's while contemplating the first mystery of the Rosary. After the tenth Hail Mary, pray a Glory to the Father, announce the next mystery of the rosary, and pray the Lord's prayer. Pray ten Hail Mary's until you have announced and contemplated the remaining mysteries of the Rosary.

## Mysteries of the Rosary

**Joyful Mysteries**
Annunciation
Visitation
Nativity
Presentation of Jesus
Finding Jesus in the Temple

**Sorrowful Mysteries**
Agony in the Garden
Scourging at the Pillar
Crowning with Thorns
Jesus Carries his Cross
Crucifixion

**Glorious Mysteries**
Resurrection of Jesus
Ascension
Descent of the Holy Spirit
Assumption of Mary
Coronation of Mary

**Luminous Mysteries**
The Baptism of Christ in the Jordan
Jesus' Self-manifestation at the Wedding Feast of Cana
The Announcement of the Kingdom Along with the Call to Conversion
The Transfiguration
The Institution of the Eucharist as the Sacramental Expression of the Paschal Mystery

# The Stations of the Cross

The Stations of the Cross commemorate the journey of Christ from the praetorium—where Pilate held court—to Calvary and the tomb. Many crusaders retraced this path, and the prayerful reflection many people experienced while retracing these steps was brought back to Churches throughout Europe.

1. **Jesus is condemned to death.**
   - Scripture reference: Matthew 27:11–31; Mark 15:2–15; Luke 23:2–25; John 19:1–16
   - Scripture reflection: "For God so loved the world that he gave his only Son, so that everyone who believes in him may not perish but may have eternal life" (*John 3:16*).

2. **Jesus carries his cross.**
   - Scripture reference: Matthew 27:31; John 19:17
   - Scripture reflection: "If any want to become my followers, let them deny themselves and take up their cross daily and follow me" (*Luke 9:23*).

3. **Jesus falls the first time.**
   - Scripture reference: none directly
   - Scripture reflection: "All we like sheep have gone astray; we have all turned to our own way, and the Lord has laid on him the iniquity of us all" (*Isaiah 53:6*).

4. **Jesus meets his mother.**
   - Scripture reference: John 19:25–27
   - Scripture reflection: "Is it nothing to you, all you who pass by? Look and see if there is any sorrow like my sorrow . . ." (*Lamentations 1:12*).

5. **Simon helps Jesus carry his cross.**
   - Scripture reference: Matthew 27:32; Mark 15:21; Luke 23:26
   - Scripture reflection: "Truly I tell you, just as you did it to one of the least of these who are members of my family, you did it to me" (*Matthew 25:40*).

**6.** Veronica wipes the face of Jesus.

- Scripture reference: none directly

- Scripture reflection: "Whoever has seen me has seen the Father" (*John 14:9*).

**7.** Jesus falls the second time.

- Scripture reference: none directly

- Scripture reflection: "Come to me, all you that are weary and carrying heavy burdens, and I will give you rest" (*Matthew 11:28*).

**8.** Jesus speaks to the women of Jerusalem.

- Scripture reference: Luke 23:27; Matthew 27:55; Mark 15:40

- Scripture reflection: "Daughters of Jerusalem, do not weep for me, but weep for yourselves and for your children" (*Luke 23:28*).

**9.** Jesus falls the third time.

- Scripture reference: none directly

- Scripture reflection: "For all who exalt themselves will be humbled, and these who humble themselves will be exalted" (*Luke 14:11*).

**10.** Jesus is stripped of his garments.

- Scripture reference: John 19:23–25

- Scripture reflection: "None of you can become my disciple if you do not give up all your possessions" (*Luke 14:33*).

**11.** Jesus is nailed to the cross.

- Scripture reference: Matthew 27:35; Mark 15:24; Luke 23:33

- Scripture reflection: "For I have come down from heaven, not to do my own will, but the will of him who sent me" (*John 6:38*).

**12.** Jesus dies on the cross.

- Scripture reference: Matthew 27:50; Mark 15:37; John 19:30

- Scripture reflection: "And being found in human form, he humbled himself and became obedient to the point of death—even death on a cross" (*Philippians 2:7–8*).

**13.** Jesus is taken down from the cross.

- Scripture reference: Matthew 27:59; Mark 15:46; Luke 23:53; John 19:31–38

- Scripture reflection: "Was it not necessary that the Messiah should suffer these things and then enter into his glory?" (*Luke 24:26*).

**14.** Jesus is laid in the tomb.

- Scripture reference: Matthew 27:59–60; Mark 15:47

- Scripture reflection: "Unless a grain of wheat falls into the earth and dies, it remains just a single grain; but if it dies, it bears much fruit" (*John 12:24*).

# Glossary

## A

**acrostic (p. 138)**—An ordered poem in which the first letters of individual lines or verses, when combined in order, form their own pattern, phrase, or word.

**allegory (p. 126)**—Symbolic characters that presents religious truths or generalizations about human nature.

**anawim (p. 157)**—A Jewish term referring to people who are in need of assistance.

**anthropomorphism (p. 35)**—The attributing of human characteristics to nonhuman realities.

**antihero (p. 161)**—A character who is placed in the role of a traditional hero but is not idealized in any way.

**apocalypse (p. 152)**—A revelation of future events.

**Ark of the Covenant (p.15)**—An ancient symbol of God's protection and presence; a portable throne in ancient times that included a seat that was believed to be occupied by God.

## B

**Babylonian Exile (p. 135)**—Period of history when the Babylonians forced most of the inhabitants of Judah to migrate to Babylon; the Exile.

**ban (p. 83)**—Ancient custom of completely destroying everything in a defeated city.

**Bar Mitzvah (p. 163)**—Jewish coming-of-age ceremony for thirteen-year-old boy.

**Bat Mitzvah (p. 163)**—Non-Orthodox Jewish coming-of-age ceremony for twelve-or thirteen-year-old-girl.

**Beatitudes (p. 160)**—Jesus' eight teachings about the meaning and path to true happiness; descriptions of the way to attain eternal blessedness, or holiness, to which God calls all of us.

**biblical Inspiration (p. 7)**—The process by which God the Holy Spirit assisted a human author in writing a book of the Bible.

## C

**canon (p.8)**—The official collection of inspired books of sacred Scripture that contain the witness and instruction for our faith.

**canonization (p. 113)**—An official Church statement by which a person is declared to have lived a holy life of heroic virtue; in the last stage of the process of canonization, the person is named a saint.

**communion of saints (p. 113)**—All faithful Church members on earth, in heaven, and in purgatory.

**covenant (p. 7)**—A sacred agreement between God and his people.

## D

**Diaspora (p. 147)**—The community of Jews in Babylonia after the Exile.

**Divided Kingdom (p. 120)**—The result of the division of Israel into two separate nations: Israel and Judah.

**divine justice (p. 124)**—The moral standard by which God judges human conduct; the realization of that standard by God; an expression of God's righteousness, pity, love, and grace.

**divine revelation (p. 7)**—God's communicating of himself and his plan of goodness throughout history.

**dynasty (p. 100)**—A succession of rulers in the same family line, frequently father to son.

## E

**epic (p.21)**—The detailed history of a hero who demonstrates bravery and wisdom and goes through a series of trials.

**epilogue (p. 196)**—The conclusion to a literary work.

**evangelization (p. 185)**—Giving witness to one's faith by proclaiming the Good News of Jesus Christ to the world through words and actions.

**exiles (p. 135)**—People banished from their home or land.

**Exodus (p. 9)**—Departure of the Israelites from Egyptian slavery under the leadership of Moses, who was led by God.

**fairy tale (p. 162)**—A myth with an earthly setting, human characters, and a happy ending.

**figures of speech (p. 24)**—Comparisons meant to be taken imaginatively, rather than literally.

**folklore (p. 21)**—Composite of traditional customs, art forms, tales, and sayings preserved among a people.

**genealogy (p. 44)**—An account of ancestry.

**hapiru (p. 65)**—A class of people living in the countryside of Canaan, some of whom were former slaves; they may have been ancestors of the Hebrews.

**Hebrews (p. 65)**—Peoples enslaved in Egypt who eventually became the community known as Israel.

**idolatry (p. 69)**—False worship; honoring and revering a creature in place of God.

**imagery (p. 23)**—Concrete sensory images that make a literary work vivid and realistic.

**irony (p. 25)**—A literary technique in which what is said or done is contrary to what is expected.

**Israelites (p. 65)**—A people who unified around 1050–1000 B.C. and included Canaanites, the hapiru, the shasu, Sea Peoples, and the original Hebrews.

**Jews (p. 66)**—Term originally used to describe the people who resettled in the area of Judah following the Babylonian Exile; most commonly used to refer to followers of Judaism.

**judge (p. 85)**—One of twelve charismatic military leaders of the Israelites during the period between the conquest of Canaan and the establishment of the monarchy who was animated by the spirit of God.

**Kingdom of Judea (p. 120)**—The kingdom south of Israel that existed from the time following Solomon's death in 925 B.C. until the destruction of the Temple in 586 B.C.

**legends (p. 175)**—Unverifiable stories that are passed down from generation to generation and accepted as true or partly true.

**matriarchs (p. 14)**—The founding mothers of Israel, particularly Sarah, Rebekah, Rachel, and Leah.

**messiah (p. 98)**—King or deliverer expected by the Jews; the "anointed one."

**messianism (p. 98)**—Belief in a messiah as the savior of the people.

**monarchy (p. 100)**—Rule by a single head of state, often a hereditary office.

**monotheism (p. 9)**—The worship of one God.

**myth (p. 22)**—A symbolic story that illuminates views of a particular people regarding the relationship between humans and the divine.

**narrative (p. 22)**—A story that illuminates a detail within a genealogy.

**natural moral law (p. 10)**—The moral order that is part of God's design for creating the law that expresses the original moral sense, enabling people to discern good and evil through the use of reason.

**novella (p. 162)**—A suspenseful tale that revolves around a specific situation.

**oracle (p. 22)**—Words of wisdom or advice given by God through a spokesperson.

**oral tradition (p. 17)**—Unwritten, memorized accounts of historical events and stories.

**original sin (p. 40)**—The human condition of the need for salvation based on the first humans' choice to disobey.

**origin story (p. 20)**—A story in which an explanation of how something came to be is given.

**parable (p. 22)**—A short illustrative story that teaches a moral or religious lesson.

**parallelism (p. 24)**—The repetition of words, phrases, or thought patterns.

**Passover (p. 68)**—Refers to when the Israelites were "passed over" by the angel of death as dictated by the tenth plague; a holiday celebrated by Jews as a day of deliverance.

**patriarch (p. 44)**—Male leader of a family or tribe.

**patriarchs (p. 5)**—the ancestors of the Israelites, particularly Abraham, Isaac, and Jacob.

**Pentateuch (p. 33)**—The first five books of the Old Testament; the Torah.

**personal sin (p. 40)**—The free choice to disobey God; to do something that is the opposite of the good.

**personification (p. 193)**—Something nonhuman is described with human characteristics.

**prologue (p. 196)**—The introduction preceding a literary work that gives information to help the audience understand the story that follows.

**prophecy (p. 121)**—The words of God, delivered through a spokesperson known as a prophet; generally calls for the Israelites to live justly and avoid idolatry.

**prophets (p. 69)**—Persons who have a close relationship with God and communicate a divine message.

**proverbs (p. 199)**—Brief statements that convey a general truth or rule of conduct.

**providence (p. 44)**—Divine guidance and care.

**polytheism (p. 14)**—The worship of many gods.

**rabbis (p. 67)**—Ordained Jewish teachers and spiritual leaders.

**remnant (p. 148)**—Exiles and former exiles who remained faithful to God.

**saints (p. 113)**—Deceased members of the Church, who have been canonized by the Church and are in heaven.

**salvation history (p. 5)**—The saving action of God throughout human history.

**satirical humor (p.161)**—Humor that exposes human frailties through a form of ridicule in order to achieve a moral purpose.

**satrapy (p. 148)**—An administrative province ruled by a governor called a *satrap.*

**sensory images (p. 205)**—Images that appeal to any of the five senses.

**sin (p. 40)**—Something spoken, a deed, an attitude, or a desire contrary to God's law.

**social sin (p. 42)**—A collective, societal act or sign that society has distanced itself from God.

**Talmud (p. 67)**—A collection of Jewish oral law and commentary; a guide for conduct in particular circumstances.

**Ten Commandments (p. 7)**—The laws given by God to Moses that prescribe moral obligations for the Israelites as part of God's covenant with them.

**theocracy (p. 97)**—A nation ruled by God.

**V**

**vocation (p. 137)**—One's call to love and serve God and others.

**vow (p. 101)**—A solemn promise.

## Endnotes

**1.** St Augustine, *De Civitate Dei*, XVII, 6, 2: PL 41, 537: CSEL 40, 2, 228.

**2.** Pius XII, loc. cit.: Denz, 2294 (3829-3830); EB 557-562.